Contents

List of Capsule Texts

Introduction

It is impossible to exaggerate the importance of the Industrial Revolution. Only the smelting of metals and the adoption of agriculture brought a comparable change in human history. Before the Industrial Revolution humanity, for all its ingenuity, lived in a precarious balance with the natural world.[1] The overwhelming majority of people were vulnerable to starvation, disease and debilitation, and were rarely able to rise beyond mere subsistence. All work was done by human and animal muscle, and life for most was a continual struggle against exhaustion and the spectre of death. There were great civilisations of course, but none ever freed its people from the threat of imminent famine or disease.[2]

In contrast the Industrial Revolution laid the foundations of a new world in which famine and want could be eliminated, where machines replaced human labour and where technology could be harnessed for the benefit of humankind. More than that, industrialisation changed the whole of human society, bringing into being new methods of social and economic organisation, new political forces and new social classes. The Industrial Revolution also had a transforming effect on human psychology, dramatically altering humanity's relation to the natural world and embedding the belief that change, not stasis, is the necessary backdrop to human existence.[3] We have seen too the malign effects of industrialisation – the despoliation of the natural world, pollution, climate change and increasing inequalities; the overthrow of that precarious balance has brought its own problems. For good or bad, so pervasive are the effects of the Industrial Revolution that it is impossible for us to comprehend human history without an understanding of this momentous episode: everything was changed forever.

What then was the Industrial Revolution? That may seem like an odd question. After all, every schoolchild knows about the spinning jenny, Samuel Crompton's mule and James Watt's steam engine, even if we are a little vague about how they worked; and we all know about cotton factories, smoky cities and steam locomotives. All these, and much more, certainly came into being in Britain in the late eighteenth century – but does this justify the claim that there was a revolutionary change in human existence?

In fact the very idea that there was an Industrial Revolution in Britain has come under attack from many quarters.[4] Historians of technology have pointed out that important inventions have occurred throughout human history, often in clusters, so there is nothing unique about Britain in the late eighteenth century. In addition, several of the major innovations associated with the Industrial Revolution – from Abraham Darby's blast-furnace technique to Thomas Newcomen's steam engine and John Kay's flying shuttle – were invented decades before that period. Moreover, Britain had been developing a strong manufacturing and commercial economy since 1650, with large numbers of people involved in production of textiles, iron and steel, tin, copper, brass, metal goods, salt, glass, shipbuilding, coal mining, brick-making and construction.

Early eighteenth-century Britain already had a large urban population, boosted by the phenomenal growth of London in particular. Urbanisation became a crucial element in the process of industrialisation but London in 1700 managed to support half a million people through trade, commerce and craft-scale manufacturing. Historians have argued that the inventions of the classic period of the Industrial Revolution were mainly concerned with the cotton industry, but this remained a small part of the British economy until the first quarter of the nineteenth century, while the factory system did not make significant inroads until after the first great phase of the Industrial Revolution had passed.

Economic historians have also pointed out that the British economy grew extremely slowly through the eighteenth century. Sustained growth – the sign of a significant change in the productive capacity of the economy – did not kick in until the middle decades of the nineteenth century, at a time when the likes of Richard Arkwright, James Watt, Henry Cort and Matthew Boulton were all in their graves.

All of this provides ammunition for the argument that Britain went through a long period of gradual and sustained change, the effects of which were felt only from the 1830s onwards. If the Industrial Revolution did bring about the alteration of human society, this process had begun much earlier and its effects were felt much later than we have been led to believe. The much-vaunted transformation begins to look less and less like a revolution and more like a gradual, centuries-long process.

And yet, the Industrial Revolution has emerged from this process of intense analysis bloody but unbowed, and in many ways stronger and more clearly defined. Historians have been forced to seek answers to fundamental questions. Firstly, if this was a revolution – i.e. an episode of rapid and fundamental change – then what exactly was that change? And second, what precisely do we mean by the word 'industrial'?

The answer to the first question is that, in a period of just three and a half decades, a series of innovations ushered in an entirely new kind of productive economy. The spinning jenny, Arkwright's frame, Watt's steam condenser, Crompton's mule, Cort's new method of iron-making, the rotary steam engine, the automatic loom and Trevithick's steam locomotive all had effects which were threefold. Firstly, they laid the foundations for the mechanisation of industrial production – the spinning frame and the mule, for example, were designed to be driven by external power not by human or animal muscle. Secondly, they brought in a new source of power for these machines – steam engines. Thirdly, they adapted steam power to locomotion, opening up the possibility of rapid transport. All of this was brought into being between the registration of patents for Arkwright's frame and Watt's steam engine in 1769, and Trevithick's successful trial of a steam locomotive at Pen-y-darren in 1804. This was, in any sense, a revolution in technology and the direct effects of these innovations were felt and appreciated at the time. Watt and Arkwright became famous in their lifetime and everyone soon saw that mechanised production powered by steam was opening up a new world.[5]

What, then, is the answer to our second question: what exactly do we mean by 'industry' and 'industrialisation'? It is important for us to pin this down at the outset since these words have long carried a host of meanings that can easily bring confusion. Beneath the mechanised production, the smoky factories, the technical wizardry and the reordering of society that began in the Industrial Revolution lay two essential forces that made Britain the birthplace of industrialisation.

The first was the emergence of an economy fuelled by coal. As we shall see, Britain had access to almost limitless amounts of cheap coal that were used in increasing amounts for heating and manufacturing during the eighteenth century. Thermal energy enabled Britain to become more prosperous and productive; but the crucial breakthrough into an industrial economy came with the use of coal to produce mechanical energy. Applying steam power to productive industry enabled Britain to break free from the constraints of the so-called 'organic economy' where everything was finally dependent on the resources of the land. In the past, expansion of production had been constrained by the amount of wood, grain and grass that could be grown, the number of animals raised and the amount of power produced by waterwheels. The new mineral or industrial economy had no such constraints – providing the coal did not run out – and could grow without fear of hitting the limits of what the land could provide. It was mechanical power from fossil fuel that drove industrialisation.

The second driving force is to do with innovation itself. Before the Industrial Revolution there had of course been important technical changes throughout human history, but these had not led to a sustained momentum of innovation, development and adaption. Yet the eighteenth-century revolution began a period of technical innovation that has lasted until the present day – the microchip is the direct descendant of the Jacquard loom, while modern dynamic feedback systems derive from Watt's centrifugal governor. We can therefore describe industrialisation as self-sustaining production powered by external energy and developed by continual innovation; this is what the Industrial Revolution brought into being.[6]

One of the most exciting aspects of this analysis is that the Industrial Revolution needed technological innovation to bring it into being. Some accounts of the period imply that the innovations were less important than the general increase in prosperity that preceded and, in their view, precipitated, the Industrial Revolution. But it is clear that there were two intertwined stories in eighteenth-century Britain. The first shows a country becoming increasingly wealthy on the back of its historical wool trade, its divergence into a host of craft manufactories, and the burgeoning of international commerce through the opening up of the Atlantic and sea routes to India. Britain was exploiting its 'organic economy' to the full. The second story shows a coal economy helping craft manufacturing to thrive, but which had not yet made the crucial transition from thermal to mechanical energy.

In fact Britain could have gone on exploiting its organic and mineral resources without ever becoming a fully industrial economy. The transition to the production of mechanical energy was not bound to happen, and any sense of inevitability comes only with hindsight. The Industrial Revolution came about because of inventors and their innovations. So, having survived a few decades in the wings of history, the great inventors – Watt, Newcomen, Hargreaves, Arkwright, Trevithick – are once again centre stage as the great movers in this historical drama. It was a single generation of British artisans who made possible Britain's transition to industrialisation and transformed the prospects of humanity.

*

Over the next few hundred pages I will explore how this momentous process unfolded, and tell of the people, inventions, industries and events that made the Industrial Revolution happen when and where it did. We will discover why there were so many crucial inventions in such a short space of time, explore the key developments that drove the revolution, and examine the immediate and lasting effects on work, life and global population.

The Industrial Revolution comprises a vast panorama of interconnected events and people; any historian of the period therefore has to choose between a straight chronological record and a thematic approach. The chronological narrative risks reducing this fascinating story to a list of individual events without providing the opportunity to understand the context within which each industry developed. So instead, this book is made up of separate sections, each covering a different aspect of industrialisation or a different industry. Each section tells its own story – often starting in the late medieval period and extending past the Industrial Revolution itself and on into the nineteenth century – while at the same time making connections to the other sections. The section on 'Power', for example, explores the development of the steam engine by Newcomen, Watt and Trevithick, while 'Invention' shows how these men came from the same social class of engineer–artisans; the section on 'Cotton' details the spectacular career of Richard Arkwright, while 'Work' shows the lasting effects of Arkwright's factory system. These focussed sections are bookended by a Prologue that describes Britain on the eve of industrialisation, and an Epilogue that examines the state of the country eighty years later. This structure will allow the reader to revel in the individual stories, while at the same time seeing them in the context of this world-changing process.

Innovation and technology lie at the heart of the Industrial Revolution. So, while many accounts of the period have skated over the details of atmospheric engines or spinning jennies, this book takes the opposite approach. Without a basic understanding of the process of spinning cotton, it is impossible to understand the enormous achievement that James Hargreaves's spinning jenny or Samuel Crompton's mule represented; without some grasp of how a hand-loom works, it is difficult to appreciate the ingenuity and the impact of the invention of the flying shuttle; and unless you know roughly how an atmospheric engine works you cannot see how James Watt's inventions changed the world. Understanding the fundamentals of these processes gives us a far richer appreciation of our own history and allows us to share in the sheer excitement brought on by discovery and innovation. The task of the historian is not to avoid the details of technological innovation but to reveal them as the thrilling focus of human endeavour and achievement.

The Industrial Revolution is the nexus through which all of modern human history flows. In a world concerned about climate change, pollution and environmental degradation, industrialisation can seem like the villain of the piece. But everyone reading this book leads a life of well-being beyond the imagining of those who lived before 1770: it is the great watershed and there is no going back. Instead we are beginning to understand that the world and the future of humanity depends on our instincts as makers and doers, as solvers of practical problems through mental and technical ingenuity. The Industrial Revolution is more relevant than ever.

Prologue:
Britain on the Verge

From 1769 to 1804 a series of astonishing innovations in iron production, steam power and textile machinery changed the prospects of humanity. Inventors and entrepreneurs seized the opportunity that history offered, and made the machines that allowed humans to move into a different kind of existence. This was the start of a deluge of technical innovation that has carried us to the present. But how did this happen? And why did it happen in Britain in the late eighteenth century? To begin to answer those questions we need to look at the state of this rapidly changing nation, standing both on the edge of Europe and on the verge of the Industrial Revolution.

While we tend to see pre-industrial Britain as an overwhelmingly rural economy little changed since medieval times, the truth could hardly be more different. By the eve of the Industrial Revolution Britain had already been through a remarkable 200-year transformation from a relatively poor agricultural society into a powerhouse of world commerce. In 1500 just 7 per cent of the English were urban dwellers; by the 1760s Britain was, along with the Netherlands, the most urban society in Europe with close to 30 per cent of the population living in towns (the equivalent figures for France and Germany were 13 and 9 per cent); Britain's workers earned more than any of their European counterparts, and prosperity at home was enhanced by a global trade network.[1] The historic shift of trade from the Mediterranean to the Atlantic had benefitted Britain more than any other nation. A series of governments had invested in naval expansion and Britain had begun to dominate trade with the North American colonies and with India.

Gains in the Seven Years War (1756–63), mostly at the expense of France, saw Britain take effective control of the world's oceans while the Dutch had been forced to concede much of their earlier supremacy. Annual exports to North America rose from £872,000 in the 1740s to £2m by the 1760s and £4.5m by 1771, while a series of Navigation Acts restricted foreign ships from trading in British ports and so increased the size and power of the British merchant fleet.[2] Investment in harbour and port facilities at Liverpool, Bristol, Glasgow, Newcastle, Whitby, Hull, Dundee, Ipswich and elsewhere brought dividends in the international trade in tobacco, sugar, tea and slaves, with cotton increasing in importance. In the mid-eighteenth century there were around 6,000 merchant ships in Britain, double that of France (which had a far bigger population), with around 100,000 men working on board.[3]

Most importantly the wealth of Britain was spread widely across its population. Previous civilisations had accumulated vast riches but few if any societies in human history had so much wealth so widely distributed. Over the previous 200 years England had grown rich on the wool trade, first selling fleeces and raw wool to the weavers of Flanders and Italy, then making its own cloth for sale across Europe and the world. Changes in land use saw English sheep grazed on the finest pastures producing wool that was famous for its quality. Wool was produced in almost every corner of England and a series of trades from farmer and fuller to spinner and weaver prospered in every county and market town. Merchants from London, Amsterdam, Paris and Leipzig would travel to the cloth markets of Exeter, Crediton, Norwich and Leeds. In 1726 Daniel Defoe described the English wool trade as 'the richest and most valuable manufacture in the world'.[4]

Wool was the backbone of English prosperity, and the widespread wealth it created enabled the English – and later the British – to diversify successfully into other trades. In Tudor times England had looked to Continental Europe for technical expertise and had imported most of its high-quality manufactured goods; but by the eighteenth century Britain led the world in metal-smelting, iron-forging, shipbuilding, chemicals, mining, pottery, glass-making, brewing and construction. Historians have estimated that by 1700 industry accounted for 30 per cent of the British economy, with agriculture standing at 40 per cent.[5]

This diversification into small-scale manufacturing was able to happen because from roughly 1600 to 1730 Britain underwent an agricultural revolution. Small farmers, protected by so-called copyholder and beneficial tenancies, brought about a doubling of agricultural productivity. Not only was each acre of land able to produce twice as much food, but this was achieved without an increase in the number of agricultural workers. In Tudor times each farm worker fed around 1.25 people, but by 1730 this figure had increased to 2.5; in other words, each farm worker could now feed herself and 1.5 others.[6] The result was a wholesale change in the structure of society. Not only did it lead to a growing number of urban dwellers, but the rural population became evenly divided between those who made their living purely by farm work and those engaged in crafts such as spinning, weaving, nail-making, iron-forging and so on. Britain saw its overall population expand but also witnessed a radical restructuring of society away from agriculture and towards craft industries and urban living.

The growth in urban population was dominated by the rapid expansion of London, which increased from around 55,000 in 1500 to 500,000 in 1700, but other towns like Bristol, Norwich, Ipswich, Liverpool and Oxford grew significantly too. And while Britain still had a smaller population than France, Italy, Germany or Spain, it was growing at a much faster rate – by 280 per cent between 1550 and 1820 compared to 50 to 80 per cent for other European countries.[7]

The rise in agricultural productivity had a variety of causes, but one highly significant element that agriculture shared with the growing crafts manufactories was the use of coal. Coal was easy to find and cheap to dig in many parts of Britain; it was transported in bulk by ship and boat to many parts of the island. Crafts like brick- and salt-making, tanning and brewing took advantage of cheap coal, and from 1710 onwards it began to be used in blast furnaces, replacing charcoal. Crucially coal was also used in making vast quantities of lime for use as fertiliser. Coal not only enabled farmers to fertilise more land, its use as a heat source freed them from their reliance on trees for fuel, thereby allowing more acres to be used for food production.[8]

Houses constructed to accommodate the increasing numbers of town-dwellers were built with new types of grates and chimneys as coal took over from wood as the principal fuel for heating. Coal was shipped down the east coast from the coalfields of Northumberland and Durham in vast quantities to supply the homes and workshops of London. Coal production increased from 227,000 tons in 1560 to 3 million tons in 1700 by which time 80 per cent of the coal mined in Europe was mined in Britain; it has been estimated by one historian that in 1700 Britain was producing five times as much coal as the rest of the world.[9] While coal helped increase agricultural productivity and therefore allowed more people to live in towns, these could expand due to massive production of bricks for houses that were in turn heated by coal. The coal trade also began to change Britain's infrastructure; the new canal system that developed rapidly after 1761 was largely created to transport coal – the Bridgewater canal, Britain's first industrial canal, was built from Worsley colliery to Manchester to ship the Duke of Bridgewater's coal to his customers.

Coal also induced British landowners to view the coming industrialisation of society as a benefit, where previously established authorities tended to stand in the way of change. This was crucial because landowners were the dominant force in Parliament and the judiciary. A principal reason for their acquiescence was the coal that lay under their land; by the mid-century landowners across the Midlands and the north of England were benefitting handsomely from the coal economy. Coal had its tentacles in every part of this changing society.[10]

The development of commerce through the wool trade, the increase in agricultural productivity, the diversification of craft trades and the growth in the urban population created a virtuous circle of increasing prosperity. The wool trade itself became more productive and efficient, developing systems that saw more and more specialisation of work. Indeed specialisation and standardisation of work, and the concentration of crafts in particular regions, were crucial developments that emerged in the eighteenth century. While originally sheep farmers had processed wool before taking it to town for finishing, by the eighteenth century merchants were operating and controlling a 'putting-out' system where they paid piece rates to rural workers for fulling, carding, spinning, weaving and dyeing wool, linen and cotton, before selling the finished products at local markets or taking them to London for shipping out. The system became highly developed in the West Riding of Yorkshire and parts of east Lancashire and Derbyshire, leading to a decline in the wool trade in traditional areas like Devon and Norfolk. Improved transport pushed forward this regional specialisation which in turn further increased efficiencies, producing higher levels of cooperation, competition, innovation and standardisation. A patchwork of late medieval regional agrarian economies was being gradually integrated into a single commercial capitalist market system.

Specialisation extended into other areas too. For most of human history households had been largely self-sufficient: families would grow, process and cook most of their own food, make their own clothes, build their own shelter, and so on. Naturally this varied through time and place, but while there were always a few specialist workers the overwhelming majority of people applied themselves to a variety of tasks, divided among the family, in order to fill their needs. Even those apprenticed to a particular trade would generally combine that work with other tasks. Another historic change in eighteenth-century Britain, therefore, was the gradual disappearance of self-sufficiency in favour of specialised occupations. This was of immense significance as it also facilitated the transition to a cash-based economy. A woman who had previously baked all her bread, butchered her meat and made her own clothes could now work as a frame-knitter and use her pay to buy in the goods and services she needed. This specialisation went hand in hand with urban growth, and it is easy to see that it was an important precursor to an industrialised economy.[11]

The medieval system of apprenticeships remained important but it too was breaking down along with the powers of the guilds and worshipful companies that had regulated much of the manufacturing trades for centuries; this transition was crucial as the Industrial Revolution would need both the skills of the time-served apprentices and the flexibility that came with the loosening of regulation.

Another important change in the nature of work was the standardisation of production. As we have seen, from the late 1600s a wide variety of crafts developed in Britain; over the course of the next century many of these crafts found ways to be more productive by standardising both methods of production and the products themselves. Bricks, iron fireplaces, nails, glass, pottery and even entire houses (think of all those Georgian terraces with identical doors, windows, fittings, firebacks and stairs) began to be made in standard forms, while people like George Ravenscroft and Josiah Wedgwood standardised the production of glass and pottery. Shipbuilders began to adopt standard methods of construction so that craft could be built and repaired in different yards and ports. In the manufacture of everything from cloth dyes to beaver-skin hats and fish and whale oil, standardisation and a degree of mechanisation were being introduced.

Crafts of all kinds were made more efficient through the increased use of water power; traditionally used for grinding corn, water-powered mills were now increasingly constructed to power fulling stocks, paper-grinders, forging hammers and bellows. This required purpose-built or adapted buildings as well as engineering skills to make driveshafts, gearings, bearings and cams to transfer power from the waterwheels to the appropriate devices; millwrights and skilled metalworkers became highly sought after.[12]

We have already mentioned the high wages earned by the

British. In 1725 workers in England earned three times as much as workers in Italy and Spain; this was a remarkable turnaround from 200 years previously when the Mediterranean had been the centre of economic power. While southern Europeans now struggled to earn a subsistence wage, the ordinary British household had money to spare. The first effect was an improved diet. The British ate meat, cheese and eggs regularly, as well as the basic requirements of bread and vegetables, and they indulged themselves with tea, sugar and beer. They also bought items of furniture, crockery, cutlery, bed linen and clothing that had been beyond the reach of their grandparents; household inventories from the mid-eighteenth century show widespread ownership of all these goods, as well as clocks, ornaments and books, all of which became more affordable through the course of the century.

Although Britain was becoming a prosperous society, by modern standards life was hard for the majority, and unremittingly harsh for the poorest. The Whig aristocracy who had emerged triumphant from the Glorious Revolution of the 1690s ruled the land, while a growing middle class of lower gentry emerged into positions of local influence. British society was, however, divided in a way that is central to our story. The civil wars of the 1640s had seen a bitter religious division into Anglicans (and their equivalents in Wales and Scotland) and those who became known as Dissenters or Nonconformists. After the restoration of the monarchy in 1660 Nonconformism was constrained in a series of parliamentary acts, which became known as the Clarendon Code. Congregationalists, Presbyterians, Baptists, Unitarians, Quakers and any others who refused to acknowledge the Church of England as the ultimate Christian authority in the land were barred from public office and military service. Nonconformist ministers were forbidden to come within five miles of incorporated towns and were not allowed to establish places of worship. The restrictions were eased only slightly by the Act of Toleration of 1689 which allowed Nonconformists to worship together; the remainder of the Clarendon Code remained in place until the nineteenth century.[13]

In practice this meant that a large swathe of respectable society was not permitted to take part in public administration or to get involved in politics or military leadership. At the same time these religious groups formed strong internal bonds fostered by mutual trust and support that led them to develop their own parallel social and economic networks. Despite, or perhaps because of, its separation from 'polite' society, Nonconformism flourished, particularly in those newly established towns in the Midlands and the north of England that fell outside the restrictions of the Clarendon Code.

Making up a large proportion of the 'middling sort', as Defoe called them, Nonconformists were noted for their lack of ostentation. Company records show how little those who went into commerce and manufacturing took out of the businesses; instead profits were reinvested to buy plant or improve infrastructure. While frugality was an important part of life, business was done on the basis of a handshake, putting great value on a reputation for decency and straight dealing.

The countervailing truth to the moral piety of the Nonconformists was the importance of slavery to British prosperity. Slave ships left Liverpool and Bristol filled with cheap goods to exchange for slaves in West Africa. Millions of Africans (the total is thought to be around 12 million over a period of 250 years) were then shipped across to the Americas in appalling conditions to work on sugar and tobacco plantations; here the ships were loaded with the produce of those plantations to be sold to an eager British market.[14] For the Africans it was a catastrophe, for the British slave merchants it was a highly lucrative system, and it was an important element in the British economy. In the second half of the eighteenth century the majority of British overseas income came from the goods traded through the Atlantic Slave Triangle. The elegant Georgian terraces of Bristol and Bath, the imposing waterfront of Liverpool, the merchants' quarter of Glasgow, all owed their existence to the slave trade.

It is important to note too that while the commercialisation of society grew apace the political and social situation in Britain was, in many ways, unstable. Governments changed with alarming rapidity – eight times between 1757 and 1770 – and successive administrations seemed not to know quite how to deal with their colonial subjects, mishandling the American colonists disastrously. From 1750 onwards the enclosure of common land was causing immense social disruption in the countryside, sending poor people into towns and cities in search of work, while prices rose steeply after the end of the war in 1763. There was chronic social unrest which regularly broke into open rebellion. Benjamin Franklin lived in Britain in the 1760s and early 1770s and observed: 'I have seen within a Year, Riots in the Country about Corn, Riots about Elections, Riots about Workhouses, Riots of Colliers, Riots of Weavers, Riots of Coalheavers, Riots of Sawyers, Riots of Sailors, Riots of Wilkites . . .'[15] The commercialisation of society was a painful process involving disruption, destitution, and a sense that no one was quite in control.

Increasing prosperity created a continually expanding demand for goods, particularly among the growing urban population. The growth of craft trades was able to satisfy this demand, while improving supply through specialisation, standardisation and more efficient systems. All this was based on the prosperity of the wool trade and the growing use of coal for fuel. The other important dynamic in British society was the emergence of thrusting artisan and merchant classes eager to better themselves – so called human capital.

The growing commercialism created a more fluid society as people saw that it was possible to gain an advantage in life through bettering yourself, not merely through the accident of one's birth. So, while British working people were able to afford better diets and manufactured items they also began to spend money on acquiring knowledge and skills, both for themselves and their families. This desire to learn was of immense significance: people bought apprenticeships for their children, learned to read and write and improved their arithmetic. In the second half of the eighteenth century literacy rates in England were 53 per cent; in southern and eastern Europe 20 per cent; in France and Germany 35 per cent. Only the Netherlands had a higher literacy rate at 68 per cent.[16] While reading was often done for pleasure – the price of books fell dramatically during the century – numeracy skills were learned for work. Engineers, traders, instrument-makers, merchants and skilled sailors all needed to be able to handle figures or geometry with confidence. People knew that skilled workers like stonemasons, iron-makers, brewers, clockmakers, shipwrights, glassmakers and carpenters could earn at least 60 per cent more than the unskilled, provided they had served their apprenticeships. Families put up money at the start of the term and in return the master would feed and house the apprentice while teaching him the skills and secrets of his trade. Nearly two-thirds of young Englishmen went through the apprentice system in the eighteenth century.[17]

While these were the main factors that encouraged change and innovation, it is also important to see how barriers to change were being dissolved. The fierce religious adherences of the seventeenth century had declined, along with fears that innovation or improvement offended against nature and the Will of God, while the death of Queen Anne in 1714 brought any serious attempts at religious persecution to an end.[18] The growth of the insurance industry from the 1660s onwards also shows how people looked to Mammon rather than God to save them from destitution. The move away from the medieval system spread to trade, where laws designed to ensure standards of quality and to give protection to artisans and workers in their native towns were gradually loosened or quietly ignored. Meanwhile, in the new towns like the unincorporated Manchester and Birmingham, which lay outside the old medieval system, trade and manufacture flourished unhindered by regulation.

As well as general prosperity and an increasingly well-trained and educated workforce, there are other aspects of mid-eighteenth-century Britain that are fundamental to our story. One is finance and banking. In the wake of the disastrous naval defeat at Beachy Head in 1690, the government had set up the Bank of England as an independent institution to raise money for the Exchequer – a strategy that proved immensely successful in stabilising the financial system. The principal debtor in the British economy had always been the state. It was therefore in the government's interests to keep interest rates as low as possible, while also allowing a decent return on investments. Governments sometimes offered high rates of return in order to be able to borrow money – especially in times of war – but as the stability of the British economy increased, the official interest rate was gradually lowered. In the 1750s the prime minister Henry Pelham consolidated all government debt into one account, which paved the way for the formation in 1757 of the Consolidated Stock (known as Consol). The long-term Consol rate of 3 per cent gave stability to the system, dictated interest rates elsewhere in the economy and encouraged long-term investment – with negligible inflation, funds could simply be left in companies to mature.

Financial investment suffered a severe setback in 1720 when speculation in the shares of the South Sea Company, which had taken on the whole of the government debt in return for a monopoly of trade in South America, inflated the market until its eventual collapse. The resulting legislation restricted joint-stock companies to those authorised by Parliament, limited the number of investors in any enterprise to six, and made all partners individually responsible for all its debts. These restrictions might have fatally restricted industrial enterprise, but they forced into being modest yet ambitious enterprises founded and supported by networks of families and trusted associates.

One of the potential barriers to a functioning commercial and industrial economy was the lack of a national banking system. In the early eighteenth century trade was the dominant financial enterprise; London banking houses were geared up to allow people to deposit money, which was then loaned to shippers and merchants. While the Bank of England was set up in 1694 to

manage the government's finances and deal with large-scale transactions with London bankers, this left the rest of the country
without a financial infrastructure.

The main financial instrument in the early 1700s was the bill
of exchange, drawn on a London bank. This could be transferred
from one merchant to another and redeemed at the bank itself.
The obvious limitation of this system was that it didn't provide
the notes and coins that were needed for everyday transactions.
This began to be overcome when merchants in country towns
started to accept the bills and give currency in exchange – taking
commission along the way – and thereby giving birth to a de facto
national banking system. Private banks operating on this principle
became widespread by the 1760s, as goldsmiths, textile-makers
and associations of cattle drovers all set up their own banks. The
foundation of joint-stock banks outside London was prohibited,
so country banks had corresponding London houses and would
lend money by issuing bills of exchange drawn on those banks.
This quasi-national system was particularly useful in directing
money where it was needed; farmers, for example, often had money
to deposit in late autumn, which was the time when manufacturers
were in need of funds to settle end-of-year accounts.[19]

By the mid-eighteenth century there were developments that we
now recognise as important stepping stones towards an industrial
economy. Iron-smelting in blast furnaces had come to Britain in
the fourteenth century and become well established in areas like
the Weald in Kent, the Forest of Dean, Staffordshire and east
Shropshire, with steel production in the Tyne Valley and South
Yorkshire. In 1709 Abraham Darby became the first ironmaster to
power a blast furnace with coal instead of charcoal, opening the
way for an expansion in iron-making, and in the 1740s Benjamin
Huntsman of Sheffield invented the crucible method of steel-
making. Craftspeople also found ways to switch from charcoal to
coal in a range of other industries like brewing, salt-making, sugar
refining, baking and distilling; the production of bricks, tiles, glass,

pottery and lime; the manufacture of chemicals including alum, copperas, saltpetre and starch; the processing, dyeing and bleaching of cloth; calendaring, paper-making and hot-metal printing. By 1750 manufacturers were using around 30 per cent of the coal consumed in Britain.[20] While coal produced heat it did not yet produce power, but this began to change with the Newcomen steam engine, or fire engine as it was then known. First installed in 1712, it was one of the greatest inventions in human history. Nevertheless, its huge use of coal limited its use to pumping water out of mines.

By the mid-eighteenth century Britain had begun to develop a manufacturing infrastructure and expertise, so that when the famous machines of the Industrial Revolution were invented, they were rapidly put into productive action. At the same time craft industries were being turned into manufactories as, for example, in the glass trade. Venice had been the centre of European glass-making for centuries, with English makers producing inferior versions of the famous cristallo. Glass-maker and merchant George Ravenscroft lived in Venice in the 1650s and on his return to England tried new methods of glass production. In 1676 he discovered that the addition of lead oxide gave the glass added brightness and lustre, and also made it easier to cut.[21] Ravenscroft was able to make lead crystal and, within twenty years of the end of his patent in 1681, more than a hundred English glass-makers were following his example. Britain soon overtook Venice as the centre of European glass-making, producing large volumes at low cost and high quality and utility.

The putting-out system that worked so well in textiles was extended into other trades. Merchants would buy pig iron, for example, and take it to forges to be made into spades, knives, plough-shares and nails, which they would later collect and take to market. But putting-out was beginning to change too, with some rural workers finding it more profitable to move into town and set up small workshops, taking on other workers or going into partnerships.

At the same time one particular product was beginning to

make its mark on British society and the national economy. Cotton cloths known as calicoes, brought from Bengal by the East India Company, grew so popular that they were banned in 1720 to protect the domestic wool trade, opening the way for home calico production from imported raw cotton. This growing trade was based around Manchester, the traditional centre of linen-making. By 1739 *Gentleman's Magazine* was telling its readers: 'The manufacture of cotton, mixed and plain, is arrived at so great a perfection within these twenty years, that we not only make enough for our own consumption, but supply our colonies, and many of the nations of Europe.'

The diversity of textiles and their origins is perfectly illustrated in Daniel Defoe's description of a country grocer and his wife in 1726:

> For his clothing . . . instead of buying the cloth from Yorkshire, perhaps he has it a little finer and so his comes from Wiltshire and his stockings . . . are of Worsted and so they come from Nottingham . . . his wife . . . not dressed over fine yet she must have something decent . . . her gown, a plain English mantua silk manufactured at Spitalfields . . . her under-petticoat, a piece of black callamanco made at Norwich – quilted at home if she be a good housewife but the quilting of cotton from Manchester, or cotton wool from abroad . . . her stockings from Tewksbury, if ordinary – from Leicester if woven . . . her muslin from the foreign trade; likewise her linen . . . her wrapper . . . a piece of Irish linen printed at London . . . the furniture of their house . . . the hangings are made at Kidderminster, dyed in the country, and painted, or watered, at London . . . the curtains from Taunton and Exeter or of camblets from Norwich . . . the blankets from Whitney in Oxfordshire; the rugs from Westmoreland and Yorkshire; the sheets, of good linen, from Ireland.[22]

The changing economy of Britain was most evident in the north of England. Along the Tyne in the mid-eighteenth century you would see hundreds of boats taking coal out to colliers moored further downstream, with shipyards among the wharves and jetties and salt pans along the river. In Coalbrookdale and South Yorkshire there were impressive ironworks, and outside Leeds and Halifax, and in Lancashire, ranks of weavers' cottages. But most craft production was hidden away – the stocking-knitters, spinners, weavers, nail-makers and iron-forgers all worked within dwellings or small workshops. Only the coal and metal mines would have stood out against the landscape. The cities of the north were small compared to London and acted principally as markets and hubs for rural industries, sending goods on to merchants overseas or in the capital. Connections between them were only slowly developing.

Nevertheless, Britain in 1750 was an international commercial powerhouse with a growing manufacturing sector; the prosperity of its people was driving efficiencies and increasing production in agriculture and in manufacture. Britain had far outstripped its European rivals in the exploitation of its natural resources and the organisation of industrial and agricultural production. Meanwhile, urban workshops were providing training grounds for engineers of all kinds. Their work and the steady improvement of lathes, stamps, draw-benches and presses, went on without much outside attention – in fact many of these incremental innovations were kept secret. But these second- and third-generation artisans – literate, numerate and with the lure of expanding demand – were everywhere tinkering with the tools and machines of their different trades, figuring out how to make things work better.

This background to the great events that were to come shows us a dynamic society in a state of continual change, far removed from its medieval roots and pushing forward into an unknown future. The condition of Britain in the mid- to late eighteenth century should help us to answer the key question: why did the Industrial Revolution happen in this place and at this time? Historians have pointed to four particular factors or trends that came together for the first time in history.[23]

Firstly, in eighteenth-century Britain barriers to change were dramatically reduced. The medieval world view had been based on the fatalism of Augustine's doctrine of predestination – believers could not alter God's will, it was their Christian duty to endure. In the eighteenth century most people still saw the world as the enactment of God's will but they no longer interpreted their faith fatalistically; instead they believed that God rewarded those who used their talents to change their circumstances. While change brings with it social upheaval and was therefore rigorously oppressed by rulers throughout history – Ming China is a stark example of this – British landowners who governed the country were not threatened by industry; indeed many stood to gain from it. Although not overly interested in industry per se, Parliament was deeply concerned with promoting commercial power and so resisted legal and physical attempts to halt innovation. Just as important, resistance to labour-saving machines was overcome by showing that saving labour did not necessarily mean unemployment, but efficiency and greater production – the cotton industry in particular, with its vast potential for expansion, was vital in demonstrating that efficiency meant more jobs, not fewer.

On an intellectual level the long-held belief that the ancient world was the most important source of wisdom was also breaking down. The breathtaking work of Isaac Newton showed that modern humanity could outdo ancient authority, while instruments like telescopes and microscopes revealed facts about the world that were utterly new. This encouraged people to believe that discovery and innovation, rather than obedience to ancient authority, was the path that humanity should follow. The Industrial Revolution was a revolution of the mind as much as a technological leap forward.

We have already discussed the second trend – the change to specialised working. From the late seventeenth century workers were able to specialise because they could buy in goods and services from others. Historians have argued that this coordination of specialised work and the availability of goods and services to buy marked the birth of modernity.

The third factor was the interplay of high wage costs, cheap capital and cheap coal. High wages provided a ready market for manufactured goods, thereby encouraging more efficient production methods, while producers were keen on innovations that used coal-fired power to reduce labour costs, and cheap capital enabled others to invest in long-term industrial ventures.

The fourth and final factor brings us back to the inventors themselves. By the middle of the eighteenth century Britain had been home to craft trades for three or four generations. Made rich on the wool trade, the British had diversified into other industries, initially lagging behind their Continental rivals, but eager to learn (partly through welcoming skilled refugees) and rapidly making up ground. Second- and third-generation artisans were steeped in the techniques of their trade, and in the needs of the markets they served. The new fluidity in society enabled those who could earn a good living from their trade to buy goods and services to get a more comfortable life for their families; these were well within reach of the skilled artisan, while the craftsman who was prepared to innovate might prosper like never before.

At no other time and place in history had these four factors coincided for a sustained period. Ancient Mesopotamia and Egypt and the classical world of Greece and Rome had produced extraordinary technical achievements as well as a thriving intellectual culture, but the separation between work and wealth and the availability of cheap or even slave labour gave little incentive to produce labour-saving devices; instead inventors like Hero of Alexandria made steam-driven toys to amuse their friends. Roman construction work was hugely impressive but iron production was low quality and sailing ships were badly rigged; there was no harness suitable for using horses as draft animals and no stirrups, while water power was used only sporadically and was inexpertly exploited.[24]

At different times in its history China had also been a centre of dazzling innovation but our medieval forebears did not wake one morning to see a fleet of Chinese steamships, complete with cannon and telescopes, and with a cargo of clocks, pistols, locks, jennies, locomotives, roller printers and cheap cotton looming on the horizon. A single powerful authority viewed innovation with suspicion because of its potential for social disruption. Both the Ming and Qing dynasties in China (1368–1917) favoured orderliness over technical advance.[25] The British experience gives good evidence that change does indeed cause social disruption; the advent of the full industrial economy brought upheaval, dislocation, and social rearrangement on a scale that had never been experienced before. The 'pandaemonium' of Milton, the satanic mills of Blake, and the 'sublime smoak' of Arthur Young, the great chronicler of eighteenth-century England, were about to be unleashed on the world.[26]

This helps us to understand why late eighteenth-century Britain was so well placed to be the crucible of the Industrial Revolution. It may be that historians in 1,000 years will be able to point to a time when the momentum of technological innovation created by the Industrial Revolution finally came to an end. But there seems no immediate prospect of that; instead technology-based industrialisation is spreading to all corners of the world. We will begin the story of the revolution by looking at the role that inventors played in this unique episode.

I. Invention

'The age is running mad after innovation; all the business of the world is to be done in a new way.'

DR JOHNSON, 1783

1. The Watershed

By the 1760s the stage was set for the great deluge that we have come to call the Industrial Revolution. While some key inventions had been made in the previous sixty or so years, the innovations, devices and processes that occured in the half-century after 1770 are those that changed the course of history. But before looking at what they were and who invented them, it is important to see them in the context of their immediate precursors.

In 1709 the ironmaster Abraham Darby of Coalbrookdale, Shropshire, developed a method for using coal to produce cast iron in blast furnaces. Up until then charcoal had been the only suitable fuel, as coal contained impurities which ruined the iron. Ironmasters had tried to solve the problem for decades, and were becoming increasingly desperate as wood for charcoal was becoming scarce and expensive. Darby was an experienced metalfounder and knew that Shropshire coal might be pure enough. He turned the coal into coke and found that, with care, he could make perfectly good cast iron – production was no longer limited by the number of trees available.

At almost the same time Thomas Newcomen, a metalworker based in Dartmouth in Devon, was putting the final touches to a single-piston engine, driven by steam, for pumping water from mines. The world's first ever continually working steam engine was installed at Dudley in 1712.

Around twenty years later, in 1733, John Kay, a textile machinery maker and serial inventor from Bury in Lancashire, patented the flying shuttle. This extraordinary device revolutionised the craft of weaving by automatically throwing the weft thread back and forth across the loom where previously it had been passed by hand. The productivity of each weaver was dramatically increased.

All three of these innovations were of primary importance. What Darby and Kay did was to increase pressure further along the productive system, while Newcomen provided the enormous first step forward in a journey that James Watt would follow. Over the next few decades increases in the efficiency of the economy, the expanding population, more investment and spending all added to the demand for technical innovations and, crucially, provided financial incentives for innovators.

The dam began to crack in the 1760s. First came the spinning jenny developed by James Hargreaves, perfected by around 1764 and patented in 1770. Kay's flying shuttle had vastly increased the capacity of cotton looms and therefore the demand for cotton yarn, which hand-operated spinning wheels could not meet. After a slow start, by the 1760s the flying shuttle had spread throughout the cotton districts of Lancashire putting yarn in continual short supply. The spinning jenny opened this bottleneck by allowing one person to operate first eight, then sixteen, then up to 120 spinning wheels at the same time.

In 1769 Richard Arkwright patented his spinning frame which achieved the same ends through a different principle, and which was powered from a waterwheel. People sometimes wonder why improving the spinning of cotton thread should have had such a major impact on industrialisation, but cotton was the shock industry of its day – the equivalent of computing and the Internet today. The cotton industry's vast potential for expansion rewarded continual innovation; it also demonstrated that rather than throwing people out of work, better machines created employment.

In the same year as Arkwright patented his spinning frame, the Scottish engineer-cum-surveyor James Watt obtained a patent for an improved steam engine. Watt's stated intention was to save on the huge fuel consumption of Newcomen engines by condensing steam in a separate chamber from the main cylinder. (Unlike the jenny and the spinning frame, Watt's engine was not yet built – he had patented an idea that he had tested, but not a fully working engine.) Once Watt's first engine was built in 1776, it became clear that while Newcomen's engine had been restricted to pumping water, this engine could be used much more widely. Mechanics all over the country began to adapt Newcomen engines with Watt condensers – either illegally or under licence.

Meanwhile, by 1772 Richard Arkwright had installed his spinning frames, together with picking, washing, carding and packing facilities, in a five-storey mill in Cromford in Derbyshire. Factories of this kind had existed before, but Arkwright opened his at a perfect time. Cotton had become more and more popular among consumers and, as mechanisation reduced prices and increased quality, the industry entered a virtuous circle of increasing demand and supply that lasted for over a century. Arkwright's pioneering powered cotton mill was rapidly copied so that the opening of the Cromford mill marked the beginning of the factory age.

Cromford was powered by a single waterwheel, in common with iron forges, grain mills, gunpowder-makers and breweries, which were increasingly concentrating their machinery in large buildings and powering them with water. Waterwheels were ideal for driving machinery as they gave smooth rotary motion, while the Newcomen and early Watt engines simply moved a beam up and down. But waterwheels needed rivers and suitable sites were fast disappearing. In 1780 Matthew Wasbrough, John Steed and James Pickard, working in partnership in Birmingham, patented a crank and flywheel device and attached it to a steam engine to run a flour mill. James Watt believed the three men had stolen his own idea and, with his colleague William Murdoch, rapidly made his own rotary device – the sun and planet gear – which was patented in 1781. Boulton & Watt (the company Watt had founded with his investment partner Matthew Boulton) now became the country's prime engine-makers, installing rotary steam engines in mills, workshops and factories.

*

It is important to understand that these inventions were not happening in a vacuum; they were propelled into being by the forces around them. The British economy was developing apace through more effective organisation, standardisation and production processes; but at each point along the way bottlenecks appeared – such as shortages of charcoal, cotton yarn and water power – that had to be cleared. Key to the period from the 1760s to the 1820s was the intensification of relations between different industries, born out of the contacts between industrialist entrepreneurs as well as the geographical proximity of the industries. Such interaction also emerged from the technologies themselves as the spread of textile machinery, for example, depended on the availability of cheap iron and steel, and Watt's steam engines depended on high-quality castings. In fact, the making of machine components was a major area of improvement and ironmasters like John Wilkinson, the Darbys of Coalbrookdale, Samuel Walker and the Carron Works in Falkirk gained a reputation for the quality and accuracy of their engineering. And it was the symbiosis between different branches of industry that allowed Watt's engine to be radically improved as soon as his patent expired.

Around 1779 Samuel Crompton, a Lancashire spinner, weaver and inventor, perfected his spinning mule. Crompton did not patent his machine for fear of infringing Arkwright's patent, but it was rapidly adopted by the Lancashire cotton industry. The mule, a highly complex hybrid of the jenny and the frame, was the final part of the answer posed by the flying shuttle – how to produce enough high-quality cotton yarn to feed the vast and growing demands of the cotton cloth-making industry. Mules could not only run 1,000 spindles off one device, they could produce the finest yarn at the highest quality. They became the dominant spinning machines in the textile trade for the next 150 years.

The next major technical breakthrough came in iron production. While Darby had shown how to make cast iron in a blast furnace using coke, making wrought iron or bar iron involved a further process that still required charcoal. Iron-forgers tried for decades to find ways round this, and in 1783 Henry Cort from Fareham in Hampshire finally came up with the answer. His method, known as puddling and rolling, allowed forgers to use coke, and finally freed iron production from its dependence on charcoal. Iron production expanded dramatically, and iron could now be put to work in the service of industry.

The demand for mechanisation and power was now reaching into all parts of productive industry, turning cottage crafts into factory-based production. Technically astute engineers moved from one field to another, looking for opportunities. The patent system, for so long a chaotic bear pit, was gradually becoming favourable to inventors as judges began to understand the value of rewarding innovation. Between 1700 and 1740 the average number of patents awarded annually was fewer than five; from 1740 to 1780 the average was nineteen; from 1780 to 1800 this increased to fifty-two.

These figures not only show an upsurge in innovation – and in the opportunities for inventors – but they demonstrate how the culture of invention had been let loose and how the patent system, once used to block invention, provided an incentive for continual improvement. James Watt, for example, managed to get his original patent extended to 1800, but he knew that he had to keep refining his engine because he was competing with other inventors and engineers. A critical momentum of innovation had been reached.

While Watt continued to make ground-breaking improvements throughout the 1780s and 1790s, including parallel motion gearing, a reciprocating engine and the centrifugal governor, the one area that he did not explore was the use of high-pressure steam, which he considered dangerous and unlikely to work. But within months of the expiry of Watt's patent in 1800 the Cornish engineer Richard Trevithick ran a carriage driven by a high-pressure steam engine up Camborne Hill. In 1804 he cemented his genius by running the world's first steam locomotive along nine miles of track at the Pen-y-darren ironworks at Merthyr Tydfil. Trevithick showed what many had believed: that high-pressure steam could be used safely, and that high-pressure engines would be light enough to be carried by the vehicles they propelled.

In time-honoured fashion, Trevithick's success led to another major improvement. The rails along which his locomotive ran were, like most trackways, made of wood occasionally topped with iron strips. This worked for horse-drawn wagons but could not bear the weight of locomotives. Cast iron was inadequate too, and the slightest incline proved difficult for engines. Into this potential bottleneck stepped George Stephenson, who combined the talents of engine builder with surveyor, rail-maker and visionary entrepreneur. It was Stephenson who, in 1825, built the Stockton to Darlington line and its locomotives, and who then built the Liverpool to Manchester railway, and who won the 1829 Rainhill trials with the most famous steam engine in history, the *Rocket*. After 1829 no one doubted that steam locomotion was the wonder of the world and the future of transport.[1]

So, by 1804 a series of inventors had shown that coal could be used to create mechanical energy: for the first time in history mechanical works could be reliably carried out by machines not powered by human or animal muscle; with cheap and plentiful coal there was no limit to the amount of energy available. Other inventions – the powered loom, the Jacquard device, the self-acting mule, the Fourdrinier paper-maker, gas lighting, the miners' safety lamp – followed rapidly as the steam-powered mechanisation of production spread into different industries and the conversion to a coal-based industry was completed. Innovations continued to come, but the essential groundwork had been laid in just forty years.

2. Inventors and Inventing

By 1760 Britain had developed a highly effective agricultural, commercial and manufacturing economy far outstripping its Continental rivals. Yet its growth was still limited by the natural resources available – timber, water, land and animals. As we have seen, these constraints were beginning to break down, particularly through the prodigious use of coal, but the great breakthrough of the next decades was converting coal into mechanical energy, and to use that energy for powering a range of mechanical devices. To do this, Britain needed inventors.

In the sixteenth and seventeenth centuries Britain had been behind the Continent in mining and metallurgy, the quality of textiles and a whole range of craft technologies. Ideas, many believed, came from abroad, along with the skills to put them into practice. It was Britain's acceptance of its own inferiority in these areas that began to change things, through successive governments welcoming skilled refugees from Europe. Flemish weavers, Italian silk-throwers and alum-makers, Huguenot glass-makers, German metallurgists and gun-makers were encouraged to settle in Britain. The 1572 St Bartholomew's Day massacre in Paris, the 1576 Spanish sacking of Antwerp, the Thirty Years War (1618–48), the expulsion of Huguenots from France in 1685 all brought skilled artisans to England. As well as the push of religious persecution and conflict, there was the pull of prosperity. Britain was a growing market for high-quality goods, and with an underdeveloped domestic industrial base immigrant workers could make a good living. In the late seventeenth century British manufacturers like Abraham Darby even visited Europe to lure workers to England.

It was this adoption of skills from abroad and the training of artisan apprentices that enabled the country to diversify from the wool trade and work its way to the forefront of technological innovation in Europe.[1]

There were several reasons why the British carried this off so brilliantly. By the mid-eighteenth century Britain had developed a large pool of skilled workshop labour, working with an increasingly sophisticated set of tools. This pool of workers was continually renewed and was geographically widespread. While we tend to focus on a few brilliant inventors, it was vital that there were able craftsmen in every part of the nation. As most inventors did not build machines for sale but licensed their use, inventions were turned into working machines by skilled mechanics, whose presence throughout the country was an important factor in the rapid spread of technology.

The characteristic British inventor and entrepreneur of the eighteenth century might be called the 'artisan plus'. These were men who were trained as artisans but were both ambitious and had access to funds for investment. By and large they were not part of the higher social orders with their traditions of public and military service, their social snobbery, and their conservative attitudes. Instead they were a distinct group of independent resourceful folk: some were the sons of craftsmen who had bettered themselves and artisans who had grown up in the trade; others came from commercial merchant backgrounds. These new men formed clubs and associations, like the Manchester Literary and Philosophical Society, and they came together in Nonconformist meetings. What kept these men in industry was often a lack of alternatives. A seat in Parliament or the highest levels of government service required wealth and connections beyond their reach, as did a career in the army or navy; and Nonconformists were still barred from both higher education and government service. In industry or commerce, however, they could become powerful people at local, regional and national levels.

Looking more closely at the most important innovators of the

Industrial Revolution we see striking similarities in background and status. Almost all of them had been apprenticed or worked in manufactories. Thomas Newcomen was an apprentice ironmonger; John Kay, loom-maker; Abraham Darby, maltster; Richard Arkwright, wig-maker and barber; Richard Trevithick, mining engineer. James Hargreaves and Samuel Crompton were both cotton spinners, Henry Cort was an iron-maker while James Watt was the son of a shipwright. Of all these inventors only James Watt had any contact with scientific experts in his field, and that came through informal academic networks in Scotland; and of the most significant inventors only Edmund Cartwright, inventor of the powered loom, had a university education. As Bernard Mandeville, one of the most acute observers of the early stages of industrialisation, wrote in 1724: 'They are very seldom the same Sort of People, those that invent Arts, and Improvements in them, and those that enquire into the Reason of Things: this latter is most commonly practis'd by such, as are idle, and indolent, that are fond of Retirement, hate Business, and take delight in Speculation: whereas none succeed oftener in the first, than active, stirring, and laborious Men, such as will put their hand to the Plough, try Experiments, and give all their Attention to what they are about.'[2]

If we spread our net wider than this small group, we find much the same social profile, but increased numbers allow us to build a more detailed picture. Recent analysis has shown that inventors were not drawn in equal proportion from every social class; instead two tendencies stand out.[3] The first is that while the aristocrats, gentry and clergy contributed little to industrial invention, wealth was a factor. Secondly, the 'middle' classes comprising both merchants and capitalists, and shopkeepers, manufacturers and artisans, made up just 25 per cent of the English population but supplied nearly 70 per cent of inventors.

So much for the inventors themselves, but other factors created a climate that helped build the momentum of innovation. One cause was that industrialisation took place in a relatively small geographical area. This area, bounded by Shropshire, Staffordshire,

Birmingham, Leicester, extended through Nottingham and Derby, up to South and West Yorkshire and across to south Lancashire, is at most a hundred miles across. Navigable waterways were plentiful and an improving road system, while not always easy to use, was available; a comprehensive network of canals was quickly added from 1761 onwards. Satellite areas such as Newcastle and Durham, central Scotland, South Wales and Cornwall were all readily accessible by coastal shipping as was the major market of London. Political unity and cohesion meant few tolls or tariffs between places of production, supply and consumption. (In France, in contrast, tolls were levied at cripplingly frequent intervals, making long-distance trade extremely difficult.)

Another factor was the financial gain to be won from innovation. We may see these inventions as contributing to a historic change in society, but the inventors' overwhelming motivation was financial reward. Either through developing their own business or by licensing or selling their patents, men like Watt, Crompton and Arkwright invented in order to make money. And even though a grounding in, say, metallurgy would seem to push an innovator towards making inventions in that industry, this was often not the case. Once they had acquired sufficient technical expertise, inventors became 'professional' and worked across different fields. As the cotton industry expanded more than any other, offering greater financial rewards, it is not surprising that it was here that the most important inventions were made.[4]

Despite the prospect of financial gains for inventors, a crucial aspect of the innovations of this classic period of the Industrial Revolution was their modest scale. The artisan inventors were not, in the main, supported by large-scale investors and had to work within severe limits. Devices like the Newcomen engine, the flying shuttle and the spinning jenny and frame could be built in a workshop or even the room of a house, while the materials – timber, brass and iron components, oakum and wire – were available to smiths and joiners everywhere at relatively low expense. Indeed the main expense was time; it took Thomas Newcomen

Eureka Moment: Thomas Newcomen

'For ten consecutive years Mr Newcomen worked at this fire-machine which never would have exhibited the desired effect, unless Almighty God had caused a lucky incident to take place. It happened at the last attempt to make the model work that a more than wished-for effect was suddenly caused by the following strange event. The cold water, which was allowed to flow into a lead-case embracing the cylinder, pierced through an imperfection which had been mended with tin-solder. The heat of the steam caused the tin-solder to melt and thus opened up a way for the cold water, which rushed into the cylinder and immediately condensed the steam, creating such a vacuum that the weight, attached to the little beam, which was supposed to represent the weight of the water in the pumps, proved to be so insufficient that the air, which pressed with a tremendous power on the piston, caused its chain to break and the piston to crush the bottom of the cylinder as well as the lid of the small boiler. The hot water which flowed everywhere thus convinced the very senses of the onlookers that they had discovered an incomparably powerful force which had hitherto been entirely unknown in nature, – at least no one had suspected that it could originate in this way.'

Marten Triewald, 1734[5]

around a decade to come up with a practical working engine, while James Hargreaves said that he 'laboured for six years' to get his jenny to work. James Watt's steam engine needed a greater invest-ment in engineering materials and the money was put up by his sole partner Matthew Boulton, while Richard Trevithick had the initial support of two investors, Andrew Vivian and Davies Gilbert.

Despite the positive factors for inventors, barriers to innova-tion remained. The horrendously complex and imprecise patent law (see Chapter 3) was a difficulty, as were the restrictions enforced by worshipful companies in industries like wool, silk, printing, instrument-making and cutlery production, which guarded their special privileges closely. Because cotton was an undeveloped industry it could thrive and innovate in the unincorporated city in Manchester, while mining and smelting and casting of metals were historically relatively unregulated.

Obstacles to innovation came from legal and social restrictions. In the late sixteenth century William Lee left England for France because of resistance to his stocking frame. In 1638 ribbon looms were banned by the Crown and in 1701 and 1720 restrictions and punitive tariffs were brought in on sales of cotton cloth and printed calico in order to protect the native wool industry. Although all of these restrictions were later overturned or amended, some hostility to innovation remained throughout the eighteenth century: the flying shuttle was effectively repressed for thirty years by threats of violence and there were fierce riots in Lancashire in 1779 and in 1792; most notoriously from 1811 to 1816 the so-called Luddites destroyed machinery throughout Britain's industrial areas. However, these attempts to halt mechanisation were ultimately unsuccessful; more and more mills were built and machines installed, and mill-workers were not inclined to support hand-spinners and weavers in their protests. And, although the list of disturbances is long, new machinery was installed for the most part remarkably calmly.

Legal attempts to resist technology were also generally unsuccessful, with courts and Parliament taking the side of the industrialists – in 1769 Parliament passed a law making destruction of machinery punishable by death. Petitions from hand-cotton-spinners in 1780 and wool-combers in 1794 to ban new machinery failed, and in 1809 ancient laws governing the wool industry were repealed. 1814 saw the repeal of the Statute of Artificers (1563), which had regulated the supply of labour, made apprenticeships mandatory and restricted movement of workers, though this was really a recognition of changed practice.[6]

A further impetus to innovation came through the growing acceptability of Nonconformism in the north of England, the

Midlands, Wales and Scotland. Congregationalists, Unitarians, Quakers and Presbyterians grew steadily more influential, while their beliefs and their outlook – hard work, lack of ostentation, seriousness of purpose, implicit trust – suited the new mix of commercialism and manufacturing that was burgeoning, particularly in the northern towns and the Midlands.

Unitarians and Congregationalists were predominant in the Manchester cotton industry while famous iron-trade names such as Rawlinson, Lloyd, Pemberton, Spooner, Parker, Fidoe, Hodgetts, Manster and Huntsman were all Quaker families. The outstanding example is the Darby family: as well as the three generations of Abraham Darbys, the managers Richard Reynolds and Richard Ford were also Quakers. The Friends were also prominent in brewing through the Barclays, Trumans, Perkinses and Hanburys, and in banking through the Lloyd, Barclay, Bevan and Gurney families.

Each denomination offered a network of mutual support and investment. People knew and trusted other members of their chapel, meeting house, congregation or sect. They invested in each other's businesses, took on each other's sons as apprentices and became suppliers and customers to one another. The old saw about marrying the boss's daughter was common enough, and for good reason: family firms depended for their continuation on male heirs or, if there were none, sons-in-law to carry on the business. Connections helped in practical ways too: Thomas Newcomen was a Baptist in Devon and his first engine was commissioned through the Baptist church in Bromsgrove.

The traditional education system had little to offer budding innovators. Grammar schools were originally attached to cathedrals and were dedicated to teaching Latin by rote (Shakespeare learned Latin and Greek at Stratford Grammar School). By the eighteenth century this had changed only a little, with new schools being founded by endowments or by guilds, as feeders for universities. Pressure was brought by parents and others to widen the curricula, and some schools began to teach arithmetic

Eureka Moment: James Watt

'It was in the Green of Glasgow. I had gone to take a walk on a fine Sabbath afternoon. I had entered the Green by the gate at the foot of Charlotte Street – had passed the old washing house. I was thinking upon the engine at the time and had gone as far as the Herd's house when the idea came into my mind, that as steam was an elastic body it would rush into a vacuum, and if a communication was made between the cylinder and an exhausted vessel, it would rush into it, and might be there condensed without cooling the cylinder.

'I then saw that I must get quit of the condensed steam and injection water, if I used a jet as in Newcomon's [sic] engine. Two ways of doing this occurred to me. First the water might be run off by a descending pipe, if an offlet could be got at the depth of 35 or 36 feet, and any air might be extracted by a small pump; the second was to make the pump large enough to extract both water and air ... I had not walked further than the Golf-house when the whole thing was arranged in my mind.'

James Watt[7]

and modern languages. Here again Nonconformism stood out. As Dissenters (as Nonconformists called themselves) were barred from England's two universities they set up their own Dissenting Academies from the 1660s, and from the mid-eighteenth century large-scale academies were founded through public subscriptions, as at Warrington, or by trust funds as at Daventry. These academies provided high-quality instruction in a range of subjects, including commercial and scientific studies, to generations of Nonconformists.[8]

In Scotland too education was quite different from the traditional English model and it is not surprising that many inventors and entrepreneurs were Scottish. Universities founded at Glasgow,

St Andrews and Aberdeen in the fifteenth century were joined in the following century by the University of Edinburgh and a second university in Aberdeen – the granite city had as many universities as the whole of England. While these started as training grounds for the clergy, from the mid-seventeenth century they offered a broad curriculum based on philosophy, chemistry, sciences, economics and medicine; by the eighteenth century Scotland had become the main centre for medical education in Britain.

The most direct effect of Scottish education was the preponderance of chemists; here networking took on a distinct character through the presence of Joseph Black, professor of medicine at Glasgow University from 1757. Black seemed to know, advise and inspire every scientist and technical innovator who passed within fifty miles of him. These included John Roebuck, an Englishman educated in Edinburgh, who invented the industrial manufacture of sulphuric acid and was involved in many Scottish industrial ventures, including the Carron ironworks and James Watt's early experiments in engine design. Charles Mackintosh, inventor of waterproof fabrics, attended Black's lectures, while Archibald Cochrane, who opened up the iron fields of Scotland, was a close friend of Black. Francis Home, an early pioneer of vaccination, was a colleague, and James Keir, perhaps the most important chemist of the Industrial Revolution, studied medicine under Black at Edinburgh, where he also taught.

The Scottish academic network, in great contrast to that in England, encouraged discussion of sciences *and* their practical applications; so, while James Watt was never enrolled as a student, he had many conversations with Joseph Black, John Leslie and others on the science of heat and steam. When Watt went south to Birmingham in the 1770s he found the city well supplied with fellow Scottish engineers, and others like William Murdoch and William Brunton followed later. Scotland itself was a thriving centre of industrial innovation. Rapid industrial development in the coal, iron and textile industries, as well as in the lucrative Atlantic shipping trade were the prelude to

Scotland becoming the world centre of shipbuilding and marine and civil engineering.[9]

Innovators benefitted from other networks including clubs in Britain's expanding urban centres. Many of these were based on the old trade guilds, giving services to members in return for subscriptions; some were more educational, often owning libraries and museums; others, like the celebrated Lunar Society of Birmingham, were informal gatherings of like-minded people. Literary and Philosophical Societies (or Lit and Phils as they were commonly known) sprang up in industrial towns and cities, providing meeting places for commercial and industrial men, and also forums where the old landed gentry could meet the new breed of entrepreneur and inventor. They played an important role in spreading information about innovation: George Stephenson first demonstrated his miners' lamp at the Newcastle Lit and Phil, established in 1793.

We take it for granted that modern inventors are motivated by the prospect of financial returns, and although eighteenth-century inventors did not write much about their motives, it is clear they were mainly economic. Thomas Newcomen, James Watt and Henry Cort were not conducting experiments simply to amuse themselves or to add to the sum of human knowledge; they each worked in a trade (or in Watt's case several) and they wanted to improve their business in order to make a better return. Of course the success of their technological innovations gave these men a great thrill, but without an economic impetus they would not have come to fruition.

This economic imperative was crucial in what is the most important aspect of the industrial innovation – its continuation. From the 1770s onwards, thanks to the ever-growing market for manufactured goods, particularly in the cotton trade, there was a continual financial incentive to innovate to produce goods quicker, cheaper and better. Some innovations were at a local, workshop or factory level, while others spread across industries.

The spinning mule, for example, was improved in small ways by almost every mill-owner who used it: Henry Stone installed toothed gearing and metal rollers; others added parallel scrolling, gears and a clutch to better control the tension and produce finer thread; in 1825 Richard Roberts patented the self-acting mule, which allowed the powered machine to work continuously with a minimum of human intervention.

In this new climate of commercial demand for technology, inventors became professionals, developing devices and processes for use in a variety of industries, and using the patent system to sell rights to their innovations. William Bundy took out ten patents from 1796 to 1830, including a cooling device, a comb-maker and a pin-making machine; John Leigh Bradbury, an engraver and calico printer, was awarded six patents from 1807 to 1824, which included an improved pin-maker, fibre spinners and engravers. Lemuel Wright, an American living in London, took out twenty patents from 1820 to 1849 for such devices as machines for making bricks and tiles, steam engines, bleaching devices and a mechanical sweeper. By the mid-nineteenth century established inventors like Henry Bessemer were being commissioned by companies to come up with solutions to problems, while big manufacturers bought up multiple patents in order to dominate their sector – Price's, for example, the biggest candle-maker in the world, bought any patent that impinged on candle manufacture.

As we have seen, inventors didn't have to sell their inventions, they could licence them. While manufacturers wanted exclusive licences in order to outdo their competition, inventors preferred to have multiple licencees, all paying a royalty.[10] Boulton & Watt and Richard Arkwright were able to dictate terms because their machines were essential to all the entrepreneurs in their industries. Arkwright, in particular, was a master at manipulating licences, restricting each licencee to a total of 1,000 spindles and thereby preventing any one mill-owner from challenging his dominance, while at the same time getting good royalties from his invention. Typically, Arkwright bent the rules by granting 'exclusive' licences to a number of neighbouring mill-owners.

So, by the eighteenth century, Britain had absorbed lessons in technological innovation from Continental Europe, and began to use the base of prosperity from the wool trade, and the plentiful supply of cheap coal and iron ore, to diversify into craft industries. The consequent demand for goods, coupled with cheap energy and high wages, gave financial incentives for inventors, particularly in the cotton industry, which was unregulated and carried the potential for enormous expansion. All this gave opportunities for inventors. And at the same time Britain's craft trades, with their tradition of time-served apprenticeships, combined with the special qualities of Nonconformism culture and Scottish education, as well as a fluid social environment, provided the human capital needed to exploit those opportunities. This was a unique combination and, while it may have come about through chance, it still took the immense dedication of a small number of technical geniuses, aided by a generation of tens of thousands of artisans, to bring about the inventions that transformed the world.

3. Navigating the Patent System

Nowadays patents exist to protect the interests of inventors, to test whether their inventions are genuinely original, and then to ensure that no one can exploit them without the permission of the inventor. So we would expect patents to have been key elements in encouraging the surge of inventions that changed the industrial landscape in the late eighteenth century. And indeed they were, at least sometimes. But patents were not the friends to inventors that they might have been. In fact the patent system had been designed and was used for entirely different reasons – and it was the inventors themselves who forced the system to adapt.

A letter patent is literally an open letter granting certain rights to its recipient. This openness is important, as it enables the public to access its contents, and informs everyone that the recipient is being granted special legal status. This status could be the sole right to exploit an invention, or the monopoly over a particular craft or industry.

The granting of protection through letters patent became the centre of English industrial policy under Elizabeth I's Lord Treasurer and chief advisor Lord Burghley (William Cecil) who used patent protection to attract foreign manufacturers to England from the 1560s. Burghley was acutely aware that England was an industrial backwater, while manufacturing processes were being developed apace in the Netherlands, Italy, France and the German states. He offered twenty-one-year monopolies to foreign makers using techniques unknown in Britain; consequently new ways of making glass, soap, paper, silk cloth and for refining ores were introduced. Immigrants were expected to teach native workers their techniques, while applicants stressed the benefit to the commonwealth rather than their own claim to have invented a new device or process. Burghley set the tone for all English patents up to the Industrial Revolution – he had no interest in the intellectual property rights of the applicant; a patent was granted in order to benefit the country and the Exchequer.[1]

Unfortunately for later inventors, patents and monopolies became fatally entangled, particularly as Stuart kings used the sale of monopolies in processes like alum-making to raise the funds that Parliament would not deliver, or handed them out to court favourites. Though Parliament enacted a Statute of Monopolies in 1624 in an attempt to clean the system, abuses continued, leaving craftsmen barred from their own trades by the corrupt granting of monopolies. Nevertheless the 1624 Act did provoke the Chief Justice Edward Coke to codify the conditions under which a patent might be granted. The three most important were: first, that the protection would be granted for fourteen years, twice the length of an apprenticeship, so an apprentice could not immediately steal his master's secrets; second, that the applicant must be the original and true inventor; and third, that the technique should not already be in use by someone else.

However, while we might assume that the granting of a patent would give legal authority to the holder, this was not the case. The Patent Office had no role in the enforcement of patents, so the process and granting of a patent was, in every case, open to legal challenge. This meant that if someone copied an invention the patent-holder had to go to court and not only prove that there was duplication, but also that the patent itself was valid in the first place. The burden was on the patent-holder continually to enforce his rights.

Consequently by the eighteenth century patents, while still the only form of protection for inventors, were widely regarded as an obstruction to fair trade, and were essentially granted on the basis of government gain rather than the novelty of an invention. To give just one example, in the 1720s there were three separate attempts to patent methods of making candles from tallow. But tallow candles were charged duty at 1d per pound and wax candles at 8d per pound; improved tallow candles would therefore represent a serious threat to government revenue, and the patents were refused. Only in the 1760s did the excise begin to lose its power to intervene in technical inventions, while financial reforms brought in by William Pitt in the 1780s meant that the excise became less protective of its sources of income.

This was a horribly difficult situation for bona fide inventors and innovators who wanted legal protection. First and foremost, the granting of patents was a slow and expensive process, going through ten separate offices of state. If at any stage a caveat, which allowed others to be warned of applications in their field, could be found it would delay the process by around six months. The costs of gaining a patent were around £100 to £120 for an English patent, with the same amount again for a patent valid in Scotland.

A second difficulty concerned the necessary specification of the invention. Often applications were disqualified because there was some minor fault in the specification; and it was possible that an application could go through every stage and then fall at the last hurdle. More seriously there was vagueness about what the specification should show – was it supposed to be a general guide to the device or process, a clear indication of the novelty of the invention or, as emerged later, a thorough technical template from which a 'typical' engineer could build the device or run the process? Inventors were understandably reluctant to reveal too much about their inventions in the specification when they could not rely on the Patent Office to fully protect them.

This leads us to a third area of difficulty, which concerned the law. The Patent Office did not enforce the law; instead, when challenged, inventors had to defend their right to a patent in a common law court. Common law depends on the development of precedents, but most judges were ignorant of case law in this area, which was in any event confusing. James Watt's lawyer noted in 1785 that in the records of case law at the time there were no entries in the indexes for Patent or Monopoly; cases had been tried but their value in law had not been recognised, therefore no future judge could avail himself of precedent.

The variation in judges' opinions was also alarming as some believed that every invention should be freely available to all, while others saw that, without protection, innovation would cease or inventors would keep their secrets to themselves (a good example of the latter is Benjamin Huntsman's method of making crucible steel). And while there seemed to be some improvement in protection from the late 1760s, this was often down to the legal and political skills of inventors and their supporters, who gradually grew more powerful.

The law became clearer through the 1780s and 90s but there was still insecurity and uncertainty. Judges disagreed over whether an invention could cover a process as well as a machine (over two-thirds of patents were for processes); others tried to differentiate between a manufacturing process, a method and a principle. Judges questioned whether a patent should apply only to an object already created, or could be granted for something that was yet to be made. And should the invention be saleable, or could it be something made just for interest? While hearing the *Hornblower vs Boulton & Watt* case in 1799 Lord Kenyon, Chief Justice from 1788 to 1802 – during the period when inventions made Britain the leading industrial power in the world – declared from the bench: 'I'm not one who greatly favours patents.'

Burghley's intentions that existing trade should be not be damaged by patents, and that they should not be granted to inventions that simply improved on existing techniques, were not officially abandoned until 1776 in *Morris vs Branson*, where Justice Mansfield concluded that their continuation 'would go to repeal almost every patent that was ever granted'.

Despite this level of ignorance and hostility from the law, the patent system *was* a crucial element in the development of inventions and innovations. We can draw this conclusion from the practice of inventors themselves: almost all the significant inventions of the late eighteenth century were patented, and most patents that were granted, were awarded to serious inventors. But why would inventors want to invest time and money acquiring protection that was so difficult to defend? The main reason was that, imperfect though they were, patents were the *only* legal support for their claims of originality. These were professional men, either improving their own business or using their expertise to make money through licensing their inventions: patents were therefore a key tool for their business. Inventors in the Industrial Revolution were motivated above all by commercial returns; the use of the patent system, the diversification of inventors into other areas and the trade in inventions through sale and licence shows that they were not lucky amateurs but astute, profit-seeking artisans. Although the system came in for a good deal of criticism and patents and patent extensions were resisted and contested by fellow inventors and industrialists, they didn't want the system abandoned; instead they wanted it safeguarded and improved.

In addition, while the patent system of the mid-eighteenth century was a rough and ready affair, the inventors themselves, through the success of their inventions and the prosperity that they brought, showed the widespread benefits of a robust patent system; this changed the views of judges and decisively altered the interpretations of the law. The figures here are stark: in the period from 1750 to 1799, of all patent cases decided at common law courts 39 per cent went to the patent-holder, 61 per cent to the objector or infringer; by the 1840s the respective figures were 76 per cent and 24 per cent. Judges finally accepted that inventions led to the growth of industry, not its constriction; if the judges' benches were the last bastion of resistance to innovation, they too eventually caved in.

The patent system was clearly not for the faint-hearted; many inventors had patents overturned while others had to go to court to protect rights that should have been upheld by statute and regulation. It is therefore a massive historical paradox that the very messiness of the patent system in the eighteenth century may, in practice, have made it ideal. The system gave just enough protection to inventors to encourage them to innovate, but not enough to stop others from working the system by pirating other people's inventions, or making small improvements that kept the momentum of innovation going. The imperfection of the system allowed ideas and innovations to spread through industries, and encouraged a vast number of technical people operating below the level of true invention to join in the changes that enabled industry to continue its relentless search for efficiency.

II. Coal

'Coal is not only used in common fires, but in most mechanic professions that require the greatest expense of fuel.'

JOHN HOUGHTON, 1682

4. Fuelling the Revolution

Medieval and early modern Europe was able to sustain a large and growing population from two principal natural resources – good land for growing crops and rearing livestock, and a legacy of vast forests. Trees provided material for housing, boats and ships, machinery, furniture, vehicles and tools, and, crucially, they provided an apparently limitless supply of fuel. But the expanding population, together with the increasing demand for charcoal from growing industries, began to put pressure on supplies. More people meant more burning of wood for fuel; it also created a growing need for land to grow crops.

Britain began to solve its energy problem during the seventeenth century with the growing adoption of coal as a fuel for home and industry. The figures are impressive: in 1560 total coal production in Britain was around 250,000 tons per year, by 1700 this had increased tenfold to 2.7 million tons and by 1750 production had reached 4.7 million tons. By 1700 the country's mines were producing nearly 80 per cent of the total coal being mined in Europe – Britain was leading the world into a new type of energy economy.[1]

The availability and easy access to vast reserves of cheap coal enabled British people to gain a prosperity unknown in the rest of Europe or indeed the world. In the early eighteenth century the estimated price of energy was around nine grams of silver per million BTU* in Beijing and Paris, roughly five grams in London and Amsterdam and less than one gram in Newcastle. Thanks to

* British Thermal Units. 3,414 BTU = 1 kilowatt

its cheap coal, the ratio of wages to energy was higher in Newcastle and the northern English coalfields than anywhere else in the world.[2]

By the 1760s Britain was prospering from its widespread use of coal to produce heat, or thermal energy; this was followed by the breakthrough into the use of coal as a source of power, or mechanical energy, triggering the great revolution in industrial production that is at the centre of this book. It is clear that this growing coal economy was a necessary precursor to the Industrial Revolution, so how did it come about?

Britain is rich in mineral resources. Its very particular geological history has bequeathed an astonishing range of rocks from every period and a bounty of coal, iron, lead, copper, tin, zinc, lime and even gravel, that enabled Britain's Industrial Revolution to be largely self-sustained. The coal is almost all from the Carboniferous period and is either exposed on the surface or available via shafts in the north-east of England, Yorkshire, Lancashire, the Midlands, Kent and Gloucestershire, as well as in South Wales and central Scotland.

Britain's position on the edge of the European continental plate brought about several episodes of volcanic and igneous activity during its geological history. Hot magma was pushed up into the earth's crust and heated the surrounding rock, sending groundwater rich in minerals percolating through the existing strata. This process was particularly productive in south-west England where, around 300 million years ago, igneous activity formed the great granite masses that underlie the moorlands of Devon and Cornwall. The subsequent heat led to hot fluids spreading through surrounding rocks and leaving metallic ores. The metals were deposited in a particular order as the liquid cooled; this was long known by Cornish miners who coined the expression 'Black Jack rides a good horse' to describe how the black zinc ore called zincblende would usually lie on top of tin and copper ores – so find Black Jack and dig down.

British coalfields: Britain had large quantities of easily available coal, particularly in the Midlands and North of England, Central Scotland and South Wales; in many places coal seams were near to rich seams of iron ore.

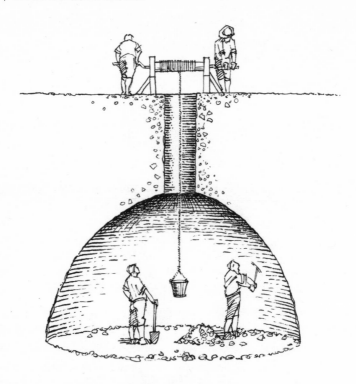

Bell pit: One of the earliest forms of mining. The mine is dug down into the seam, which is hollowed out in a dome or bell shape. Once the danger of roof collapse is imminent the mine is abandoned and another dug nearby.

The earliest mines were drifts cut into the side of hills, following the coal seams downwards into the earth, or bell pits dug vertically downwards and then out as far as possible before the roof was in danger of collapse. As the demand for coal increased miners realised that more reserves could be reached by sinking vertical shafts. They then worked outwards from these shafts, using either pillar and stall or long-wall methods, robbing the seams as they went.[3]

Before the sixteenth century coal was largely local fuel, restricted to certain parts of the country; difficulties in transport and the plentiful amounts of wood available in most areas, together with its unsuitability for tasks like heating houses (see pp. 63–7) diminished its importance. But there were early indications

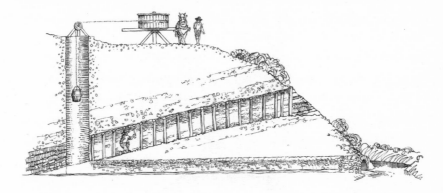

Adit mine: A vertical shaft is sunk to where it meets the sloping coal seam, which is then worked out. The coal and miners are taken up the shaft in baskets. An adit is dug out from the seam to the hillside to drain the mine. As shafts were sunk deeper drainage became a major problem.

that supplies of wood for fuel were running low in some places. As early as 1255 there had been concern that two limekilns in Wellington Forest in Somerset had consumed 500 oaks; while in 1559 stocks of timber had fallen so low around Worcester that a law forbade the felling of timber for iron production within fourteen miles of the Severn. In medieval London occasional shortages of charcoal forced lime-burners, brewers and dyers to use coal, leading to intermittent complaints about coal smoke in the capital. Although these were local problems they hint at a delicate balance between manufacturing and fuel resources.

Charcoal produced an intense clean heat that was widely used in iron-making, baking and brewing. But as craft industries grew and intensified the supply of wood for charcoal, alongside the demand for timber for house-building, shipping and all manner of vehicles and implements, native woodlands simply could not replenish themselves. Timber simply became too scarce and too expensive, and so British craftsmen began to turn towards coal as an alternative source of heat.

The principal obstacle to switching was transport. This was easiest solved through rivers and coastal shipping; in 1530 the

Crown granted a monopoly of coal shipping on the Tyne to the city of Newcastle's Quayside, showing that the area was already developing its coal trade. For the next 300 years river boats known as keels took coal out to flat-bottomed ships known as colliers, which sailed down the east coast. The colliers returned with sand ballast which turned the Tyne and Wear valleys into centres of glassmaking. The amount of coal brought from the Durham and Northumberland coalfields to London increased from around 500,000 to 2 million tons in the course of the eighteenth century; and while a collier carried 140 tons in 1700 by 1840 capacity increased to 580 tons. The trade sustained shipbuilding centres right along the east coast from South Shields to Sunderland, Whitby and Lowestoft. Ipswich, for example, owed its prosperity to the trade with many shipowners building grand houses in the town.[4]

Coal was shipped along the Severn between Bristol, Shropshire and Staffordshire, around the coast of Kent to the Thames Estuary, along the Clyde and Forth in Scotland and the Humber and Trent in the English Midlands. Cardiff, Swansea, Newport, Newcastle, North and South Shields, Hartlepool, Hull and Grimsby all owed their prosperity to coal shipping. And it was the demand for coal that drove the coming revolution in transport (see Chapters 18 and 19) with canals and steam locomotives developed to move the fuel that powered the new economy.

Coal consumption in different crafts shows just how varied the industrial landscape was before the great events of the late eighteenth century, and how far removed it already was from a rural subsistence economy. Most manufactories had few problems in changing from charcoal while some that had traditionally used coal increased capacity markedly during the eighteenth century. Lime was perhaps the key example of the latter. Limestone was burned in kilns to produce lime, which was of crucial importance in agriculture; applied to the soil it encourages plant growth and increases the efficiency of manuring. With the value of wheat and barley steadily increasing through the seventeenth century, lime became ever more important. In 1625 Walter Blith wrote that lime 'is of excellent use, yea, so great that whole countries, and many counties, that were naturally as barren as any in this nation . . . doth and hath brought their land into such a posture, for bearing all sorts of corn, that upon the land not worth above one or two shillings an acre, they will raise (well husbanded with lime) as good wheat, barley and white and grey peas, as England yields'.[5]

Lime was also used for mortar and lime washes in the building trade. Huge quantities of coal had been used to produce lime for building projects like Conwy and Caernarvon Castles in the thirteenth century and Rochester Castle in the fourteenth, as well as for the Tower of London and Windsor Castle, but these isolated projects were dwarfed by the building boom of the seventeenth and eighteenth centuries during which wood was replaced by bricks and mortar. Every town had limekilns to supply its builders, while the countryside was dotted with kilns. The voracious needs of London builders were supplied by kilns grouped at Gravesend and Northfleet on the Thames Estuary with other concentrations of kilns on the Tyne, Forth and Severn.

Brick production required yet more fuel. More bricks were 'spoiled' in a coal firing than a wood or charcoal one but this loss was soon compensated by the low price of coal. In London, the south-east and the east, where there was a lack of stone and timber and plentiful supplies of good clay, bricks were the prime building material. By the 1660s brick was in use in most parts of the country and clay and wood buildings began to disappear. Clay roof tiles were also made in coal-fired kilns, as was the growing amount of pottery.

The salt industry was another huge consumer of coal. After being self-sufficient in salt up to the twelfth century, English saltmakers lost out to cheap imports from Aquitaine, which England ruled from 1154 to 1453. But political disruption in France in the 1500s led to a massive surge in output in Britain. In places like Sunderland it was the salt works that drove the need for coal, and brought about the opening of new collieries. Tyneside, with its cheap coal and good transport links, now became a prime centre of salt production; by 1644 there were 222 salt pans along the

Tyne, consuming an estimated 95,000 tons of coal a year. By the 1720s the process of evaporating seawater to obtain salt was made more fuel efficient, but it still took between six and eight tons of coal to produce one ton of salt. By the early eighteenth century salt-making consumed between 7 and 10 per cent of the coal produced in Britain.

Other industries had to make adaptations if they were to replace charcoal with coal. One technique was to use coked coal – coal that had been slowly baked to drive out water and other impurities. Where this wasn't possible the principal requirement was to separate the fuel and its harmful smoke from the products themselves, although this could not be done in an iron blast furnace, and special coke derived from low-sulphur coal had to be used. But in steel-making, food-processing, brewing, dyeing and the burgeoning chemical and textile trades, makers successfully adapted their processes and equipment to the new fuel. Cheap coal and growing demand enabled these trades to expand prodigiously, and enter a virtuous circle where they could reduce prices and encourage yet more demand. The brewing trade is a case in point; in the middle of the seventeenth century Derby malters started using coke to replace charcoal, and Derby malt and beer became highly sought after. A London brewing house could use as much as 1,000 tons of coal a year and most brewing towns – Burton, Derby, Tadcaster, Nottingham, Shrewsbury, Bridgnorth, Lichfield, Plymouth – had access to cheap coal.

Food industries like sugar-making and baking, which were increasingly being carried on outside the home by specialist producers, as well as production of salt meats, tallow, vinegar and the like, all increased greatly and used significant amounts of coal. The growing chemical industry was a significant consumer too; by 1647, for example, around 8,000 tons of Sunderland coal were sent to the Yorkshire coast alum industry each year.

In 1611 Thomas Percival gained a patent giving him the exclusive right to manufacture window glass using coal as fuel; he converted furnaces to coal use by using enclosed clay crucibles

Soap making: Coal was used in vast quantities in industries like soap-making, where chemicals were boiled in open pans.

which prevented contact between coal fumes and the raw materials of the glass. Three years later another patent banned the use of any other fuel except coal in glass-making – the Crown awarded itself a royalty on the licence, glass-makers were coerced into using coal. In the seventeenth century the smelters of copper, lead and other metals had also adapted to using coal and in the 1730s Benjamin Huntsman's crucible method allowed coke to replace charcoal in steel-making.

While manufacturers benefitted from the availability of cheap coal, people were keen to do the same in their homes. Coal was used for making bricks but houses were traditionally heated by wood. A medieval cottage usually had just one room with a hearth in the centre, surrounded by stone or tile to constrain the wood

Climbing Boys

The advent of narrow chimneys brought in one of the enduring symbols of industrial Britain: the climbing boy. Flues were narrow (usually nine inches by fourteen inches), and were often built with angles in the belief that this would help the fire to draw. Chimney sweeps therefore hired or acquired boys from workhouses to climb up the flues to remove the soot. It was a dangerous, filthy job with soot full of carcinogens and the flues often left hot. Boys died of cancer, suffocation or heat exhaustion. From 1803 effective brushes and even a mechanical sweeper were available, but these were not taken up by most sweeps, who continued to use children. The following is from evidence taken at the Parliamentary Committee on Climbing Boys held in 1817 (the committee recommended ending the use of boys, but this continued until 1875):

'No one knows the cruelty which a boy has to undergo in learning. The flesh must be hardened. This is done by rubbing it, chiefly on the elbows and knees, with the strongest brine, close by a hot fire. You must stand over them with a cane, or coax them by the promise of a halfpenny, if they will stand a few more rubs. At first they will come back from their work with their arms and knees streaming with blood: then they must be rubbed with brine again. Some boys are awkward and suffer more, but all are scarred and wounded.'

Mr Ruff, a Nottingham sweep

'On Monday morning, 29 March 1813, a chimney sweeper of the name of Griggs attended to sweep a small chimney in the brewhouse of Messrs Calvert and Co. in Upper Thames Street; he was accompanied by one of his boys, a lad of about eight years of age, of the name Thomas Pitt. The fire had been lighted as early as two o'clock the same morning, and was burning on the arrival of Griggs and his boy at eight. The fireplace was small, and an iron pipe projected from the grate some way into the flue. This the master was acquainted with (having swept the chimney of the brewhouse for some years), and therefore had a tile or two broken from the roof, in order that the boy might descend the chimney. He had no sooner extinguished the fire than he suffered the lad to go down; and the consequence, as might be expected, was his almost immediate death in a state, no doubt, of inexpressible agony. The flue was of the narrowest description, and must have retained heat sufficient to have prevented the child's return to the top, even supposing he had not approached the pipe belonging to the grate, which must have been nearly red hot; this however was not clearly ascertained on the inquest, though the appearance of the body would induce an opinion that he had been unavoidably pressed against the pipe. Soon after his descent, the master, who remained on the top, was apprehensive that something had happened, and therefore desired him to come up; the answer of the boy was, 'I cannot come up, master, I must die here.' An alarm was given in the brewhouse immediately that he had stuck in the chimney, and a bricklayer who was at work near the spot attended, and after knocking down part of the brickwork of the chimney, just above the fireplace, made a hole sufficiently large to draw him through. A surgeon attended, but all attempts to restore life were ineffectual. On inspecting the body, various burns appeared; the fleshy part of the legs and a great part of the feet more particularly were injured; those parts too by which climbing boys most effectually ascend or descend chimneys, viz. the elbows and knees, seemed burnt to the bone; from which it must be evident that the unhappy sufferer made some attempts to return as soon as the horrors of his situation became apparent.[7]

fire; smoke went up into the rafter space and out through a hole or louvre in the roof. Grand houses might be bigger but the hearths were essentially the same type. This was a safe arrangement for timber houses; it kept the fire away from the walls, and allowed everyone to get round the fire.

By the sixteenth century English houses had more rooms, and fires began to be placed against stone walls. Hoods were put over the fires to guide the smoke, and these hoods or mantles were made into decorated features. The practice of having several fire-places in one house spread from the great houses to the gentry, to yeoman farmers and merchants. These houses had chimneys protruding from the rooftops to help the smoke disperse.

In his *Description of England* (1576-7), William Harrison reports the changes that had happened in the village of Radwinter in Essex during his lifetime: 'the multitude of chimneys lately erected' was one of 'three things to be marvellously altered in England' within the 'sound remembrance [of] old men yet dwelling in the village where I remain . . . In their young days there were not above two or three [chimneys], if so many, in most uplandish towns of the realm (the religious houses and manor places of their lords always excepted, and peradventure some great parsonages), but each one made his fire against a reredos in the hall, where he dined and dressed his meat.'[6]

Hand in hand with the move to place fires against walls, and to build chimneys, came attempts to heat houses with coal rather than wood. While wood fires were big structures with the fuel held in an open basket and the flues often a yard across, coal needed to be kept in a small mass, and to have a strong draught to generate enough heat for it to keep burning. Just as important, coal smoke, being denser than wood smoke, needs to be drawn upwards; the flue must be specifically designed for this purpose.

However, converting to coal was easier said than done; the problems of smoke and stench were notorious and pioneers often had to call in 'smoke doctors' to save themselves from choking to death in their own homes. Hearths were reduced in size by building brick hearths within old hearths, or by the use of cast iron 'cheeks' (i.e. side baffles) and firebacks. These were among the most common cast-iron products made before the eighteenth century.

Probate inventories show the growing popularity of iron coal hearths, as well as the tools that went with them. In the coal region of Gloucestershire hearths were common by the seventeenth century; around Telford by the late seventeenth century almost every household had at least one coal-burning grate while bigger houses had more. In 1673, Zachary Kyrke, a gentleman of Lichfield, had a grate in his great chamber, one in the hall and another in the kitchen. By the seventeenth century tongs and a shovel were common household items while houses started adopting fenders to protect floors from cinders. The fireplace was only part of the system needed to burn coal. Chimneys had to be narrow and high with the opening away from the roof or from other buildings.

The rapid increase in urban populations led to a boom in house-building with most houses built to be heated by coal. Builders experimented with different designs of hearth. Georgian houses put up in London, Bath, Bristol and fashionable spa towns around the country, as well as the brick terraces of workers' dwellings, all had coal-burning fires, vastly increasing the demand for coal. Indeed, coal fires and coke boilers remained the main source of heat in British homes until the second half of the twentieth century.

By the 1760s, therefore, coal had become central to the British economy and the lives of most British people. Its use enabled the country to produce more food, to improve the efficiency of its manufactories and to keep their houses heated at relatively low cost. But there was only one device in existence that was able to use coal to produce mechanical, as opposed to thermal, energy. That was the Newcomen fire engine, which by then was approaching the venerable age of fifty. The engine was a device for pumping water out of mines using the suction induced by condensing steam. It consumed huge amounts of waste coal kept in heaps at the shaft heads, though its use also spread to the tin and copper mines of Cornwall. The power of the Newcomen engines was evident to writers like William Brownrigg who visited Whitehaven

The Energy Equation

The conversion of Britain from an economy based on natural resources derived from the land – timber, crops, animals – to an economy based on coal took around 200 years to complete. When coal began to replace charcoal as a cheap fuel for manufacturing and domestic heating, the land previously used to produce timber could be put to growing food instead; it is estimated that it would take around 100,000 acres of woodland to make 10,000 tons of iron, so freeing the land from the need to provide fuel was a huge bonus. By 1820 the huge quantity of coal used was the equivalent of adding another 15 million acres to the nation's productive land.[8] In addition coal increased the energy input into agriculture through the use of lime and other minerals produced by using coal.

In a wholly organic economy the number of people that can be fed, given shelter, clothed and kept warm is limited by the amount of material that can be produced by the land; and while this can be increased, it will inevitably reach a limit leading to a stagnant economy. The energy input into agriculture in the form of machinery, fertilisers, transport and so on therefore becomes crucial: in the industrial countries of the twenty-first century such external energy input allows the population to be fed by the labour of just 2 per cent of the workforce.

At an individual level the fundamental change brought by external energy is just as stark. If a coal miner in the late eighteenth century consumed around 3,500 calories a day mining around 200 kilos of coal, the coal contains 500 times as much heat energy as the food he has consumed. And if the fuel is used in an engine with even 1 per cent efficiency he is delivering many times the mechanical energy he is expending. This mechanical energy is then available to the mill-worker in a steam-powered factory who is able to expand the work he can perform by a factor of ten or a hundred because of the energy that the miner has placed at his elbow. Calculations for other industrialising countries reveal that by the nineteenth century coal-derived energy produced the equivalent of a workforce increased by 250 per cent.[9] In contrast, people in subsistence economies where there is no ready supply of energy in the form of fossil fuel are at a huge disadvantage. As it takes about three calories of fuel to cook one calorie of food, the fuel that is required in the form of timber takes up space needed for crops and diminishes the overall amount of calorific energy that can be gained from the land. Having coal-derived energy is therefore a double bonus.

in the early 1750s: 'It would require about 500 men, or a power equal to that of 110 horses, to work the pumps of one of the largest fire-engines now in use . . . As much water may be raised by an engine of this size, kept constantly at work, as can be drawn by 2,520 men, as is said to be done in some of the mines in Peru.'[10]

Despite this power, and the improvements carried out by engineers like John Smeaton, the Newcomen engines were not adopted by other manufacturers, and remained part of the mining trade. But then, in 1769, James Watt patented his idea for an improved steam engine, which would use far less coal to produce the same results. The first working Watt engine was built in 1776 and Britain began its historic conversion to a completely coal-based economy. Steam engines for mills, mines, furnaces, forges and factories, locomotives, steamships and barges, all consumed vast quantities of coal and the development of gas lighting (first demonstrated by William Murdoch at the Soho foundry in Birmingham in 1802) further increased demand – annual production rose to 15 million tons by 1800, 50 million tons in 1850 and 250 million tons by 1900.

Rising demand led to improvements in mining techniques.

Iron casing of shafts allowed deeper mining – in 1780 one shaft at Wallsend colliery reached 183 metres deep – and ventilation techniques allowed mines to spread further out from their shafts, while the replacement of men by ponies in the Northumberland coalfield brought down wages, making coal even cheaper. Industrial innovation did not, however, radically improve the productivity of coal mining itself. A seventeenth-century miner could produce around 150 to 200 tons a year, while in the early twentieth century a miner could fetch 250 to 300 tons. However, the number of men in the industry grew to cater for the vastly increased demand, and the surrounding transport infrastructure made the industry as a whole more efficient; the simple building of trackways, for example, allowed an ox and driver to move more than five times as much coal per day as a road wagon previously, and once steam locomotion was introduced from the 1820s coal could be moved as fast as it could be mined.

Nor did technology radically improve conditions for underground workers. Miners descended the deep shafts by holding on to the chain that was used to haul the corves or baskets of coal up to the surface; twelve hours later they were hauled up in the same way. Access to the face was often along a tunnel dug just big enough to crawl through, and at the face itself the coal was dug out with pick and shovel, often with the miner lying on his side. The coal was then hauled away either by dragging the corves, or later on wagons running on rails. The hauling was often done by children with straps from the baskets tied around their foreheads.[11] One early method of dispersing the lethal firedamp gas (chiefly methane) involved a miner crawling along the tunnels dressed in sacking soaked in water. He would then lie in a pit dug in the floor of the tunnel, cover himself with boarding and pull a lighted candle along after him; the candle was intended to explode any small pockets of gas. To aid ventilation miners dug two shafts and burned open fires at the foot of one, in order to draw air through the workings. This was highly dangerous and in some places furnaces were built at the top of the shaft as a safer alternative.

Despite all the dangers and the physical toughness of the work, there was no shortage of miners; they earned better wages than most workers. In 1800 a Northumberland miner received 2s 6d a day for a four-and-a-half-day week – around double the pay of an army sergeant. Pay was often deducted for broken tools, and miners were forced to buy candles and other goods from the manager above market rate (managers regarded this profit as a legitimate perk). But miners got free coal and a house for their families, as well as beer, bread and cheese for any additional work outside their routine labour. Mining families were eager for their children to work in the mines too, both for the income and (for the boys) as a first step into the mining life. Boys and girls as young as five or six were used as trappers, to sit by the large wooden doors that helped to control the air flow, opening them to let the coal trucks through. In order to save on candles they generally sat through a whole shift in the dark.

Safety lamps were first introduced in 1815, designed independently by Humphry Davy and George Stephenson; both worked on the recent discovery that a flame burning within a gauze or mesh filter would not ignite firedamp. As Humphry Davy wrote: 'In plunging a light surrounded by a cylinder of fine wire-gauze on to an explosive mixture I saw the whole cylinder become quietly and gradually filled with flame; the upper part of it soon appeared red-hot, yet no explosion occurred.'[12] While this was excellent in theory, accidents continued due to rusted gauze or broken glass, and many miners did not like the lamp because of its low light, so preferred to stick with candles and take precautions. Underground explosions brought a heavy toll of lives lost right up to the present day: this has been the human cost of the coal economy.

The increasing demand turned coal into big business. Landowners with the good luck to have coal seams under their land did well from the centuries-long boom in production. In the seventeenth and early eighteenth centuries many landowners effectively supervised their mining interests themselves, using their existing stewards as managers. But soon some of these stewards became expert in prospecting for coal, setting up mining facilities, digging shafts, hiring miners and arranging transport, and became highly sought after. Hugh and Thomas Taylor were employed by the Duke of Northumberland, John Curr by the Duke of Norfolk, Joshua and Benjamin Biram were used by the Fitzwilliam estates in South Yorkshire, James Spedding worked for the Lowthers of Cumbria, Alexander and Robert Bald for Lord Mar and W. S. Clark for the Earl of Bute – all became renowned for their brilliance as mining engineers. Spedding oversaw the digging of undersea pits off Whitehaven; John Curr used underground railroads, while Benjamin Biram developed a system of rotary ventilators.

As demand expanded and exploiting reserves became more complex, coal mining as a business became more sophisticated, requiring a higher level of investment to open or dig new shafts. From around 1750 onwards, landowners began to hand over the entire responsibility for mining to others. These professionals would buy the rights to mine on a lease and pay a royalty on the coal they extracted. As in other areas, therefore, building an effective commercial structure went hand in hand with the revolution in industrial production. The Northumberland and Durham coalfield was the most productive and it was here that a standard system of leasing was worked out. From 1726 an alliance of George Bowes, Sir Henry Liddell and Edward Worthy set precedents for regulating and negotiating mineral leases; and where earlier arrangements were based on royalties paid in coal, landowners now insisted on payments in cash.

If we had to give a one-word answer to the question 'What made Britain uniquely placed to bring about the Industrial Revolution?' it would be 'coal'. In the century leading up to the 1760s Britain had built a prosperous economy by combining her traditional wool trade with craft manufacturing. This manufacturing sector made a gradual and historic shift from wood to coal as its primary fuel. At the same time the growth in prosperity and the expansion of towns and cities brought about a building boom and a switch to using coal for domestic heating. Underpinning both rural manufacturing and the growth of Britain's towns was an agricultural revolution that was also crucially dependent on coal as a source of energy through the manufacture of fertilisers. Britain, by the 1760s, was utterly dependent on coal and was consuming coal in vast quantities compared to every other European nation. It was this dependence, and the presence of coal in every sphere of life, that made the great revolution possible. The breakthrough that saw coal being used to produce mechanical energy could really only have happened in a coal-based economy like Britain's. Nevertheless it took the enormous determination of a handful of men to bring that historic change to fruition.

III. Power

'We remove mountains, and make seas our smooth highway; nothing can resist us. We war with rude Nature; and, by our resistless engines, come off always victorious, and loaded with spoils.'

THOMAS CARLYLE, 1829

5. Watermills and Wheels

The Industrial Revolution brought about the mechanisation of industrial production. Machines were devised to save labour by doing the work of several and sometimes hundreds of men, but these machines needed power to run. Machinery plus power was the magic formula. So what was the major source of industrial power during the heroic age of Watt, Arkwright and Trevithick? The answer is water.

Between 1760 and 1820 the number of waterwheels in England increased from an estimated 70,000 to 120,000; this was the result of the Industrial Revolution creating machines, mills and factories that ran off a single power source.[1] Supplying that motive power from steam engines, although first pioneered in 1781, took time to spread through the manufactories of Britain and, in the meantime, water power filled the gap. In fact, most of the machines of the Industrial Revolution – the spinning frame and mule, the power loom, the blast-furnace bellows and powered forge hammers – were built to run on water power. It took James Watt years to make rotary steam engines run as smoothly and safely as waterwheels, so mill-owners even used steam engines to pump water to power waterwheels.

Water-powered mills, including old corn mills, are a crucial element in our story because they were prototype factories. Their model of raw material storage, machinery building and maintenance, transfer of mechanical power, purpose-built structures and throughput of work all informed the textile mills that were the basis of the factory system. Water power made Britain ready for the transformation that steam power was to bring. We will

therefore look briefly at the history of water power before examining how it was used as the midwife of the industrial economy.

The earliest known watermills in Britain date from the Roman
occupation – both the mill at Ickenham in Kent built around
AD 150, and mills at Haltwhistle Burn and Chesters on Hadrian's
Wall dating from the third century, used vertical wheels. A handful
of Saxon waterwheels have also been discovered, mostly using
horizontal wheels. The first documentary evidence dates from 762
and by the ninth century mills were commonly mentioned in
monastic charters. By 1300 there were between 8,000 and 9,000
water-powered corn mills in England with a further 2,000 to 3,000
windmills.[2] When the monasteries lost power in the sixteenth
century their exclusive rights over milling were taken up by newly
built private mills, while in some places the local manor retained
milling rights until the mid-nineteenth century.[3]

The engineering and technological nous involved in mill
building and maintenance should not be underestimated – indeed
eighteenth-century industrial engineers were very familiar with
mill technology (Watt borrowed the steam governor from a device
used on windmills). Most mills diverted natural streams into leats
or mill races; streams were occasionally dammed, either with
straight or angled weirs (low dams that allow water to flood over),
or with a combination of dams and sluices.

The vertical waterwheel came in three types: undershot, where
the stream flows into the bottom of the wheel, which is driven by
the force of water; overshot, which feeds water into buckets from
above using gravity to turn the wheel, and was used when more
power was needed; breast shot, where water comes into the wheel
at the midpoint, was used where conditions did not allow for an
overshot to be built.[4] As well as the type of wheel, size was an
important engineering decision, affected by the speed and volume
of water and the uses of the mill. Where water gradients were small,
large wheels were used – seventeen feet in diameter on the River
Tame in Staffordshire and as large as twenty feet in Suffolk. Fulling
mills needed smaller wheels than corn mills, and most waterwheels

were between ten and fifteen feet before the Industrial Revolution.

So what did industrial engineers learn from watermills? The gearing and drive systems were typically arranged to send power at right angles and also to speed up the rotation – in corn mills the stones turn faster than the waterwheels. Cams, shafts, wheels, cogs, lantern gears and trips were all employed, as well as offset cranks and striker plates for fulling. Millwrights had to be able to work as wheelwrights, carpenters, turners, stonemasons, builders and smiths; adaptability was a key part of the engineer's skills.

As well as setting engineering precedents, watermills influenced later factory design through their internal layout; the upper floors were used to receive and store the raw materials which were hoisted up externally using a lucam (a projecting beam with a winch); the material then flowed through the working processes and out of the lower doors as the finished product. The financial workings of mills were important too; their method of operating through a toll system created a pattern of licence and finance that Thomas Newcomen and Boulton & Watt both followed.

The influence of watermills became more direct with the building of the first silk factory at Derby around 1702–4. This first effort was unsuccessful but was followed in 1721 by the Lombe brothers' Derby mill, powered by a twenty-three-feet-diameter waterwheel with a horizontal driveshaft running the length of the building with regular take-offs to the different machines. Other silk mills were built in Stockport, Macclesfield and Congleton in the 1730s to 1750s.

The use of water power in the iron industry expanded with the increased use of powered bellows for blast furnaces, and hammers for finery forges. Blowing and crushing ore needed power, as did the cutlery and tool-making trades with their use of hammers and grinding wheels. By 1794 there were 111 waterwheels being used by cutlers in Sheffield alone. Other industries using water power, including paper-making, seed-crushing for oil and making gunpowder, all increased in capacity during early industrialisation.

The increased demand for power increased the number of waterwheels but it also forced mill-owners to look for alternatives. The cotton industry, in particular, expanded rapidly from 1780, and mill-owners found suitable sites more difficult to come by. Early pioneers converted old corn mills or, as at Strutt's mill at Milford in Derbyshire, reused old iron-making sites. Lancashire was a good location with early mills clustered along Pennine streams at Mottram, Royton, Chorley and the like. But suitable locations soon filled up – at one time there were sixty water-powered mills of different kinds on a three-mile stretch of the Mersey near Manchester – and Lancashire cotton masters had to look to North Wales or the Lancashire coast. By that time Watt's improved steam engine had become a more attractive prospect, despite its running costs.

Water power lasted longest at locations with particular characteristics – steady year-round high-volume streams coupled with the inconvenience of being a long way from coal supplies. New Lanark on the Clyde was the first mill to power the spinning mule by water, while the Quarry Bank mill at Styal in Cheshire, on the River Bolin, powered 9,600 spindles from a thirty-two-feet-diameter, twenty-one-feet-thick breast-shot wheel, installed in 1820. Catrine Cotton Mills on the River Ayr were perhaps the apogee of water power in the textile industry. New wheels were installed at the site in 1827; Sir William Fairbairn wrote thirty-five years later: 'They have not lost a day since that time, and they remain even at the present day, probably the most perfect hydraulic machines of the kind in Europe.'[5]

Water power kept the dwindling wool industry going in the West Country and in rural Wales and Scotland; in fact the water-powered Welsh wool industry grew through the nineteenth century. The Ulster linen industry similarly managed to keep afloat utilising water power.

However, the main problem with water power in the industrialised textile market was its availability and fluctuation. Unlike the corn mills processing the autumn grain harvest, textiles were produced year round and the industry needed a continual power supply. Water power played a decisive role in the mechanisation of industry but it was part of the organic economy; indeed the boundaries of its expansion demonstrate perfectly the limits of an organic system. Industrialisation could only expand and be sustained by the introduction of motive power based on steam. This was to be the great leap into a new age.

6. Steam before Newcomen

The development of steam power took three distinct stages, each led by one of the great heroic figures of British inventive genius: Thomas Newcomen, James Watt and Richard Trevithick. In view of our analysis that the move from an organic to a steam-powered economy was one of the great watersheds of human history, the importance of these three men can hardly be overstated. But before we get to their stories, we need to look further into the past and see how previous generations and cultures had viewed the possibilities of steam.

In fact, the power of pressurised steam was well known to people in the ancient world, while in the sixteenth and seventeenth centuries Europeans began to use steam to unlock the power of the atmosphere. These two applications – steam under pressure and atmospheric engines – were to be the driving forces of the Industrial Revolution.

Pressurised steam had been used to make toys in ancient Greece by the likes of Hero of Alexandria and Ctesibius, and in seventeenth-century Europe it powered fountains and garden ornaments.[1] But its application to industrial purposes first surfaces with the career of David Ramsay, a Scot who came to London in 1603 on the accession of the Scottish king James VI to the English throne, and was appointed Groom of the Bedchamber to James's heir Prince Henry. Ramsay was a clockmaker by profession and a prolific register of patents.[2] These included Patent No. 50 of 1631 containing the following inventions – or at least intentions:

To Raise Water from Lowe Pitts by Fire

To Make any Sort of Mills to goe on Standing Waters by Continual
    Moc'on without the Helpe of Windes, Waite or Horse.

To make Boates, Shippes and Barges to goe against stronge
    Winde and Tyde.

There is no evidence that Ramsay made headway in any of these, but the patent application is a milestone because it shows that men were thinking of practical applications for steam beyond fountains and garden ornaments. The hugely wealthy Edward Somerset (later Marquis of Worcester) was another investigator of steam connected to the Stuart court. In 1654 he set up an engineering works at a cannon foundry in Vauxhall. There, in partnership with his colleague Kaspar Kalthoff, Worcester built a large-scale machine following which a 1663 Act of Parliament allowed him to 'Receive the Benefit and Profit of a Water-Commanding Engine by him invented' for ninety-nine years. Was this 'Water-Commanding Engine' a continually working steam engine? In a 1659 pamphlet Worcester described the machine as follows:

> I have taken a piece of a whole Cannon, whereof the end was burst, and filed it three-quarters full of water, stopping and scruing up the broken end, as also the touch-hole, and making a constant fire under it; within 24 hours it burst, and made a great crack; So that having a way to make my Vessels, so that they are strengthened by the force within them, and the one to fill after the other. I have seen the water run like a constant Fountaine-stream forty foot high; one Vessel of Water rarefied by fire driveth up forty of cold water. And a man that tends the work is but to turn two cocks, that one Vessel of Water being consumed, another begins to force and refill with cold water, and so successively, the fire being tended and kept constant, which the self-same Person may likewise abundantly perform in the interim between the necessity of turning the said Cocks.[3]

The steam from the boiler (in this case the enclosed end of a cannon) was released into a tank of water with a narrow pipe, from which water would shoot, pointing upwards. Water would be drained from another tank down into the boiler to keep it topped up; when steam was achieved it could then be released into either of the water tanks and the cycle restarted. It is unlikely that Worcester was able to make the device self-sustaining, nevertheless he is describing the use of high-pressure steam from a cylinder (in this case a cannon barrel) to drive a continuous spout of water. As cylinders form the basis of almost all engines in use in the world today, this was a significant step.

In 1675 Sir Samuel Morland (1625–95), 'Master of Mechanicks' to King Charles, bought the Vauxhall Foundry used by Worcester, which had in the meantime become a sugar factory. Like Ramsay and Worcester, Morland is one of those people who inhabit the byways of history but who deserve much greater interest. For it was the likes of Morland who began to combine contemporary knowledge about the natural world with an innate desire to make things. He devised and built adding and trigonometry calculating machines – including one for pounds, shillings and pence – metal fire hearths, barometers, a machine for weighing anchors, water pumps and, central to our story, both an internal combustion chamber and a steam-driven pump. A patent was granted to Morland in March 1674, which stated: 'We are fully satisfied [that the apparatus] is altogether new and may be of great use for the clering of all sortes of mines, and also applicable to divers kinds of manufactures within our dominions.'[4] The state papers from 1682 tell us that: 'Sir Samuel Morland has lately shown the King a plain proof of two several and distinct trials of a new invention for raising any quantity of water to any height by the help of fire alone.'[5]

It was long doubted whether a machine was ever built, but in 1936 H. W. Dickinson, James Watt's biographer, discovered a sketch in the diary of the eminent seventeenth-century MP, lawyer and biographer Roger North (1653–1734). While the sketch is frustratingly vague, and North's accompanying description shows that he was recalling something he had seen without much understanding of exactly how the machine was working, it is the earliest record of steam from a boiler being used to move a piston in a separate cylinder from the boiler. It is also the first mention of a self-acting valve gear – the falling bar being used to 'shut out the steam . . . by a stop cock'. However, there is no indication of how the downward plunge of the piston was achieved after the steam was shut off, and there is no record of anyone building directly from Morland's design, which was probably unknown to later inventors.

Morland took the work on pistons a stage further by exploding a small charge of gunpowder in a cylinder in order either to force a piston to move, or to create a vacuum that would suck a piston in; Christiaan Huygens was experimenting with that idea at about the same time. Neither of these were steam-powered devices, but their use of a moving piston in a cylinder was important to the story of steam.

All these machines used steam under pressure. And while most of us would now assume that this was the simplest and most obvious way of harnessing its power, this wasn't how steam was first used in engines. In fact the world had to wait until 1801 for Richard Trevithick to build a full-scale working engine powered by pressurised steam. In the meantime a different characteristic of steam was employed in the engines that powered the early Industrial Revolution.

These were static engines, driven by the effect created when steam is rapidly condensed, or turned back to water. These so-called atmospheric engines worked on the basis that, firstly, nature abhors a vacuum, and secondly that the atmosphere has weight. The third premise was that, when steam condenses, the volume of water it makes is around 1,800 times smaller than the volume of the steam, thereby creating the possibility of a vacuum. The knowledge of these fundamentals came not from those interested in building mechanical devices for entertainment or decoration but from philosophers observing natural phenomena.

It was an article of faith among medieval philosophers that the universe was full of God's creations, and therefore a vacuum could not exist. This carried the stamp of classical authority, from Aristotle's explanation of how water pumps work: if you attempt to create a vacuum it will become filled with water and this will enable water to rise. But then, in 1641, engineers working at the villa of Cosimo de'Medici in Florence created a vacuum, which they planned to use to pump water from a well fifteen metres deep. They expected the water to travel up a long pipe to fill the vacuum they had created in the upper chamber. But however much they tried, the water would not rise more than ten metres. The men sought the advice of Galileo, by then living at Arcreti near Florence. The elder statesman of science was mystified too, but after his death in 1642, his pupil Evangelista Torricelli decided to investigate the problem.

Torricelli saw that, rather than being sucked upwards by the vacuum, the water was pushed up the vertical pipe by the weight of the atmosphere pressing on the water at the bottom of the well. The vacuum was essentially an absence of atmosphere: so the water rose until the weight of the water in the vacuum section of the pump equalled that of the atmosphere acting on the water in the well. The vacuum was held in balance by the weight of water and the counteracting weight of the atmosphere.

Torricello realised that, if this were true, then a heavier liquid would rise to a lower height than the ten metres achieved by the water, and when, in 1643, he and his pupil Vaviani tested the effect of a vacuum on a column of mercury they found that it rose just 80 cm. In doing so he invented the mercury barometer, but more important, this seemed to support his theory.

When the French philosopher Blaise Pascal heard about Torricello's mercury column he took the experiment a step further. He suggested that the weight of the atmosphere at sea level should be greater than at high altitudes, and as Pascal was living in the low-lying Normandy city of Rouen, he asked his brother-in-law, Florin Périer, to test his hypothesis. On 19 September 1648 Périer climbed the 1,500-metre Puy de Dôme near Clermont-Ferrand carrying a glass tube containing mercury. Sure enough, on reaching the summit, the mercury had risen by just 71 cm, 9 cm less than at sea level – this was proof that the weight of the atmosphere diminished with height.

While Otto von Guericke of Magdeburg was probably unaware of Torricello's work, he was also fascinated by the effects of vacuums. In an early experiment he pumped air out of a copper sphere, and was surprised at the force of air that rushed in when he opened a tap in its side. Encouraged by this he then placed two copper hemispheres together, connected only by an airtight seal, pumped the air out of them and then challenged two teams of horses to pull them apart. They failed, showing the extraordinary power generated by a vacuum inside a vessel. Guericke's next experiment, conducted in the 1650s, showed this power not just as a passive resistance, but as a powerful dynamic force. First, he built a metal cylinder with a tightly fitting piston. A group of men then pulled on a rope attached to the piston rod, thereby creating a partial vacuum in the cylinder. Guericke now connected a sphere, which held a vacuum, to the cylinder and opened a valve between them. The small amount of air that was left in the cylinder rushed into the vacuum in the sphere and the piston was sucked inwards, overpowering the best efforts of twenty men to prevent it. The creation and destruction of a vacuum could generate power previously unknown to humanity.

In the 1660s the English scientist Robert Boyle toured Europe where he learned of the work of Torricelli, Pascal and Guericke. His work on gases became the foundation of a new science but his experiments also required improved devices for pumping air, which he developed. Other experimenters too looked for better ways to create a vacuum. Sir Samuel Morland, Christiaan Huygens and the Frenchman Jean de Hautefeuille all experimented with using gunpowder to blow air out of a cylinder, but the most significant step was taken by Huygens's French assistant Denis Papin.

Papin was a Huguenot who had left his native France in 1675 to make a career as a scientist and inventor in England. In common with his predecessors he understood that the creation of a vacuum provided a source of power. Sometime between 1690 and 1695 Papin abandoned the idea of a gunpowder charge and instead placed a small amount of water in the bottom of a cylinder, with a piston at the top. He heated the water, which drove the piston upwards, and the resulting steam pushed most of the air out of the cylinder. When the fire was removed, the steam condensed and the piston was pulled down by the resulting vacuum and the weight of the atmosphere. Papin thus hit upon the two applications of steam that were to drive the Industrial Revolution – the ability of steam to create a vacuum, as used by Thomas Newcomen and James Watt in their atmospheric engines, and the pushing force of steam under pressure, which would drive Richard Trevithick's locomotives.

The story of steam before the great breakthrough by Thomas Newcomen culminates in the figure of Captain Thomas Savery, a wealthy gentleman from Devon with a keen interest in mechanical devices. On 25 July 1698 Savery was awarded a fourteen-year patent for 'Raising water by the impellent force of fire', which was extended in 1699 for a further twenty-one years. Savery's apparatus was a pump rather than an engine, but it was the first steam device known to have been used on a large scale. The pump was not an experimental model nor a playful garden ornament but a practical device for taking water out of mines, a problem that bedevilled the coal and metals miners of Britain.

The pump had no moving parts other than valves and used both properties of steam that we have been tracing: its use in creating a vacuum, and the power of steam working under pressure.

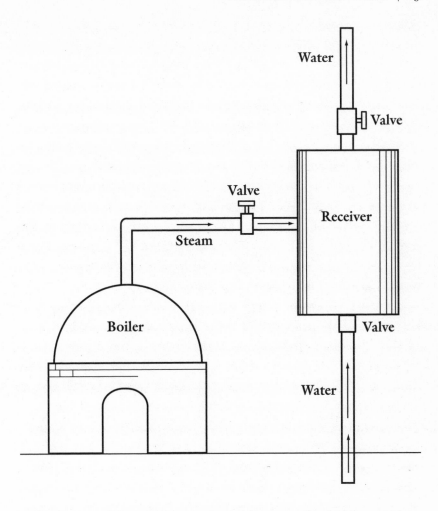

Savery pump: Firstly steam was sent from a boiler into a vessel called a receiver. Once filled with steam the valve between the two was shut off and cold water was poured over the outside of the receiver. This condensed the steam inside and created a vacuum. A different valve was then opened on a pipe leading from the receiver down to the water in the mine. The presence of the vacuum caused the water to be forced up the pipe, which could then be closed off. The next stage was to force the water now in the receiver up through a third pipe and out of the mine. This was done by sending yet more steam into the receiver from the boiler and opening a valve in the third pipe to allow water to be expelled under the pressure of the steam. The process of sealing off the receiver and condensing the steam was then begun again.

Savery improved his pump in 1699 by using two receivers working alternately from the same boiler: he then developed it further by using a wheeled valve so that when one receiver was open the other was closed. His 1702 book *The Miner's Friend* revealed the final improvements – a sector plate in the shape of a fan, which was later adapted by Newcomen and Watt to automatically open and close steam valves. He also added a second 'feeder' boiler to keep the so-called 'great boiler' continually topped up with water via a clack (or one-way) valve. Savery could have omitted the third phase of the process (in which steam is driven upwards under pressure) and simply allowed the water to be drained off at the level of the receiver, but he would have faced the same problems as Torricello in Florence – the water forced up the original pipe would never be lifted more than thirty feet or so.

The use of steam under pressure had its dangers, as John Desaguliers later described in 1744: 'I have known Captain Savery, at York Buildings make steam eight or ten times stronger than common air; and then its Heat was so great that it would melt common soft Solder; and its Strength so great as to blow open several of the Joints of his Machine; so that he was forc'd to be at the Pains and Charge to have all his Joints solder'd with Spelter or hard Solder.'[6]

The Savery pump was installed in a few mines, but without much success. The need to heat and cool the receiver during every cycle made it slow and inefficient and it found wider use in the ornamental gardens of the nobility. In 1729 the garden designer Stephen Switzer commented: 'How useful it is in gardens and fountain works ay or might have been seen in the garden of that right noble peer, the present Duke of Chandos, at his late house at Sion Hill, where the engine was placed under a delightful banqueting-house, and the water being forced up into a cistern on the top thereof, used to play a fountain contiguous thereto in a very delightful manner.'[7]

The duke's guests might have been less delighted if they had known that, for all his engineering ingenuity, Savery had never come up with a safety valve.

Despite their failure as pumps for draining mines, Savery pumps were adapted for other uses – they were made until the 1760s, and were still in use in the early 1800s. Developers got round the problem of high-pressure steam by using the pumps only as suction devices, with the water that was pulled into the receiver being drained into a cistern that could then drive a waterwheel. Joshua Rigley of Manchester built this type of pump in Lancashire in the 1760s, while in 1827 John Farey described an adapted Savery engine driving lathes at a works in St Pancras. But the real importance of the Savery pump comes from its proximity to its successor, the Newcomen engine.

7. The Newcomen Engine

However much we are able to trace the development of steam power through the preceding centuries, and however much ingenuity was shown by the likes of Worcester, Papin and Savery, the engine developed by Thomas Newcomen was such a bold and brilliant advance that it deserves a place among the greatest inventions in human history. Not only did Newcomen show great technical imagination and flair, he also worked tirelessly to make his invention into a practical working engine. This was the first machine that replaced human, animal and water power; its effect on the world could hardly have been greater.

Little is known about the life of Thomas Newcomen. His father Elias was a freeholder in the town of Dartmouth in Devon, but there is no documentary evidence of his working life. Thomas was born in Dartmouth and christened on 24 February 1664 – birth records were not commonly kept but it is fair to assume that he was born in January or February. His family were Nonconformists, probably Baptists, and had connections with the scholar John Flavel of Bromsgrove, a place that was to feature in Newcomen's career. The historian Thomas Lidstone (1821–88) wrote three pamphlets about Newcomen and included the fact that he was apprenticed to an ironmonger in Exeter, but no record of this has been found.[1]

When aged twenty-one Newcomen is likely to have completed his apprenticeship and returned to Dartmouth. We know from contemporary accounts that he set up business with his fellow devout Baptist John Calley (sometimes known as Cawley) in the ironmongery trade. Newcomen married in 1705 and his son Elias was born the following year – he would later take on his father's business. In 1707 Newcomen took a lease on a large house where he conducted his ironmongery business, with part of it used as a place of worship; by this time he had become the preacher of the local Baptist congregation.[2] While the house was the base of the business it seems that Newcomen and Calley used a nearby workshop for the practical side of their work, and it was here that they carried out their experiments with steam and built their prototype engines. Calley was a plumber and glazier, Newcomen a blacksmith–ironmonger. This term described the making and repair of more or less anything made of metal including tools, receptacles, fire irons and the like, but possibly also more sophisticated instruments and guns.

So how did Newcomen, a Dartmouth ironmonger, become interested in steam power? We can only speculate, but his proximity to the tin and copper mines of Cornwall and Devon may have been crucial. He certainly visited the mines in the course of his business (he also travelled the locality as a Baptist preacher) and knew the problems they had with drainage. There may have even been a Savery pump working in one of these mines, but although Savery and Newcomen came from the same county there is no evidence that they met before Newcomen had built his engine. Suggestions by nineteenth-century historians that Newcomen knew about Papin's and Worcester's work or that he was in correspondence with Robert Boyle have all been discounted; the likelihood of a Devon tradesman reading the *Philosophical Transactions of the Royal Society* is indeed negligible. It may have seemed unbelievable to Victorian historians that an untutored artisan could have made such a groundbreaking invention without the help of scientists and aristocrats – but in that sense he was more typical than they knew.

In fact Newcomen did not follow in direct line from any of his predecessors; he took findings from each (while unaware of their origins) and created something quite different. It is clear that the problem of water in mines was sufficiently pressing to engage a number of people, so it is perhaps not surprising that developments happened in parallel. And while we can make reasonable conjectures as to why Newcomen became interested in solving the problem using steam power, there is no explanation for his extraordinary dedication to making a working engine. Newcomen simply embodied that necessary combination of inspiration and perspiration.

The most reliable witness to Newcomen's work was a young Swedish engineer called Marten Triewald who came to England in 1716 – after the first Newcomen engines had been built – and stayed for the next ten years. He visited Newcomen and Calley in their workshop and later helped to erect a Newcomen engine at Byker colliery near Newcastle, before himself building an engine at Dannemora mines after his return to Sweden. In 1734 he gave an account of the motivation behind Newcomen's work:

> Now it happens that a man from Dartmouth, named Thomas Newcomen, without any knowledge whatever of the speculations of Captain Savery, had at the same time also made up his mind, in conjunction with his assistant, a plumber by the name of Calley, to invent a fire-machine for drawing water from the mines. He was induced to undertake this by considering the heavy cost of lifting water by means of horses, which Mr Newcomen found existing in English tin mines. These mines Mr Newcomen often visited in the capacity of a dealer in iron tools with which he used to furnish many of the tin mines.[3]

According to Triewald and another contemporary writer, Stephen Switzer, Newcomen and Calley began serious work on their engine in 1698 at the latest. But the first fully working Newcomen engine was not installed until 1712 – so what happened in the intervening fourteen years? As we don't have any documentary evidence, we have to make assumptions from the end result. It seems certain that both men worked part time on the idea while carrying out their normal business. And once Newcomen had conceived the central idea of the engine it is likely that they made scale models; while this was an essential step it could have caused problems due to the 'scale effect' whereby heat loss and friction are more exaggerated at small scale.

Newcomen's first requirement when building a model was to have a cylinder and piston with a reliable seal. He probably used the seven-inch-diameter cast-brass pump cylinders that were common at the time, applied a leather seal round the piston head, and then put water on top of the seal to improve its resistance to leaks. It was a relatively simple process to introduce steam into the cylinder, but the next phase in the engine's cycle required the steam to condense. To allow this to happen naturally (as Papin had done) would have been too slow for a working engine. It seems that Newcomen first poured cold water over the cylinder, as Savery had done on his pump. But he soon revised this method and instead built a jacket around the cylinder, through which he circulated cold water. This would have got the engine to work but probably not to a satisfactory level. Even with the beam and rods working in the right way the engine would have struggled to maintain a continuous action.

Though the cooling of the cylinder might seem a secondary matter compared to the generation of power, it was of fundamental importance. In fact the removal of excess heat from engines is still a prime concern of engineers: around 90 per cent of the heat in steam engines, and 70 per cent in internal combustion engines, is waste. Newcomen knew that the cooling needed to be both efficient and rapid, otherwise all his work would be in vain.

The next advance therefore was dramatic: Marten Triewald described (see capsule text p. 39) how a pin-hole in the brass allowed cold water to shoot directly into the cylinder, creating an immediate vacuum and pulling the piston down with such force that it crushed the bottom of the cylinder sending water flying everywhere.

We can imagine the scene in the small workshop. Did

Newcomen and Calley turn to each other, perhaps first in panic and amazement, and then with the realisation that they had, through their immense perseverance and ingenuity, stumbled on something extraordinary and transforming? Did they then pick through the pieces and discover how this had happened and immediately take steps to reproduce the 'accident' under controlled conditions? Something like that surely happened.

This was a happy accident but it never would have come about without the years of tenacity that preceded it. Newcomen still had to solve other fundamental problems, including how to rid the cylinder of the condensed steam (now water) and of the air that entered with the steam – he no doubt had to rebalance his beam in order to take account of the different level of force, and later developed a system of rods and levers so that the engine operated its own valves automatically – but now he must have known that once he solved those technical problems, his engine would run continuously. Human labour was about to be replaced, for the first time in history, by a mechanical device driven by energy derived from the earth.

Writing in 1844, William Pole asserted that the first Newcomen engine was installed in Huel Vor mine in Breage, Cornwall, around 1710, but there is no documentary evidence of its existence.[4] The first fully working commercial Newcomen engine that we can be certain about was erected in 1712 at Dudley Castle colliery; Newcomen had been introduced to the manager of the colliery by a fellow Baptist. This first engine was an extremely sophisticated machine in which all the essential technical problems had been solved; it even included a system of automatic valves. Marten Triewald tells us that: 'The cylinder of this machine measured 21 inches in diameter and was 7 feet 10 inches high. The boiler was 5 feet 6 inches in diameter and 6 feet 1 inch high. The water in the boiler stood 4 feet 4 inches high and contained 13 hogsheads; besides, the machine delivered at every rise or lift (12 lifts in a minute) 10 English gallons of water, and the mine was 51 yards or 25½ fathoms deep.'[5]

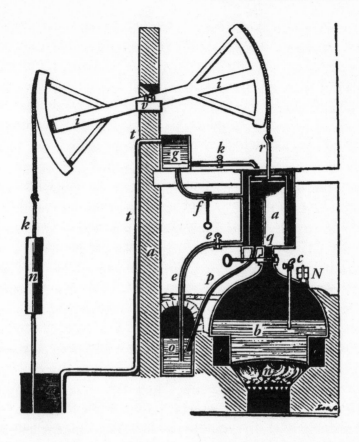

Newcomen's first engine: A metal cylinder [a] with a piston forming an airtight seal at one end and closed at the other, is filled with steam injected from a boiler [b]. Cold water is then injected into the cylinder via a valve [f], condensing the steam. The resulting vacuum pulls the piston down into the cylinder. The top of the piston is attached to one end of a balanced beam [i]; drawing the piston down pulls up the other end of the beam. When the vacuum is released the beam tilts back under gravity. The power is therefore provided by the force of the vacuum created when the steam in the cylinder is turned to water – which occupies only 1/1600th of its volume. This power in turn comes from the steam, which is heated by burning coal. This, therefore, was the first successful conversion of the thermal energy of coal into the mechanical energy of movement.

As Triewald was trying to promote the engine to his fellow Swedes he was inclined to inflate the effect it had: 'As the rumour of this magnificent art soon spread all over England, many, who were anxious to make use of this invention at their mines, in the country and abroad, and who exerted themselves to acquire the necessary knowledge for the purpose of constructing a similar wonderful machine, came from all parts of England and abroad to Dudley Castle.'[6]

In fact, in view of its historical importance, the engine and its successors were remarkably little reported. And while colliery managers immediately understood its value, the commercial exploitation of the engine was hampered by one important factor. Thomas Savery's patent of 1698 stated that he had invented the means of 'raising water by the impellent force of fire' and this was considered broad enough to encompass Newcomen's engine, even though the two devices were entirely different. As we have seen, at this time the patent system was still a way of protecting or granting monopolies over entire industries rather than protecting inventions.

Stephen Switzer wrote in 1729: 'I am well informed that Mr Newcomen was as early in his Invention as Mr Savery was in his, only the latter being nearer the Court, had obtain'd his Patent before the other knew it, on which account Mr Newcomen was glad to come in as a Partner to it.'[7] As Savery's patent had been extended to 1733, Newcomen was forced to seek the other inventor's permission to install his engines and to come to an arrangement over payments, the details of which have been lost to history. Only then was Newcomen able to go ahead and start building. From 1712 the spread of his machines was localised but rapid; by 1716 a Newcomen engine was at work at Hawarden in Flintshire; in 1725 Henry Beighton published a map of Warwickshire showing engines at Hawkesbury, Fackley and Griff collieries; and between 1724 and 1727 colliery owner Richard Beach ordered four cast-iron steam engine cylinders from the Coalbrookdale company.

Rather than constructing them himself, Newcomen sold licences and plans to the builders of these engines. In fact, one of the great attractions of the Newcomen engine (as opposed to the later more sophisticated machines designed by Watt and Trevithick) was that they could be made and maintained by any competent local engineer. An early example of such an arrangement appears in a licence with James Lowther of Whitehaven in Cumbria, dated 10 November 1715: 'Thomas Newcomen, ironmonger, of Dartmouth, Devon, and others covenanted with Mr Lowther to set up a fire-engine with a steam barrel of at least 16 inches diameter within, and eight feet in length . . . and that such engine had accordingly been erected and since continued to be wrought there.'[8]

The parts for the machine were sent by sea from London. At this time the Whitehaven mines had reached a depth of fifty fathoms (300 feet) with the Newcomen engine probably tipping water into an adit halfway up the shaft. Dr William Stukeley described the machine when he visited the site in 1725:

> At last the famous fire-engine discharges the water, which is a notable piece of machinery working itself entirely; it creates a vacuum by first rarefying the air with hot steam, then condenses it suddenly by cold water; whence a piston is drawn up and down alternately, at one end of the beam: this actuates a pump at the other end, which, let down into the works, draws the water out: it makes about fourteen strokes a minute, so that it empties 140 hogsheads in an hour with moderate working.[9]

Let us pause here to marvel at this. Even at the very early stages of the machine's working life, when some historians have characterised it as inefficient, Newcomen had got his engine moving a sixteen-inch-diameter piston through a stroke of eight feet once every four and a half seconds. This was a stupendous engineering achievement, brought about by alternate injections of steam and cold water, using nothing more than the waste coal piled at the pithead; it enabled the engine to pump over 33,000 litres of water every hour. By 1755 the Whitehaven mines were the deepest in the world, using four Newcomen engines to drain a depth of 800 feet.

In 1714 or 1715 a Newcomen engine was also built at Moor Hall colliery in Leeds, the birthplace of the engineer John Smeaton.

Those were the mines that we know, from firm documentary evidence, had Newcomen engines at the time of Thomas Savery's death in 1715; this was an important date, because the rights in his patent now passed to a syndicate – and the development and spread of Newcomen's machines had made the Savery patent much more valuable.

The Newcomen engines now spread across English coalfields and into metal mines in Cornwall and Derbyshire. Often towering above pitheads, they drew a range of curious eighteenth-century travellers. The engine at a lead mine at Yatesstoop in Derbyshire was described by the Reverend James Clegg:

> September 28th 1730 – I set out with Mr Tricket to see some remarkables in several parts of ye Peak . . . came to Winster about noon. Saw 3 curious Engines at work there, which by ye force of fire heating water to vapour a prodigious weight of water was raised from a very great depth, and a vast quantity of lead ore laid dry. The hott vapour ascends from an iron pan, close covered, through a brass cylinder fixed to the top, and by its expanding force raised one end of the engine, which is brought down again by the sudden introduction of a dash of cold water into ye same cylinder which condenseth the vapour. Thus the hott vapour and cold water act by turns, and give ye clearest demonstration of ye mighty elastic force of air.[10]

Newcomen left no records of his own work, so we have to appreciate his genius at second hand. He made small additions to his engine design while other engineers improved such things as the shape of the boiler. The admission valve that let steam from the boiler into the cylinder was almost certainly developed by Newcomen and Calley; its intricate mechanism using a tumbling bob is evidence of huge attention to detail by the original pair of workers. Newcomen also developed a mechanism called a buoy which slowed the engine down so that it would not suck too much steam out of the boiler at each stroke, thereby halting the rhythm of the engine. This was present in the Dudley Castle engine, but once boilers were enlarged and improved the buoy became unnecessary. Newcomen was also the first to develop a valve that used gravity acting on a weight to open it, and upward pressure (by steam) to close it. The piston seals were also improved by using hemp rather than leather. New techniques were used in the pumps themselves to cope with the power of the engines. As the rods could be immensely long, timber 'spears' or masts were used.

Engineering firms were well aware that Savery's patent was to expire in 1733, leaving them free to build their own engines and to make improvements and adaptations. Richard Ford, Abe Darby's son-in-law and successor as head of the Coalbrookdale Company, wrote to his partner Thomas Goldney in March 1733: 'As ye patent for ye Fire Engine is about expiring, that business will consequently more increase.'[11]

However, the basic Newcomen engine stayed remarkably constant until the revolutionary changes wrought by James Watt. While this was partly due to the social and commercial currents of the time, it seems that Newcomen's engine was such an enormous leap into the technological future that it took a couple of generations for other engineers to understand fully its technical implications.

By far the most important adaptation was the widespread use of cast iron rather than brass for cylinders, which allowed them to be made ever bigger: in 1763 a cylinder seventy-four inches in diameter and of ten-and-a-half-feet stroke was built at Coalbrookdale. By then the Northumberland coalfield – the most productive in Britain – was dotted with Newcomen engines. Jesmond, Heaton and Tynemouth collieries each ran four engines, Long Benton five, and Byker six. Using multiple engines increased running costs but on Tyneside coal was extremely cheap. In 1752 the first iron cylinder on Tyneside was installed at Throckley, owned by William Brown, who was the most noted engine builder in the region. This first engine had a gigantic forty-seven-inch-diameter cylinder and Brown put up another twenty-two engines on Tyneside and others in

Scotland. He also erected the biggest Newcomen engine ever built: the gigantic seventy-four-inch engine at Walker colliery was fed by four boilers, and its cylinder, which was built at Coalbrookdale, weighed six and a half tons.

In 1769 John Smeaton asked William Brown to make a list of the engines in the north of England and Scotland. There were then ninety-nine engines in total; twenty-one had cylinders of sixty inches or greater in diameter, almost certainly all recently made of iron.

While coal was cheap in collieries and at metal mines near northern coalfields, in the lucrative mining districts of Cornwall it was expensive. But this situation was eased in 1741 when the duty on coal was lifted. While there had been just one Newcomen engine in 1740, William Borlase, the Cornish naturalist, reported thirteen engines in Cornish mines by 1758; in 1769 John Smeaton listed eighteen, and by 1775 there were more than sixty.[12] The Cornish connection was crucial for the development of steam power. First, the particular needs of the mines in the south-west of England made Cornish engineers develop their own ideas and adaptations, leading eventually to Richard Trevithick's revolutionary work. The second reason was Cornwall's connection to North America.

One of the main builders of Newcomen engines in the county was the Hornblower family – Jonathan Hornblower together with his sons Jonathan and Josiah. It was Josiah who introduced the atmospheric engine to America via Colonel John Schuyler, who opened a copper mine at North Arlington, New Jersey, in 1715. After sinking a deep shaft in 1735, Schuyler was unable to go deeper due to lying water; he travelled to Cornwall in search of a solution. In 1753 Josiah Hornblower sailed from Falmouth to London, where he oversaw the loading of the components for a Newcomen engine; on 6 June 1753 the *Irene* sailed, reaching New York in September. The bad weather on the voyage made Hornblower swear he would never sail again, and he stayed in America for the rest of his life. At North Arlington it took eighteen months to quarry the stone to build the engine house, which needed a strong so-called 'fulcrum wall' to support the overhead beam, but in March 1755 the first ever steam engine in America was fired up and, with modifications, ran until the early nineteenth century. The lower part of the iron cylinder, thirty inches in diameter and eight feet long, is now in the Smithsonian Institution in Washington. Schuyler would go on to build an engineering works next to the mine and it was here that the first steam engine to be entirely forged and built in America was made.

Thomas Newcomen died aged sixty-five on 5 August 1729 in London at the lodging house of a Mr Wallin. By that time he had seen his engines installed across a swathe of Britain. He did not outlast the patent taken out by Thomas Savery, nor did he live to see the steam engine take over the world; nevertheless, he had accomplished his aim of devising an engine that would lift water out of mines. He almost certainly did not realise that, in doing so, he laid the grounds for the transformation of human existence. Newcomen was buried, unmarked, in a common vault at Bunhill Fields Nonconformist Cemetery on City Road, Finsbury, London.

His only obituary appeared in the *Monthly Chronicle*: 'About the same time (7 August 1729) died Mr Thomas Newcomen, sole inventor of that surprising machine for raising water by fire.'[13]

The Engineering Profession

Accounts of the Industrial Revolution naturally focus on the inventors who made the most important breakthroughs. But thousands of mechanics and engineers were at work in eighteenth-century Britain erecting, maintaining and improving Newcomen engines, building roads, bridges, harbours and canals, and constructing mine workings. Engineering began to be recognised as a profession, with engineers able to turn their hand to a variety of tasks. Engineering, which became a crucial part of Britain's conversion to an industrial economy, emerged from a generation of artisan mechanics; however, the most distinguished engineer of the time came from a different background.

John Smeaton was born in Leeds in 1724, attended Leeds Grammar School and entered his father's law firm. But Smeaton gave up the law in order to pursue his scientific and engineering interests.[14] Beginning as a maker of mathematical instruments, he became a skilled and successful engineer, specialising in public works such as harbours, bridges, lighthouses and canals. From the 1750s until his death in 1792 he designed and oversaw a huge array of building projects from the Calder Navigation to Charlestown harbour, including the Eddystone Lighthouse (known as Smeaton's Tower) which now stands on Plymouth Hoe. He called himself a civil engineer, and was probably the world's first. What distinguished Smeaton was his interest and skill in pursuing the theoretical and mathematical aspects while also working as a practical engineer. He made significant contributions in every field he investigated; he was elected a fellow of the Royal Society in 1753 and won the Society's highest award in 1759 for his work on waterwheels and windmills.

From the 1750s Smeaton began to study Newcomen's engines and in 1765, at his workshop at Austhorpe, Leeds, he built a working model of an engine incorporating an oscillating wheel instead of a beam, an internal flue in the boiler, and a small but long cylinder. In 1767 he applied the lessons from the model to an engine installed to pump water up to a high-level reservoir at New River Head in Islington, London. The machine didn't work as well as he hoped, and this provoked Smeaton into undertaking a thorough scientific investigation of all the Newcomen engines in the north of England and Cornwall.

In order to compare their workings Smeaton invented a standard measurement of their efficiency, which he called the Duty – this was the number of millions of pounds weight of water raised through one foot using one bushel of coal. Smeaton also invented a measure of power, which he called the Great Product – this is the volume of water raised through one foot in one minute. This could be expressed in units of horsepower (a concept developed by James Watt), and Smeaton found that the power of an engine with a seventy-five-inch cylinder was 37.6 h.p., while the sixty-inch cylinder produced 40.8 h.p. Against the received wisdom of the day, he found that a larger cylinder, or even higher pressure exerted by the piston, did not necessarily lead to a higher Duty or Great Product.

Smeaton saw that the variations in performance could be ironed out by more care being invested in construction, maintenance and operation – using the full length of stroke, firing the boiler correctly, maintaining the cylinder bore, and so on. He adjusted the beam so that the pistons were slightly resistant to the introduction of the steam, which ensured that air did not enter the cylinder at the same time; he increased the height of the cold-water header tank so that the injection of condensing water was a fine spray. The engine water was usually taken direct from the pumped mine water, which led to corrosion and scaling, so Smeaton used only rainwater. He introduced regulatory devices, including a pet-cock to allow in some air when necessary, and a cataract or 'Jack in the Box' to make the supply of water intermittent. These enabled the engines to run at less than full

load without making them less efficient by, for example, short-
ening the piston stroke. The first engine built by Smeaton with
all these improvements was installed at Long Benton colliery in
Northumberland in 1772. The Duty figure was 9.45 million, a
huge improvement on the 7.44 million achieved by the most
efficient engine. He went on to build other Newcomen engines,
including one used to empty the docks at Kronstadt in Russia.

Other engineers made improvements to the Newcomen
engine and adapted it to different uses. Joseph Oxley used a patent
ratchet device in 1763 at Hartley colliery in Seaton Delaval,
Northumberland, to turn a 'whim' or cable drum, but the movement was too irregular so was converted to a waterwheel. John
Stewart patented a ratchet in 1766 and in 1768 he built a
Newcomen engine in Jamaica to power a sugar mill; all before
the breakthrough made by Matthew Wasbrough and James
Pickard (see p. 131). Improvements to the boiler by recycling heat
were made by James Brindley and Sampson Swaine. All of these
preceded the revolution brought about by the work of James Watt;
though even during Watt's dominance of steam power other engineers continued to improve old Newcomen engines. In the 1790s,
the firm of Bateman and Sherrat of Salford supplied engines to
Lancashire cotton mills with two cylinders working alternately,
which drove an overhead 'rocking shaft'. In 1795 Hornblower and
Maberley connected two cylinders to an overhead pulley, while
Francis Thompson of Derbyshire used two forty-inch cylinders,
each with a six-foot stroke, arranged vertically with the top one
inverted. In 1790 John Curr of Sheffield placed boilers in a separate
location at Attercliffe Common colliery.

All these adaptations and improvements made Newcomen
engines more efficient and fit for purpose. However, the
combined ingenuity of these and a thousand other engineers
could not make the Newcomen engine into a multipurpose
power source; to do that took the special genius of James Watt.

8. James Watt's Revolution

Every schoolchild knows that James Watt invented the steam engine. In fact he didn't, but strangely enough the fact that Watt was not the originator of steam power makes his achievements all the more remarkable. He had the vision and the engineering genius to adapt an engine with limited application, and use it to open the way for the industrialisation of Britain. Watt went well beyond the level of brilliant inventor to become the guiding spirit of the age; he was able to isolate and solve engineering problems in ways that no one else could, and thereby ushered in the powered mechanisation of industry.

Watt's role was central because, as we have seen elsewhere, the transition from an advanced organic economy to one based on power derived from fossil fuel was far from inevitable. It took a special combination of scientific curiosity and inventive genius to understand the possibilities that steam power offered, and to work out how to exploit them. Watt was one of the few inventors of the eighteenth century to show an interest in solving theoretical as well as practical problems; this double facility enabled him to meet a series of challenges with apparent ease and dazzling success.[1]

By the 1760s steam power in the form of Newcomen engines had been around for more than half a century without radically changing the power source of most manufacturing; put in context, that is like us still using the room-sized computers of the 1960s to carry out a few specialist tasks. It was the series of adaptations devised and brought in by Watt, encouraged by his backer Matthew Boulton, that put steam power within reach of every factory and mill. This allowed mechanised industry to shed its reliance on water power and relocate from isolated valleys with fast-flowing rivers to towns and cities, coalfields and iron-mining districts. The resulting double concentration of industrial production – into large factories located in specific regions – changed the nature of work and human society. More than that, Watt's demonstration that steam could be an efficient and effective power source led directly to the development of steam locomotives and the advent of the powered economy.

James Watt was born in 1736 in the town of Greenock, a seaport on the outer estuary of the Clyde. At that time the Clyde region was, even by the standards of the day, lacking any significant industrial development. The main occupations were fishing and farming, with shippers carrying on a steady trade with Ireland and a growing trade with the Americas. The Clyde had not yet been deepened to allow ships access to Glasgow, then a city of 12,000 inhabitants described by Daniel Defoe in 1724 as 'the best built city in Britain, London excepted'.[2] The Act of Union in 1707 gave Scottish towns access to English markets and to international trade through growing British sea power; by law all colonial trade passed through Britain and, though the lucrative Atlantic trade was still in its infancy, the west of Scotland was to benefit mightily.

Although Greenock was a small town of around 3,000 inhabitants, it had enough trade to support Watt's father James, who trained as a wright or carpenter before becoming a house- and shipbuilder, ship's chandler and merchant. James Watt Jnr excelled at mathematics at the local grammar school but his education was underpinned by the time he spent in his father's workshop. Here, in the words of his biographer George Williamson, he would have seen 'the carving of ships' figure-heads, the making of gun-carriages, of blocks, pumps, capstans, dead-eyes . . . the adjusting and repairing of nautical instruments [and] . . . the first Crane made at Greenock, for the convenience of the Virginia tobacco ships then frequenting the harbour'.[3]

In view of Watt's practical ingenuity and dexterity the value of this experience can hardly be overestimated; Watt is the great example of the eighteenth-century inventor – a third-generation artisan steeped in the experiences of the professional workshop, with enough education to enhance his practical skills. After James left school he was given a bench in his father's shop, which he used for making models and helping to repair instruments. After his mother's death in 1753 the young man went to Glasgow in search of work as an instrument-maker. In need of formal training Watt was drawn to London, the world centre for making barometers, thermometers, balances, forceps, armillary spheres and all manner of technical and scientific equipment. So in 1755 Watt made the twelve-day journey south; by this time he was too old to start an apprenticeship, and was fortunate to find a master willing to provide a short, intense training.

Watt left London the following summer with a copy of the Frenchman Nicolas Bion's 1709 manual *The Construction and Principal Uses of Mathematical Instruments* (translated into English in 1723) and set up shop in the precincts of Glasgow University, styling himself 'Mathematical-instrument-maker to the University'. While Scotland may have been in the infancy of its economic growth, its universities were highly advanced and the curricula were far more scientifically based than England's. Watt was something of an autodidact: he never went to college but learned German and Italian for his work and acquired enough mathematics to hold his own with academically trained scientists.

Watt made little money in his time in the university grounds but he did make useful friends, including Joseph Black, professor of chemistry, and the noted scientist and philosopher John Robison. Watt travelled to London again in August 1759 to drum up trade and his business began to flourish when he received the financial support of one John Craig, who became his partner. He moved his shop to bigger premises in the Saltmarket and, under his arrangement with Craig, was paid £35 a year and half the profits of the partnership.

James Watt

We know that around this time Watt was carrying out experiments with steam. In 1761 he took a device known as a Papin Digester – a round boiler with a narrow tube in the top for escaping steam – and fitted a piston in the form of a syringe to the top. A steam cock was put between the boiler and the syringe to allow steam to be diverted; when it was allowed into the syringe, the piston could lift a weight of fifteen pounds. But rather than encouraging Watt, the pressure he had generated made him fearful of the dangers of steam under pressure and he abandoned that line of enquiry.

On 1 December 1763 an advert in the *Glasgow Journal* read: 'James Watt has removed his shop from the Sautmercat to Mr Buchanan's land on the Trongate where he sells all sorts of mathematical and musical instruments, with variety of Toys [iron and steel ornaments and goods] and other goods.' This was a settled and productive time for Watt; he invested in the nearby Delftfield Pottery and in 1764 he married his cousin Margaret Miller. In 1765 he worked with Joseph Black on a new way of making soda by treating lime with seawater; this came to naught but it brought Watt into contact with John Roebuck, an industrial entrepreneur with many connections.

Watt, then, was a man with a business to run and with interests and contacts in a variety of fields. Then, an incident in the university brought his mind back to the phenomenon of steam power. Some time in the academic session of 1763-4 Professor John Anderson, tutor in natural philosophy, brought Watt the scale model of a Newcomen engine, made by Jonathan Sisson of London. The engine would not run more than a few strokes and Anderson asked Watt to investigate its malfunctioning.

While Watt was typical in many ways, he was also exceptional. Even the most adept artisan innovators of his time were essentially interested in solving practical problems through experience and trial and error; Watt, on the other hand, combined the skills of a practical artisan engineer with the inquisitiveness of a scientific investigator. When presented with the Newcomen engine he began to examine the properties of steam: its volume relative to water (which he got roughly right); the heat needed to convert a body of water to steam; and the effects of a vacuum on the boiling and condensing point of water (he discovered that condensation takes place at a lower temperature and therefore the engine cylinder had to be cooled well below 212°F). Watt mulled over the workings of the engine and experimented with using different liquids other than water, calculated how much coal was needed to convert one gallon of water to steam, how much cold water was needed to condense a fixed amount of steam, and so on. He later wrote:

> . . . being employed to put in order a small model of a fire engine
> belonging to the natural phil. Class & made by Jonathan Sisson
> I met with considerable difficulties in the execution owing to
> the very bad construction of some of its parts but having at last
> overcome all difficulties I was surprised at the Immense Quantity
> of fuel it consumed in proportion to its Cylinder which was only

2 in. dia. & which I imputed to the heat lost thro the Metallic
Cylinder. Mr Robison being now returned it was hinted in some
of our conversations together that if the Cylinder was made of
wood it would not occasion the loss of so much heat being less
susceptible of heat or cold than Mettals.[4]

Watt saw, as others had before him, that the engine's principal
inefficiency came from the necessity to have hot steam enter the
cylinder which then had to be cooled in order to condense in the
same cylinder in every cycle. But while others tried to improve this
process through better use of cooling jackets, the injection of water
under pressure or, in Robison's case, different materials, Watt came
to realise that a more radical solution was needed. By legend and
by his own account (told to the historian Robert Hart fifty years
later), the revelation came to him one day in the spring of 1765,
while walking across Glasgow Green (see capsule text p. 42).

Watt decided that the only way to create an efficient engine was
for the steam to condense in a separate vessel – a so-called cold
condenser. This would obviate the need for the main driving cylinder
to be heated and cooled in each cycle; the main cylinder could remain
hot, which would require less fuel and create higher efficiency. Though
other inventors saw the heating and cooling of the cylinder as one
drawback of the Newcomen engine, they had not regarded it as the
principal difficulty to be overcome in improving the efficiency of the
engine. Watt, in contrast, isolated this as the overriding problem,
and was willing to sacrifice the simplicity of the Newcomen engine
in the search for a solution. While the attachment of a cold condenser
made the engine more complex, requiring a higher level of engineering, Watt was convinced that it would repay these difficulties.

Watt immediately set about making a model engine with two
brass cylinders: one upside down with a piston inserted at its
lower end, and connected by a pipe to a second cylinder (to act
as the cold condenser) with an air pump attached: the second
cylinder was submerged in cold water and had cold metal 'straws'
running its internal length. Each cylinder was about ten inches

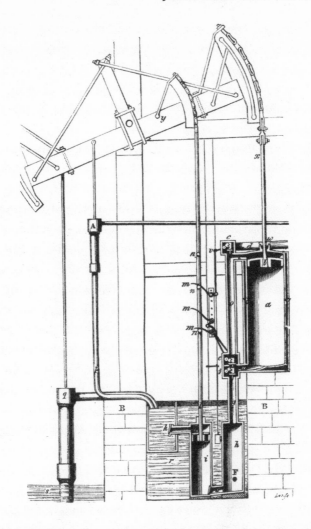

Watt's engine: Based on the same principles as the Newcomen engine, Watt added a separate condensing cylinder [h] which necessitated an air pump [i] to draw steam into the condenser from the main cylinder [a]. The main cylinder could then remain hot throughout the cycle. The boiler is not shown in this drawing.

long. Watt set his boiler going and fed steam into the first cylinder; the piston remained at the bottom of the cylinder. He then closed the steam cock and opened the valve on the pipe connecting the two cylinders, before activating the air pump that drew the air out of the second cylinder which in turn pulled the steam out of the first cylinder. The steam then immediately condensed around the cold metal straws creating a vacuum in both cylinders and causing the piston in the first cylinder to rise. When he attached a weight to the bottom of the piston, Watt found that his engine, which had a cylinder capacity of around one pint of water, could lift the equivalent of two gallons.

In April 1765 Watt wrote to his friend James Lind, 'I can think of nothing else but this Machine. I hope to have the decisive tryal before I see you.'[5]

By the summer Watt had convinced himself that his idea of a separate condenser could deliver practical results; the next step would be to build a full-scale engine, but for that he needed financial backing. He now approached John Roebuck. The son of a Sheffield cutler, educated at the Dissenting Academy in Northampton and trained as a doctor in Edinburgh, Roebuck was a technical man. In the 1740s he had devised a new method for making sulphuric acid and opened large chemical works in Prestonpans near Edinburgh; in 1759 he had also set up the Carron ironworks near Falkirk with his partners, and he held a patent for a method of making bar iron. Roebuck agreed to pay off Watt's debts to Joseph Black, who had sponsored Watt's investigations, and to fund the expenses of building a machine that would, Watt promised, halve the fuel required by a steam engine; in return Roebuck would take two-thirds of the profits.

Progress for the next two years was frustratingly slow. Watt got as far as making a full-scale experimental engine in a cottage in the grounds of Roebuck's property Kinneil House, but getting it to work properly was extremely difficult. The new engine required much greater accuracy in the construction of the cylinder and piston in order to maintain an adequate seal. Newcomen had used a layer of water lying on top of a leather collar, but this was impractical for Watt's cylinder which needed to remain hot at all times. The search for a substance that would seal the piston effectively continued for months. In addition, a cylinder made for the engine at the Carron works proved to be wholly inadequate. Watt became dispirited at the poor quality of components that were available, particularly as he needed to build an engine that others would be able to replicate.

There was a further delay while Watt worked on methods of transferring the power from the piston to where it was needed. Instead of using a balanced beam he explored two different ideas. Firstly he saw that if he turned the engine upside down the piston could operate the rods directly, without the need for a beam. But the engine would need to be a so-called reciprocating engine in order to make the cycle work. More ambitious still was his idea for a rotary engine, or steam wheel – essentially a proto-steam turbine. Although Watt worked on these two ideas for about two years, they were too advanced for the engineering of the time, and he decided to return to the balanced beam.

While Roebuck was paying the expenses for the construction of a prototype engine, Watt still needed to make a living. In the mid-1760s canals were the new boom industry, so in the summer of 1766 this multi-talented man set up as a canal surveyor. His report of a survey for a canal between the Firth of Forth and the Firth of Clyde was published in 1767; he also travelled to London as part of a campaign to win approval for the scheme, but it was refused, much to Watt's disappointment.

For the next few years Watt continued to earn a living from surveying, while intermittently working on the Kinneil engine. Not surprisingly he was being badgered by Roebuck to devote more time to the latter: 'You are letting the most active part of your life insensibly glide away. A day, a moment, ought not to be lost. And you should not suffer your thoughts to be diverted by any other object, or even improvement of this, but only the speediest and most effectual manner of executing one of a proper size according to your present ideas.'[6]

By late 1768 Watt's work on the steam engines had developed to such a degree that Roebuck decided it was time to apply for a patent. This would protect his investment and help to bring earnings when the engine was complete. Roebuck put up the money to register a patent (around £120) and Watt travelled to London to receive patent No. 913 for 'A new invented method of lessening the Consumption of Steam and Fuel in Fire Engines', which was sealed on 5 January 1769.

On his return journey Watt called at Birmingham where he met the man with whom he was to change the face of Britain. Matthew Boulton's ostensible occupation was toy-maker – a word that described a whole range of activities. According to a contemporary reference book:

> . . . these Artists are divided into several branches as the Gold and Silver Toy Makers, who make trinkets, Seals, Tweezer and Tooth Pick cases, Smelling Bottles, Snuff Boxes and Filligree work, such as Toilet, Tea Chests, Inkstands &c. The Tortoiseshell Toy maker makes a beautiful variety of the above and other articles; as does also the steel; who make Cork screws, Buckles, Draw and other boxes; Snuffers, Watch Chains, Stay Hooks, Sugar knippers &c. and almost all these are likewise made in various metals.[7]

In 1759 the Birmingham toy trade employed 20,000 people. The city grew from 15,000 in 1730 to 35,000 in 1760 and 70,000 by 1800. Distance from major rivers had pushed its tradesmen towards small-scale metal-working; the toy trade was the lifeblood of Birmingham and Boulton was at its heart.

Boulton was not a Nonconformist but, through lack of a local grammar school, he was educated at a Dissenting Academy in Deritend. His father had been a buckle-maker and within two years of leaving the academy Boulton had invented a method of inlaying enamel into buckles. He became a partner in his father's successful business and also married into money. In the 1750s and early 60s he expanded his fortune further.

Like Watt, Boulton was a practical man with a strong technical basis to his thinking. In 1761 he and his partner John Fothergill had built the Soho Manufactory on heathland north of Birmingham.[8] Unusual for the city, which was the home of the small workshop, at its heart was a space with around 600 employees, powered by

A Tea-Kettle Business

'There was a story current in my earlier day, which appeared generally credited, that [Newcomen] conceived the idea of motive power to be obtained by steam, by watching his tea-kettle, the top or cover of which would frequently rise and fall when boiling.'

A. H. Holdsworth, *Dartmouth, the Advantages of its Harbour as a Station for Foreign Mail Packets* (1841)

'An excellent example of our wrong thinking about the past is the stubborn persistence of the legend that the youthful James Watt "discovered" the power of steam by observing the lifting lid of a kettle as it boiled on the hearth of his home in Greenock. A precisely similar legend about Thomas Newcomen was once current in Dartmouth.'

L. T. C. Rolt, *Thomas Newcomen: The Prehistory of the Steam Engine* (1963)

'When John Wilkinson, the great iron-founder who bored the cylinders for Watt's engines, referred to the activities of a rival engineer as "a tea-kettle sort of business" was he being witty or just careless in his phraseology? Watt in his notebook of steam experiments at Doldowlod drew attention to the common "tea-kitchen" as the best boiler ever designed, and pointed out that we owed this invention to the Chinese. He himself quite commonly used a tea-kettle in his experiments, sometimes securing the lid with oatmeal porridge, and in the very notebook mentioned above there is a little sketch of a kettle in Watt's own hand being used in an experiment which led to his observing for himself the phenomenon of latent heat. The story about Watt as a boy sitting in the inglenook holding a spoon to the steam issuing from the kettle and watching the vapour condense derives from his cousin, Mrs Marion Campbell, who was his playmate when he was a child. Thus the myth which has so often been ridiculed by historians has, as other myths have, a basis in fact, and we merely need to sift the truth from the falsehood. The "tea-kettle sort of a business" in which Watt himself engaged led to the transformation of the Western industrial scene, and it seems to me no accident that out of everyday articles and experiences of life a man of genius may derive lessons of universal importance. In middle life Watt used a seal which portrayed a human eye and the single word "OBSERVARE". This was the keynote of his life.'

Eric Robinson, 'James Watt: Engineer by Act of Parliament' (1969)

waterwheel. Boulton was both an artisan innovator and a good salesman who attracted customers from across the world; in the 1760s and 70s his firm received orders from cities across France, Germany, Austria and as far away as Turkey.

When Watt visited Soho in early 1769, with a brand-new patent in his pocket, Boulton was already a major figure in British manufacturing. The two men instantly knew they could work together. Perhaps Watt saw that Boulton was the necessary complement to his own gloomy character – an energetic optimist who would carry him through his difficulties – while Boulton surely recognised the seriousness of Watt's character. When he returned to Glasgow Watt proposed to Roebuck that Boulton come in as a partner by buying one-third of the interest in the patent. Roebuck and Boulton already knew each other, having worked together on a plan to manufacture thermometers.

Watt was delighted not just by the prospect of investment but especially by Boulton's personal enthusiasm. As he wrote soon after his return to Glasgow: 'It gave me great joy when you seemed to think so favourably of our scheme as to wish to engage in it.' Boulton on the other hand was both excited about the project and in need of money – the building of Soho had nearly ruined him and he was often better at spending than making money. However, while Roebuck was open to outside investment in the engine he was reluctant to surrender his ownership of two-thirds of the patent; he offered Boulton a licence to build the engine in the three industrial Midlands counties. Boulton wrote a long letter to Watt explaining why he could not take Roebuck's 'three-counties' offer, and invited Watt to Soho where he would be given his own engineering works. In Boulton's ringing phrase: 'It would not be worth my while to make for three counties only; but I find it very well worth my while to make for all the world.'[9]

Watt knew that he could get better components and technical support in Birmingham and the Midlands than in Glasgow and central Scotland. Birmingham was a burgeoning centre of engineering with experienced ironmasters in nearby Staffordshire and Shropshire. But he was tied to Scotland by his work, family and Roebuck. And Watt could not agree to anything while Roebuck owned the majority of the patent. By then he was once again immersed in canal-building in order to earn his living. He didn't care for the work: 'Nothing is more contrary to my disposition than bustling & bargaining with mankind,' he wrote, 'yet that is the life I now constantly lead . . . I am also in a constant fear that my want of experience may betray me into some scrape, or that I shall be imposed upon by the workmen.'[10]

Watt was, by his own admission, inclined to periods of melancholy, frustration and inactivity. 'Of all things in life,' he said at this time, 'there is nothing so foolish as inventing.' From autumn 1769 until 1772 Watt was engaged as an engineer on the Monkland to Glasgow canal at £200 per annum. During this time he devised a method for ensuring that the surveyor's level stayed static while taking readings, using a combination of spirit levels; he also dallied with a method for estimating distances using a telescope. But Watt was a chronic pessimist and was dissatisfied with his work. In January 1771 he wrote: 'Today I entered the 35th year of my life & I think I have hardly done 35 pence worth of good in the world but I cannot help it. I do as much as indolence and ennui permit & I think myself less indolent than I once was.'[11]

Although a full-sized engine had been put up at Kinneil in late

1769 Watt was unable to spare enough time to work on it. In the meantime John Roebuck found himself in serious financial difficulties. He had developed a colliery at Bo'ness to supply the Carron ironworks, but this had become prone to serious flooding, while another chemical project had come to nothing. These misfortunes coincided with a catastrophic collapse in Scottish banking following the crash of Neal, James, Fordyce and Down in 1772, and the following year Roebuck was declared bankrupt. Watt blamed himself for his partner's plight and pleaded for Boulton to step in and buy Roebuck's share in the 1769 patent. Roebuck had no alternative but to sell: on 17 May 1773 Boulton bought his share, while Watt wrote off the money he was personally owed, as Roebuck's financial support had dried up after the initial payment of £1,000. Watt now dismantled the Kinneil engine (which was valued at precisely zero by the estate's creditors) and sent the parts down to Boulton at Soho.

In September 1773 James Watt's wife died leaving him with two young children. With Boulton now owning his patent, his ties to Scotland were becoming even less important. 'The engineering business is not a vigorous plant here,' he wrote in December 1773. 'We are in general very poorly paid, this last year my whole gains do not exceed £200 though some people have paid me very gentily. There are also many disagreeable circumstances I cannot write, in short I must as far as I can see change my abode . . . I am heartsick of this cursed country.'[12] By April 1774 he had finished his contract to survey the route of what was to be the Caledonian canal and in May, aged thirty-eight, James Watt gave up his surveying business, left his children with relatives and moved to Birmingham.

Let us pause here on the brink of the watershed. In 1774 Newcomen engines were being used in coal and tin mines for pumping water; they had been gradually improved but were limited by their size and fuel requirements to coal and metal mines. At the same time men like John Wilkinson and the Darby family of Coalbrookdale were refining techniques for iron-making, producing better materials and higher quality engineering components. In the early

1770s another revolution was under way in Derbyshire where Richard Arkwright opened a cotton-spinning mill housing his new spinning frame, driven by water power.

Matthew Boulton was not a mining man; he was a well-travelled metal-maker familiar with every aspect of manufacturing. While Watt was intent on building an engine to do the same work as Newcomen's, but more efficiently, Boulton will have known that the industrial world was desperate for a better source of power to drive its machinery. Mill-owners, ironmasters, forges and textile mills were increasingly frustrated with the limits of water power on which their enterprises depended. Britain was approaching the limits of what its natural resources could offer.

In May 1774 James Watt was installed in Boulton's old house in Newhall Walk, Birmingham, and the Kinneil engine was re-erected at the Soho works where Watt was given a large workshop. One of the reasons why Watt had come to the Midlands was to source high-precision components; he immediately showed that, once he had the right materials and support, he was as adept at making machinery as he was at inventing. But Watt's problems with the engine were far from over. The continuing difficulty was the need to fit a good seal around the piston head along the whole length of the stroke; keeping the seal needed a combination of a true cylinder and a flexible seal. Seals made of wool, felt, strawboard, pulp and horse muck were all tried and failed; a solution began to appear only when Boulton asked John Wilkinson, who had just patented a boring mill for producing true cylinders for cannon, to make iron engine cylinders for Watt. By around the end of 1774, with improved cylinders and effective seals made of oakum and hemp, Watt finally had a working engine.

However, the original patent for a new engine had been granted in January 1769 for just seven years, and so had only a little over a year to run. There were plenty of good engineers around who might have been able to build an engine on the basis of information provided in the patent, so Matthew Boulton knew he had to either seek an extension of the 1769 patent or apply for a new one.

The application for an extension was presented to Parliament on 23 February 1775. Watt described the improvements he was intent on making to the Newcomen engine and supplied a drawing in support, while Boulton argued that he did not request a monopoly over all steam engines, but the possibility of a decent return. Boulton was a good political operator and prolific networker and over his years in industry he had cultivated enough people with influence to persuade Parliament to extend Watt's patent. The bill granting a twenty-five-year extension and extending the patent to Scotland was passed on 22 May 1775; the Act described Watt as 'Engineer, by Act of Parliament'.

The patent extension remains the most controversial aspect of James Watt's career. Because his original patent was so widely drawn, from 1769 to 1800 no other engineer felt legally secure in publicly proposing improvements to steam engines. Watt had been required to submit a specification within four months of the granting of the 1769 patent; at that time his friend Dr Small had advised him to 'give neither drawings nor descriptions of any particular machinery, but specify in the clearest manner that you have discovered some principles'.[13] The patent was for a 'new method of lessening the consumption of steam and fuel in fire engines' and could therefore be used to cover almost any new development in steam engines. The decision was criticised at the time and historians have accused Watt of misusing a system that was designed to protect inventions, not block innovation.

A number of points should be made in Watt's defence. First, in 1769 patents were routinely overthrown, leaving their specifications open to use by others; so the deliberate vagueness of Watt's specification should be viewed in that light.

Second, the state of patent law at the time made it essential for any inventor to get as wide a protection as possible but, as we have seen, even then the granting of a patent offered no guarantees, since it could be challenged in the courts (see Chapter 3). A patent gave you permission to enter the arena of the court, but did not mean you would win your case. Third, Watt did not sit on his laurels and just wait for his earnings to roll in. He worked assiduously to improve his engine, making adaptations and improvements that rendered it workable in a huge range of situations; his engines brought great benefits to the Cornish mining industry and to iron, pottery, glass and metal-production. Finally, while Watt deliberately turned away from the use of high-pressure steam, and stands accused of obstructing developments by William Murdoch and Richard Trevithick (see Chapter 9) his position is unlikely to have made a huge difference: the high-grade materials and engineering skills necessary for high-pressure application were not available much before the 1800s, the decade of Trevithick's great breakthroughs.

Immediately after the patent was extended Boulton and Watt came to a financial agreement. Boulton discharged all existing debts on the project, agreed to meet all costs of experiment and pay Watt £300 a year, in return for two-thirds of the earnings for the duration of the patent. Boulton immediately urged Watt to draw up plans for a pumping engine for Bloomfield colliery at Tipton in Staffordshire, which would contain a fifty-inch-diameter cylinder, a huge step up from Watt's twelve-inch experimental engine. They also drew up plans for a thirty-eight-inch cylinder-blowing engine for the blast furnace at John Wilkinson's ironworks at New Willey in Shropshire. Wilkinson was commissioned to supply the iron cylinders; the Bloomfield engine was built to Watt's satisfaction and set running on 8 March 1776. The blowing engine for Wilkinson's ironworks began powering the furnace at about the same time; both machines were successful. They used a fraction of the fuel of Newcomen engines and, while the early installations needed constant repair, they provided useful experience for Boulton and Watt and evidence to the wider world that Watt's engines really did work. It had taken Watt eleven years to construct the first working engine – about the same time as Newcomen had spent on realising his idea. The year 1776 saw the birth of the nation that was to epitomise the modern world; it also saw the first running of a machine that was to change the fate of humanity.

*

When Boulton invited James Watt to Birmingham he had envis-aged the mass production of engines at his Soho works. But it soon became clear that the engines would need to be put together on site, from drawings and specifications provided by the firm of Boulton & Watt, who would also supply most of the key compo-nents. Watt's design was more complicated and intricate than the Newcomen engine, and the parts had to be made more precisely. The firm introduced conditions into their licences specifying that the valve assemblies had to be made and supplied by Boulton & Watt and, in some cases, refused to sell licences unless the cylinders were supplied by John Wilkinson.

Customers considering a Boulton & Watt engine needed convincing: the Newcomen engines were no longer covered by any patent, so anyone was able to construct them for free. Boulton & Watt offered either to convert existing engines or build new ones, and licence agreements specified a royalty based on the amount of fuel saved by the user compared to their existing Newcomen engine. The promised reduction in fuel was a massive incentive, especially in the mining districts of Cornwall where coal was expensive. Even the most efficient Newcomen engine, John Smeaton's at the Chacewater mine at Wheal Busy, was converted to the Watt system; and once Watt's patent expired in 1800 almost all the Newcomen engines were converted or replaced.

However, even as James Watt's ambitions were finally begin-ning to be realised, his financial standing was still in question – at least in the eyes of his prospective father-in-law. In 1776 the inventor travelled back to Glasgow to propose marriage to Ann, daughter of James McGrigor, a dyer. But McGrigor would not give consent without seeing the financial agreement between Boulton and Watt that guaranteed Watt's income. Unfortunately the agree-ment had been agreed on a handshake, and so Watt had to bluster while writing a speedy request to Boulton to bodge up a legally binding letter. After marrying Ann, Watt moved to a new house in Regent's Place in Birmingham.[14]

The First Watt Engine

'On Friday last a steam engine constructed upon Mr Watt's new principles was set to work at Bloomfield colliery, near Dudley, in the presence of its Proprietors . . . and a number of scientific gentlemen whose curiosity was excited by so singular and so powerful a machine and whose expectations were fully gratified by the Excellence of its performance. The Workmanshop of the Whole did not pass unnoticed, nor unadmired. All the iron foundry parts (which are unparalleled for truth) were executed by Mr Wilkinson; the Condensor, with the Valves, Pistons and all the small work, at Soho, by Mr Harrison and others, and the Whole was erected by Mr Perrins, conformable to the Plans and under the Directions of Mr Watt. From the first Moment of its setting to Work, it made about 14 to 15 strokes per minute, and emptied the Engine Pit (which is about 90 Feet deep and stood 57 Feet high in Water) in less than an hour . . .

'This engine is applied to the working of a Pump 14 Inches and a Half Diameter, which it is capable of doing to the Depth of 300 Feet, or even 360 Feet if wanted, with one Fourth of the Fuel that a common Engine would require to produce the same Quantity of Power. The Cylinder is 50 inches diameter and the length of the Stroke is 7 Feet . . .

'They [the principles of the design] were invented by Mr Watt (late of Glasgow) after many years Study, and a great Variety of expensive and laborious Experiments; and are now carried into Execution under his and Mr Boulton's Directions at Boulton and Fothergill's Manufactory near this Town; where they have nearly finished four of them, and have established a Fabrick for them upon so extensive a Plan as to render them applicable to almost all Purposes where Mechanical Power is required, whether great or small, or where the Motion wanted is either rotary or reciprocating.'

Aris's Birmingham Gazette, 11 March 1776[15]

Boulton was confident that, having proved the engine's efficiency, there was a potentially limitless market in Britain and Europe. When James Boswell visited Soho in 1776, then filled with 700 workers, Boulton told him, 'I sell here, sir, what all the world desires to have – power.'[16] Engines were rapidly built for a distillery at Stratford-le-Bow in London, for Bedworth colliery, Coventry, and at Torryburn in Fifeshire. Each time he designed an engine Watt made improvements, either in component quality or innovations like jackets for the cylinder and condenser. Early signs of the difficulty of enforcing the patent came when the French engineer Jean-Claude Périer approached John Wilkinson directly about

Engine construction: Steam engines under construction at the factory of Boulton & Watt, Soho, Birmingham.

supplying components for an engine that he wanted to build in France; Wilkinson refused but the request showed the need to extend protection to other countries. Consequently Boulton & Watt obtained a fifteen-year patent in France in 1778, and it was Périer who built two Watt engines at Chaillot on the outskirts of Paris. But once engineers could examine the engines, there was the danger that the most talented and unscrupulous among them would try to make their own.

It was Cornwall that was the most promising location for Watt's engine in those early days. The Cornish mining industry was a difficult but lucrative trade. Tin, copper, lead and zinc had been mined there since Roman times, but access to deeper seams through the use of gunpowder to blast the hard granite, which required Newcomen engines to pump out water, had led to a significant expansion of the industry.

Boulton knew that Cornwall was the place where the most money could be made; he also saw that there would be a struggle to overcome the independence and hostility of Cornish engineers, so he invited a group of mine-owners and engineers to visit the Bloomfield engine. This had the desired effect and orders began to arrive from Cornwall. In fact the Cornish owners were desperate to save costs; the 1768 rediscovery of the main seam of copper ore at Parys Mountain on Anglesey had challenged their supremacy. Though the Parys ore was low quality, it was so plentiful and easy to extract that it caused a huge drop in ore prices. To the Cornish miners Watt seemed like a godsend.

In 1777 Watt took the four-day journey from Birmingham to Cornwall to oversee the installation of engines at Ting Tang and Wheal Busy. The Cornish mines and their miners were something to behold. The mining country around Redruth and Camborne was a bleak site with spoil-heaps, piles of rubble, sheds, windings and tracks showing evidence of the centuries of exploitation of the rich seams of copper and tin. The miners bought ropes and candles off the mine-owners and were paid for the ore they brought to the shaft. The shafts themselves could be between 500 and 1,000 feet deep and were reached by ladder, with the baskets of ore being hauled to the surface by horse-powered winches. The miners' wives and children then smashed the ore with hammers into grains ready for treatment or transport. The ore was taken in sacks to the auction market in Redruth, from where it would be transported to the coast and on to Swansea and Bristol for smelting. Gunpowder was used to loosen the ore beneath ground, increasing the already terrifying risks of rockfalls and flooding; Cornish miners did not work much beyond thirty.

By the time of Watt's first visit in 1777 there were around sixty Newcomen engines working in Cornwall. While the mine-owners might have been keen on Watt's engine design, the local engineers – including Richard Trevithick Snr – were suspicious of Watt's claims and Watt also found that the existing engines were not kept in good repair. Jonathan Hornblower Snr told Watt that Cornwall had 'good Engine smiths . . . & some bad ones (all of them love drinking too much)'.[17]

Watt was determined to overcome any suspicions about the engines' performance by measuring the strokes – he had devised a counter to assess the premium to be paid – the weight of water pumped and the amount of fuel used. He calculated that the best duty from his engines came from a cylinder of smaller size than that employed in the Newcomen engines.

In 1777 Boulton & Watt took on a young Scottish engineer named William Murdoch, who was sent to Cornwall and soon became the best engine fitter in the land. Murdoch was to play a vital role in the future of steam power.

By September 1777 the Wheal Busy engine was working. Boulton & Watt then received an order for a sixty-three-inch engine for Tregurtha Downs at Marazion, but Richard Trevithick Snr, at a public meeting, accused Watt of inventing the fuel savings: 'I was so confounded with the impudence, ignorance, and overbearing manner of the man,' wrote Watt, 'that I could make no adequate defence, and indeed could scarcely keep my temper, which, however,

I did to a fault.' Despite the engineers' hostility, the mine-owners recognised the efficiency savings and ordered more Watt engines as fast as they could be made. Cylinders continued to be supplied by John Wilkinson, valves and nozzles were produced at the Soho works, with other parts made locally, and the on-site construction supervised by Murdoch or Watt. Cornwall was conquered.

With the engine in such demand in the West Country and else-where these should have been prosperous days for the firm of Boulton & Watt. But in 1778, when a recession hit the English economy, the firm was ill prepared. Success brought cash-flow problems: it cost hard cash to employ men and to buy components, while royalties from licences came in much later, and often had to be chased up. As Boulton couldn't raise capital through shares, he approached Cornish banks and raised capital against future earnings. He also borrowed £17,000 against the engine patent and kept harassing Watt to build more engines. At one point Boulton had to reduce his workforce from 700 to 150.

News of the improved engine soon spread through Britain's industrial community. In 1781 Samuel Walker, ironmaster of Rotherham, wrote to Boulton & Watt:

> We have some Works upon a River which in general supplies us with Water. In order to make up this defect, in some measure, we are intending to build a Fire Engine, either in the old or common manner or under the Sanction of your Patent . . . We have coal of our own getting laid down at the Works at about 2¾d cwt and are thinking of a Cylinder 36 or 43 inches diameter and eight foot stroke and suppose we may work the engine 3 to 6 months in the Year according as the Seasons are wet or dry.

Watt's reply in May 1781 showed that the market in areas where coal was cheap was still hard to crack, principally because royalties were paid to the firm on the basis of how much fuel had been saved by replacing the Newcomen engine: 'The Coal Mines in Yorkshire will not pay us for our attention on that business and we have declined engine orders where Coals are of less value than 4s or 5s a ton.'

Nevertheless Boulton & Watt were happy to supply an engine to the Rotherham firm. Samuel Walker's diary records: 'Pull'd down two shops to make room for a new Fire Engine and rebuilt 'em in the same yard: built and cover'd in a new fire engine house (this is a very heavy job).' And by September: 'The Fire Engine completed to blow our three furnaces and began to work this month.'[18]

By the early 1780s, therefore, Boulton & Watt managed to navigate the financial perils of industry while gradually attracting more customers. But they remained restricted. Their engines still used the same principle of the balanced beam that Newcomen had designed in 1712 and, like Newcomen engines, they were mostly used for pumping water and blowing blast furnaces. Boulton realised that steam engines needed to be able to imitate the rotational power of waterwheels if they were to be of use to other industries. He had been pressing Watt to build engines with a rotational motion for two years, and in June 1781 he betrayed his impatience in a letter to Watt, who by now spent much of the year in Cornwall: 'The people in London, Manchester and Birmingham are steam mill mad. I don't mean to hurry you but I think in the course of a month or two, we should determine to take out a patent for certain methods of producing rotative motion from . . . the fire engine . . . There is no other Cornwall to be found, and the most likely line for the consumption of our engines is the application of them to mills which is certainly an extensive field.'[19]

Turning the motion of a beam into rotational motion seems a trivial matter – hook up a crank and flywheel and away you go. But the practice was more complex. The stroke of the engine was irregular in time and length; a short stroke might send the crank turning back while a long stroke risked pushing it out of kilter. In addition the notion that a flywheel would help to control and smooth its motion had not been fully explored. The engines were single acting, only having power in one stroke, so a counterbalance would be needed to pull the piston out each time. How could such a counterstroke be arranged?

In 1779 James Pickard, the owner of a flour mill at Snow Hill in Birmingham, asked the Bristol engineer Matthew Wasbrough to build an engine to turn the machinery in his mill. Wasbrough's solution was a Newcomen-type engine with the addition of racks and pinions to deliver a rotational motion. When this did not work to Pickard's satisfaction he fitted a crank and flywheel; the result was the world's first working rotational engine. It was the flywheel that was crucial, but when Pickard applied for a patent in 1780 he instead specified a crank with a wheel with weights on it. James Watt was furious; this had been one of his ideas and he believed Pickard had stolen it through a spy in the Soho works. Watt immediately realised that he had to patent the range of devices being worked on at Soho, including the sun and planet gearing for translating linear into rotational motion, the swash plate for raising the beam of the engine, the eccentric wheel acting inside a circular yoke, and the counterweighted crank. All these patents were granted in October 1781 but there is some controversy as to the origin of the most important device – the sun and planet gearing. While Watt claimed that William Murdoch, who first built the mechanism, revived an old idea of Watt's, others believe that it was Murdoch who invented the sun and planet system.

In March 1782 Watt was awarded a patent for a double-acting engine with each cylinder being pulled first one way then the other – the need for a counterstroke was solved and by condensing steam on each side of the piston in turn, the engine produced smooth motion and used less fuel. This required a different connection to the beam, which had to be rigid enough to be pushed – the previous motion had been pulling only, by using a flexible chain – while maintaining the flexibility needed to allow for the curved motion of the beam end. Watt came up with the system known as parallel motion, which was patented in 1784. As Watt later

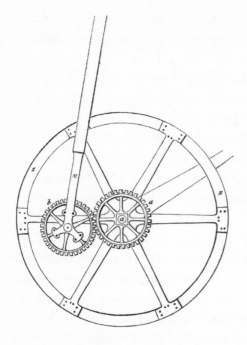

Sun and planet gearing: The drive arm [x] is pushed back and forth by a traditional Watt engine; this pushes the toothed wheel [b] around the cog [a] which turns the wheel [z] thus converting linear into rotary motion.

wrote: 'Though I am not over anxious after fame, yet I am more proud of the parallel motion than of any other mechanical invention I have ever made.'[20] Controversially, however, the 1784 patent also granted Watt protection for the invention of a steam carriage using 'the elastic force of steam to give it motion'. Given Watt's intention not to follow this course, it seems that this was a purely obstructive tactic. Watt also blocked William Murdoch from pursuing the idea within the firm, writing to Boulton in September 1786: 'I am extreamly sorry that W. M. still busys himself with the Stm carriage.'[21]

Watt finally built a rotative engine to his own satisfaction in 1783, which was supplied to John Wilkinson to drive a steam hammer at Bradley ironworks. The next rotative engine was not constructed until the following year, as Watt was engrossed in perfecting his double-acting engine. But by the late 1780s the design had become standardised with double-acting engine, sun and planet gear, parallel motion, valves and connecting rods all being supplied to customers. Steam power had become available to any sizeable industrial concern.

The final commercial breakthrough came in 1789 when Peter Drinkwater ordered an eight-horsepower engine for his Manchester cotton mill. Cotton was the great new industry and Manchester was its commercial centre; steam power had finally arrived at the heart of industrial production. Boulton & Watt rapidly appointed a Manchester agent who in 1791 was able to report: 'Mr Barton [manager of the Simpson cotton mill] desires me to inform you, that they intend taking down their old engine and putting one of yours in its place – They have set at present 4,000 spindles & preparation in the Mill and they mean to put 1,000 or 1,500 more in it.'[22]

For their beam engines Boulton & Watt charged a royalty based on the amount of fuel saved from the use of a Newcomen engine. But the rotative engine was taking them into new markets that had never used steam, so they needed a different measure of power output. People had talked about horsepower before – Smeaton commenting that his engine at Kronstadt was equal to the work of 400 horses – but in 1783 Watt quantified an engine's power, working out by rough estimate that a horse's strength was equal to raising 33,000 lb, one foot high, per minute. The firm would then rate their machines as, for example, a '20-horse engine'. Watt developed a pressure gauge to measure the power attained by his rotative engine and his assistant Southern came up with the idea of attaching a pencil and a roll of paper on which to trace the changing pressure in the cylinder over time; this allowed them to see whether the engine was performing to its proper capacity.

The firm's horizons expanded further in 1788 when Boulton & Watt invested in Albion Mill, a huge flour mill to be built on the south bank of the Thames near Blackfriars Bridge. The firm was to supply three engines to unload wheat from barges and carry out hoisting, milling and sifting. John Rennie worked on the milling side and became a famous engineer in his own right. When the mill burned down just three years after opening arson was suspected, particularly as millers had been hostile to mechanisation, but no one was ever put on trial. Between them Boulton and Watt lost around £9,000 – a fortune at the time – showing them both to be wealthy men.

The 1786 commercial agreement between Britain and France (the Eden Treaty) opened up new possibilities for British indus-trialists abroad. Both countries, after centuries of restricting trade, agreed to reduce tariffs on each other's goods. Boulton and Watt visited Paris after the French finance minister Charles de Calonne had invited the firm to tender to pump water from the Seine to Versailles. Though this never came about due to the revolution of 1789, Watt did meet France's leading scientists including Antoine Lavoisier, Pierre-Simon Laplace and Claude-Louis Berthollet.[23]

Watt continued to improve his engines and in 1788 the first steam engine to employ a centrifugal governor was built at Soho. Boulton had earlier written to Watt about an old technique being used at Albion Mill: 'for regulating the pressure or distance of the top millstone from the bed stone in such a manner that the faster the engine goes the lower or closer it grinds and when the engine stops the top stone rises up . . . this is produced by the centrifugal force of 2 lead weights.'[24] Watt didn't claim to have invented the governor but its adaptation was his final contribution to the devel-opment of the steam engine.

In 1790 Watt was prosperous enough to acquire forty acres of land on Handsworth Heath and build a substantial mansion, known as Heathfield (it was pulled down in 1927). As the prospect of the patent expiring in 1800 came nearer, Boulton realised that the firm would need to build complete engines in competition with others. In 1795 he bought land at Smethwick, only a mile or so from the Soho Manufactory, and built the Soho Foundry along-side the Birmingham and Wolverhampton canal.

By that time Boulton & Watt had become the victim of its own success: there was more demand for rotative engines than one firm could design, let alone build. Sometimes to avoid paying royalties, and sometimes out of desperation, manufacturers turned to other engine makers. In 1796 Boulton & Watt took out a writ against Hornblower & Maberley, who had taken the double-cylinder engine patented by Isaac Mainwaring and made it into a double-acting engine.[25] While this was legitimate, Watt regarded the engine's separate condenser as an infringement of his patent.

'The rascals seem to have been going on as if the patents were their own,' he wrote to Boulton. 'We have tried every lenient means with them in vain and since the fear of God has no effect upon them, we must try what the fear of the devil can do.' But Boulton was unperturbed, telling Watt: 'If we do suffer ourselves to be pissed upon by that family we deserve to be sh–t upon. For God's sake don't lose a moment's peace upon that head, but proceed, get the Engines erected & Money in our pockets.'[26]

But Watt was adamant and told Boulton that he 'should not lose the battle before you fight it'. He sent James Law to spy on the engine house at Radstock colliery where Hornblower's first engine was built, but when he couldn't get in Watt went to Bristol to confront the owner, Major Tucker, 'a potato-faced, chuckle-headed fellow with a scar on the pupil of one eye. In short I did not like his physiog'.[27] Tucker palmed him off by saying he would look into Watt's complaint. By this time Richard Arkwright had just lost his carding patent (which covered the preparation of cotton for spinning) in a sensational trial, and Watt was rightly nervous that his patent would also be overturned for lack of a precise specification.

The court initially found for Boulton & Watt, but Hornblower counter-sued arguing that the original patent was invalid because of its inadequate specification. This case was not settled until January 1799, when the patent was reaffirmed; by then it had only just over a year to run. Nevertheless the victory gave Boulton & Watt thousands of pounds in fees and damages, while those who had withheld regular royalty payments until the trial's outcome was known, particularly in Cornwall, now had to pay up.

Printing press: Rotary steam power drove the mechanisation of a vast range of activities. This printing press from the 1840s has a belt drive to draw power from a steam-powered drive shaft.

Watt handed over his responsibilities at Soho to his son and lived out his final years at his estate in Wales. When he died in 1819 aged eighty-three, he was worth around £60,000 and was a famous as well as a wealthy man. By that time James Watt had given humanity a new source of mechanical energy, steam power had been adapted for use in dozens of different industries, and the economic, physical and social revolution that this brought about was beginning to take effect.

9. Richard Trevithick: Steam into Motion

Newcomen and Watt had developed steam engines that worked under atmospheric pressure and, while these machines kickstarted Britain's conversion to a coal-based economy, they had limitations: the amount of power produced depended on enormous cylinders and pistons and, though they were great beasts capable of powering mills and huge water pumps, their size and weight meant that they remained static. The next great leap forward freed the steam engine from these shackles, put it on wheels and sent it powering across the world. The new age was announced in flamboyant and dramatic fashion on Christmas Eve 1801 when Richard Trevithick drove his *Puffing Devil* up Camborne Hill.[1]

It is no surprise that the next great breakthrough happened in Cornwall. Cornish mines had bred generations of engineers skilled and experienced in dealing with the most difficult challenges of deep mining. It was Cornwall that was the most important early market for Boulton & Watt's engines: the county's distance from the coal areas of the Midlands and north made fuel expensive, while the deep tin and copper mines needed machines to pump out water. But Cornish engineers were resentful of Watt's monopoly of improved steam power and believed his extended patent prevented their own trade from flourishing.

James Watt's steam engines followed Thomas Newcomen's central principle of using condensing steam to create a vacuum, which then drew the piston down into the cylinder. Because the essential power came from the weight of the atmosphere working on the vacuum, these are known as atmospheric engines. William Murdoch, the brilliant engineer who was entrusted by Boulton & Watt with erecting engines in Cornwall in the 1780s, experimented with using steam in a different way. It was well known to engineers at the time that water heated in a closed vessel caused a massive build-up of pressure, which could be released through narrow tubes or valves. As we have seen, Watt believed that the use of steam under pressure was highly dangerous and unnecessary, and he discouraged Murdoch from pursuing this line. But Murdoch seems to have carried on despite this. In 1784 his colleague Thomas Wilson wrote to James Watt that Murdoch had a plan for 'drawing carriages along the road by steam engine' and in 1785 Murdoch built a working model of a high-pressure steam carriage.[2] Another model followed in 1786 but he was discouraged by Matthew Boulton from pursuing this further and from registering a patent, which would have set him in opposition to his employers. However, in 1797 Richard Trevithick became Murdoch's neighbour and it is likely that the two discussed steam locomotion; it is certainly possible that Murdoch showed his model to the young Cornish engineer.

In the meantime, working practices and developments across the Atlantic were free from the obligation to respect Watt's patents. High wages, specialisation in work and openness to change all made America ripe for technological innovation. In 1787 John Fitch used an atmospheric steam engine lying on its side to power a set of twelve oars on a riverboat. Powering a boat by steam was a fertile line of development, since it could carry the weight of an engine much more easily than a road carriage. Fitch unsuccessfully tried to get a legal monopoly over the use of steam for transport and the next American steam pioneer, Oliver Evans, took its application one step further. Evans understood that 'the more the steam is confined . . . the greater will be the power obtained by the fuel. For every addition of 30 degrees of heat to the water doubles the power, doubling the heat of the water increases the power [of the engine] 100 times.' In other words, a vastly more powerful engine could run on only a small increase in fuel.[3]

Evans came up with the idea of placing the furnace inside the boiler, which had remained more or less unchanged since Newcomen's time. Being able to produce the same power with a smaller engine opened up the possibility of putting the engine on a wheeled carriage, but Evans found little enthusiasm for this project, as roads were poor and tramways not as highly developed as in Britain. Evans resorted to making stationary engines for mills but his work on high-pressure steam may have had an intriguing legacy. By his own account, written in 1805, 'In 1794–95, I sent drawings, specifications, and explanations, to England to be shown to the steam engineers there, to induce them to put the principles into practice.'[4] These were taken to England by Joseph Stacey Simpson, who died there, and we don't know the fate of Evans's papers. It is possible that they were seen by British steam engineers, but there is no firm evidence. However, strong steam and its use for transport was being openly discussed in Britain well before 1794 and was released into the world, almost as soon as Watt's patent expired, by the intoxicating figure of Richard Trevithick.

Trevithick was born in 1771 in Carn Brea in Illogan parish in the heart of the Cornish mining industry. His father, who clashed so memorably with James Watt (see p. 128), was the mine captain – a combination of manager and chief engineer – at Wheal Treasury mine. While receiving some formal education at Camborne School, Richard received most of his learning in and around mines. By 1786, when Trevithick was fifteen years old, there were twenty-one Boulton & Watt engines in Cornwall and he learned every detail of how they worked.

Trevithick was in some ways the opposite of James Watt. A huge man of six feet and two inches – he became known as 'the Cornish giant' – he was confident, outgoing and wildly enthusiastic, full of physical and mental energy and prepared to throw himself into every project. He took his first job at the age of nineteen, at East Stray Park mine near Camborne, probably working for William Bull. Bull had been hired by Cornish mine-owners to build engines different from Watt's, in order to get round the inventor's patent. In 1793 Boulton & Watt sued Bull over breach of their patent and Trevithick was implicated through his work with the Cornish engineer. Trevithick became a Cornish celebrity when he appeared as an expert witness in Jonathan Hornblower's defence against Boulton & Watt, which further exacerbated Watt's hostility to Trevithick's work.

During the late 1780s and 1790s, with engineers eager to make improvements to steam engines, some were clearly pursuing the idea of making an engine driven by high-pressure steam. In his discouragement of his employee William Murdoch, Watt wrote to Boulton: 'I wish William could be brought to do as we do, to mind the business in hand, and let such as Symington and Sadler throw away their time and money chasing shadows.'[5] William Symington had patented an improved engine in 1787, using strong steam to push the condensate out of the condenser, which then powered a second piston. He built engines for mines and mills but is best known for installing steam engines on boats, leading to the world's first successful steamboat journey by the *Charlotte Dundas* in January 1803. James Sadler was a famous balloonist who developed the 'table-top steam engine', and it is thought that Arthur Woolf, a native Cornishman who later patented the compound steam engine, was working on high-pressure steam in London in the 1790s. The clear implication of Watt's comments is that he thought these innovators were simply following the wrong tracks. What is unclear is how much Richard Trevithick learned from them (and his one-time neighbour William Murdoch) and how much he figured out for himself.

Like Watt, Trevithick was not a wealthy man and in 1796 he joined forces with his cousin Andrew Vivian, who invested money in his ideas. He also met Davies Gilbert, MP for Penzance and then Bodmin, and an eminent Cornish scientist who later

(1827–30) succeeded Humphry Davy as president of the Royal Society. It was Gilbert who answered one of Trevithick's most pressing questions. Trevithick saw that if an engine was powered by the force of steam pushing a piston, then there would be no need for a separate condenser, and the waste steam could be pushed out of the cylinder by the piston on the return stroke. But he needed to know whether all the pressure in the cylinder would be lost in each cycle, or whether some would be retained. Gilbert believed that the pressure lost would be the same as the outside atmospheric pressure, and that any additional pressure would be retained inside the hot cylinder. This meant that the steam could be pushed out straight into the atmosphere without robbing the engine of all its power at each stroke.

By 1796 Trevithick had built a model of a new steam engine, usable both as a stationary machine and for powering a locomotive. A boiler produced steam which was then directed under pressure into a cylinder; the pressure pushed out a piston which was connected directly to a crank and thereby used to drive a shaft. The rotation of the shaft, with a flywheel attached, pushed the cylinder back down at the opposite end of the cycle, and the steam was expelled through an opened valve. This engine was far simpler than the Newcomen or Watt engines: there was no beam, no condenser and no apparatus for feeding the steam into a separate condenser. Not only that: much more power could be generated from the same size of piston thereby allowing the cylinders and pistons to be made smaller. In addition, with no need for condensation and because of the simple cycle of input and exhaust the engine could be run much faster than a Watt engine. Moreover, Trevithick's design housed the engine cylinder within the boiler, so saving space and keeping the outside of the cylinder continually heated. The new engine was probably first used at full working scale in 1800 for turning the shaft of a winding wheel at the Wheal Hope mine at Dolcoath, Camborne. But Trevithick knew that the new engine, with its small size and lightness, could be used to drive a vehicle.

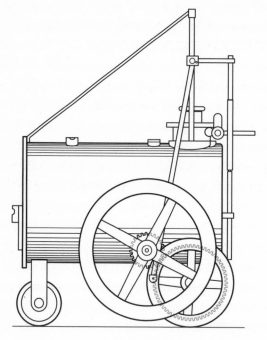

Trevithick's Puffing Devil: The single cylinder drove a piston rod connected to a flywheel, which was also connected to one set of road wheels. The vertical cylinder is located inside the large boiler.

We need to understand what a huge step this was: until this moment humanity had been able to travel only at the speed of a fast horse. Trevithick was about to make the means of propulsion part of the carriage itself and thereby break down any technical barrier to speed. But there was one major concern: the engine would power the wheels of the carriage, but would powered wheels simply slip on the road surface while the engine turned them round, leaving the carriage standing still? To find out, Trevithick and Vivian hired a one-horse chaise and moved it along the roads near Camborne by laboriously turning the wheels by hand.

The stage was set, but no one outside a small circle seemed aware of what was about to happen. Then, on Christmas Eve 1801, Richard Trevithick and a group of friends appeared on Camborne Hill propelled along on board a wooden-framed carriage driven by a single-cylinder engine with a tall chimney. The *Puffing Devil* made its first journey from Camborne Hill to nearby Beacon Hill, travelling around one kilometre. As one of the passengers recalled: 'Captain Dick got up steam, out in the high-road, just outside the shop at the Weath. When we get see'd that Captain Dick was agoing to turn on steam, we jumped up as many as could, maybe seven or eight of us. 'Twas a stiffish hil going from the Weight up to Camborne Beacon, but she went off like a little bird.'[6]

The length of journey was limited by the need for a continual water supply; nevertheless the maiden trip was a success. The vehicle itself came to grief just three days later when Andrew Vivian lost control of the steering handle, and the *Puffing Devil* was stranded. Davies Gilbert described what happened next: 'The carriage was forced under some shelter, and the Parties adjourned to the Hotel, & comforted their Hearts with a Roast Goose and proper drinks, when, forgetfull of the Engine, its Water boiled away, the Iron became red hot, and nothing that was combustible remained of the Engine or the house.'[7]

The end of the *Puffing Devil* marked the beginning of a transport revolution. Freed from the constraints of other inventors' patents, on 24 March 1802 Trevithick and Vivian jointly took out a patent 'as for improving the construction of steam-engines, and the application thereof for drawing carriages on rails, turnpike roads, and other purposes'.

Trevithick adapted his engines to work more smoothly by adding another cylinder, with the piston rods of the two cylinders working a quarter-turn apart. The firebox and the cylinder were both located within the boiler, which was made cylindrical to bear high pressure. The early locomotive engine could work with steam at a pressure of sixty to eighty pounds per square inch (atmospheric pressure is around 15 psi), and a second safety valve was fitted.

In 1803 Trevithick decided to show the world his steam carriage and a vehicle was shipped from Plymouth to London. The engine, about the size of an orchestra drum, was fitted between the rear wheels of a phaeton carriage. Trials were carried out at Lord's cricket ground before the steam carriage was taken down New Road and Gray's Inn Lane. Despite this spectacular demonstration there were setbacks which caused Trevithick's backers to doubt the engine's potential. That same year a high-pressure Trevithick engine used to pump water at a corn mill in Greenwich exploded, killing four men. The accident was due to careless operation, as Trevithick wrote to Davies Gilbert:

> It appears the boy that had the care of the engine was gon to catch eales in the foundation of the building, and left the care of it to one of the Labourers; this labourer saw the engine working much faster than usual, stop'd it without takeing off a spanner which fastned down the steam lever, and a short time after being Idle it burst. It killed 3 on the spot and one other is since dead of his wounds. The boy returned at the instant and was going to take off the trig from the valve. He was hurt, but is now on recovery; he had left the engine about an hour . . . I believe that Mr B. [Boulton] & Wat is abt to do mee every engurey in their power for they have don their outemost to report the explosion in the newspapers and private letters very different to what it really is.[8]

The comment about Boulton & Watt shows the bitterness that still lingered between these competitors. In response to the accident Trevithick introduced further safety measures, including duplicate safety valves; a pressure gauge filled with mercury, which blew out under excess pressure allowing the steam to escape; and a lead plug that would melt once the temperature reached dangerous levels.

Fortunately help was also about to arrive from an unexpected quarter. Samuel Homfray, the owner of the Pen-y-darren ironworks near Merthyr Tydfil, and an early believer in steam locomotion, came to an arrangement with Trevithick, taking a share of the patents in return for a financial investment. Just as significantly, Homfray made a bet of 500 guineas with his fellow ironmaster Anthony Hill that a steam locomotive could pull a full ten tons of iron along the ten miles of tramway from Pen-y-darren to the Merthyr–Cardiff canal at Abercynon. He was relying on Trevithick to deliver.

This was another hugely significant moment. Like other steam enthusiasts, Trevithick had envisioned an age of steam-powered vehicles running on roads. But Homfray's business, in common with many ironworks and collieries, depended on shifting bulk freight along tramways, using horses to pull specially built wagons. He wanted Trevithick to build not a steam carriage, but a steam-powered rail locomotive.

Trevithick set to work immediately and by February 1804 had built this new steam-driven vehicle. The engine used a horizontal cylinder with divided or forked connecting rods from the piston to allow room for a crank to rotate within the fork. The single cylinder engine was eight inches in diameter with an eight-foot flywheel. The exhaust steam was run up the chimney (the same chimney as the fire) thus creating a draft that made the fire burn better. On 13 February the engine ran for ten miles pulling the equivalent of ten tons of iron, at five miles an hour without stopping for water. Then two weeks later, on 28 February, came the decisive moment: the two ironmasters witnessed a repeat performance and Homfray won his bet. Trevithick described the historic journey in a letter to Davies Gilbert the next day: 'Yesterday we proceeded on our journey with the engine; we carry'd ten tons of Iron, five waggons, and 70 Men riding on them the whole of the journey. It's above nine miles which we performed in 4 hours & 5 mins, but we had to cut down some trees and remove some large rocks out of the road. The engine, while working, went nearly 5 miles pr hour; there was no water put into the boiler from the time we started until we arriv'd.'[9]

Just four years after the expiration of Watt's patent, Trevithick was capable of producing engines lighter, smaller, more powerful and of wider application than those built by Watt over the previous twenty-five years. And crucially, the reduction in weight and increase in power allowed the engines to be carried on the vehicles that they themselves powered. The Pen-y-darren locomotive had most of the essential features of steam locomotives that would transform the world over the next 150 years.

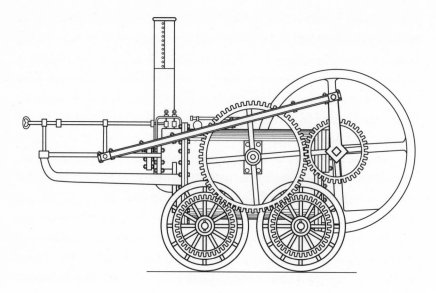

Pen-y-darren locomotive: The world's first steam locomotive used a single cylinder to drive a flywheel which transmitted power, via an intermediate cogged wheel, to the wheels on the track.

While the Pen-y-darren engine would not immediately convert the world, it made significant inroads into the area that was to be the heartland of railway engineering – the north-east of England. A Trevithick locomotive was built for a colliery in Newcastle in 1805 and a young colliery engineer named George Stephenson began making locomotives nearby in the following decade. Trevithick's own final attempt to launch the locomotive on the world came with an elliptical railway installed in Euston Square in London. Advertised as 'Catch Me Who Can', the vehicle ran for two months, July and August 1808, to crowds of spectators who paid one shilling to travel at 12 mph.

Trevithick also turned his attention to building high-pressure static steam engines. He designed engines for boring, milling, rolling, crushing, stamping, blowing as well as pumping water; he put a high-pressure engine on a barge to drive paddle wheels and built a steam-powered dredger.

Further innovations followed in 1812. Trevithick greatly improved the 'Cornish boiler' in which the steam was heated by tubes carrying hot exhaust through the boiler – 'Others have put the boiler in the fire,' Trevithick declared, 'I have put the fire in the boiler.' His 'Cornish engine', which combined high-pressure steam with a condensing process, would be used all over the world. That same year Trevithick built a high-pressure rotative engine to drive a threshing machine – it worked for seventy years and is preserved in the Science Museum in London – and went on to make a rotary-powered cultivator with a four-wheeled chassis that could be towed across a field while a series of blades cut up the earth.

Perhaps his final great invention of this extraordinary period was the 1815 steam turbine and propeller. Trevithick called his device a recoil engine; it worked on the principle of Hero's aeolipyle, being powered by pushing steam out of a series of vents like a huge Catherine wheel. The central driveshaft was then connected to a screw-like device, which was an embryonic ship's propeller.

Steam was only one of this extraordinary man's interests. Trevithick developed the use of iron tanks for storage on ships and built a small works at Limehouse to produce them. A patent of 1809 specified a huge range of inventions for use on ships, ranging from telescopic masts and bowsprits to diagonally ribbed hulls, iron floating docks and iron buoys. But Trevithick was less successful at managing his financial affairs; in 1808 he entered into a doomed partnership with Robert Dickinson; both were made bankrupt in 1811, though Trevithick managed to clear his outstanding debts within three years.

Trevithick's energetic life became even more colourful when in 1816 he set sail for South America with the hope of making his fortune in mining. He began work as an engineer in Lima but was soon caught up in the wars of independence that were sweeping the continent. Joining the army of Simón Bolívar he promptly designed a new type of carbine (a shortened rifle) made of brass, with the stock and barrel forged in one piece. The conflicts scuppered his chances of realising his mining ambitions so he went north, becoming one of the first group of Europeans to cross the isthmus of Nicaragua. When he reached Cartagena on the Caribbean coast of Colombia in 1827 he was penniless, and lucky to meet Robert Stephenson, son of George, who paid for his journey back to England.

In London George Stephenson, then a successful locomotive engineer, petitioned Parliament to give the penniless inventor a pension in recognition of his work; but this request was refused. Trevithick's last projects included building a huge ball-and-chain pump for dredging canals in Holland, and a design for a cast-iron tower 1,000 feet high to commemorate the Reform Bill of 1832; neither came to fruition. Richard Trevithick died aged sixty-two in 1833 in Dartford, Kent.

While others were to develop and improve the high-pressure stationary engine and the steam locomotive, all the essential elements of steam power had now been put in place by the triumvirate of Newcomen, Watt and Trevithick. While James Watt is famed as the great inventor of the Industrial Revolution, Thomas Newcomen and Richard Trevithick deserve to be placed alongside him as the giants of steam power.

IV. Cotton

'We saw our persons of quality dressed in Indian carpets.
The chintzes were advanced from lying on their floors to
their backs, and even the Queen herself was pleased to
appear in China and Japan. I mean China silks and calicoes.
Nor was this all, but it crept into our houses, our closets
and bedchambers; curtains, cushions, chairs, and, at last,
beds themselves were nothing but calicoes or Indian stuffs.'

DANIEL DEFOE, 1726

10. The Rise of Cotton

The cotton industry is the bellwether of the Industrial Revolution. Here the separate strands of money and power, innovation and ingenuity, labour and organisation came together in a sudden rush that launched the world into modernity. Cotton provided the vehicle for the historic change from an organic to an industrial economy. But how did a minor industry concentrated in a small, remote part of England become the driving force of a revolution in work, finance, management, business practice and technological innovation?

We will begin to answer that question in the next few chapters, but behind the stories of the world-changing machines, the huge mills and the colossal entrepreneurs lies a unique phenomenon that made this the most important industry in world history. People had always invented tools, devices and processes for doing work more easily, but at no time in the previous millennia had the need or desire for technical improvements produced an unstoppable momentum of continuing change. Once the cotton industry took off in the 1770s, it set in motion a period of transformation that has arguably lasted until the present. The Industrial Revolution was not a sudden change followed by a reversion to stasis: the jenny, the spinning frame and the steam condenser were the start of a process that has led to the microchip and the iPhone. The cotton industry provided a model for others to follow, so that eventually all branches of manufacture saw the need for continual innovation and joined the revolution.

So, why cotton? Here a number of factors came together to produce the conditions for industrial take-off. First, cotton was a worldwide trade, often described as the first global commodity, and second, the potential for expansion of British production was vast. In 1750, when all cotton was still spun by hand, Britain was producing around 3 million pounds of cotton yarn a year, while Bengal's output alone was 85 million pounds. By the end of the century, thanks to the mechanisation of spinning, the British were producing most of the world's yarn and British spinning machines were so efficient that even Indian producers were using them to save labour costs. The third factor was that the market for cotton kept growing. In 1790, 4 per cent of clothing in Europe was made of cotton (in a population of under 200 million); by 1890 it had grown to 73 per cent while the European population had roughly doubled to 400 million.[1] And finally, there was the trade on which England's wealth had rested for centuries and which, in the eighteenth century, gave birth to the cotton industry.

It was the wool trade that had made Britain a nation of craft workers and artisans well before industrialisation.[2] From around 1100 to the middle of the eighteenth century the wool trade employed more people and made more money at home and abroad than all other trades combined. It was the foundation of English and later British prosperity, directly responsible for the wealth of its citizens, the commercial success of its market towns and the grandeur of its buildings; it paid for the abbeys and monasteries of Yorkshire and the wool churches of East Anglia and the West Country.[3] But how did this trade develop? When European commercial networks began to emerge in the twelfth century, textiles became the backbone of regional, national and international trade. Fine cloths were produced in northern Italy, while a corridor of trade from Italy through the Rhine lands, Burgundy and Flanders stretched to the Baltic and Britain. Flanders and Italy imported wool from all over Europe and English abbeys and estates sold vast quantities of fleeces to merchants from the Continent. Long-term contracts were not uncommon: in the fifteenth century an Italian merchant bought all the wool produced by Kirkstall Abbey in Leeds for ten years.

It was the transition from a supplier of fleeces to a producer of woollen goods that marked the beginning of England's prosperity. In the 1330s the European trade was in a cyclical period of decline, partly brought on by political unrest in the Low Countries, which was choking off demand for wool. Edward III invited discontented Flemish weavers, fullers and dyers to settle in England and many followed his call. More importantly, however, the Black Death, which arrived in England in 1348, brought huge disruptions. The loss of population caused a shortage of labour in the countryside, which in turn encouraged landowners to turn over arable land to sheep pastures.

Previously sheep were grazed on poor soil or used to manure land in open-field systems. Now the grazing of sheep on good pasture led to a huge expansion in production: while in the mid-1300s England exported around 5,000 cloth pieces per year, by the mid-1500s this had grown to 100,000 pieces of higher quality wool with longer fibres. This enabled English producers to specialise in a new type of cloth, known as worsted, which was lighter and smoother than traditional wool fabric. The trade in worsted cloth, also known as 'new draperies', now became the engine of English prosperity, making its way to every wool market in Europe and further afield.

The most important aspect of the wool trade was its ubiquity: hand spindles, spinning wheels, looms, combers, fulling mills, drying tenters and dyeing houses were spread across the country. While the denizens of farmhouses and country cottages washed, fulled, combed, spun and wove the wool, artisans in country towns finished cloth by dyeing, teaselling and rolling before selling it at markets. Different parts of the fleece have different qualities and so sorters separated up to twelve different types of wool – the shoulder wool being the best. Scouring or fulling removed the impurities through the use of fulling stocks to pummel the wool while it stood in stale urine, the ammonia helping to remove the natural grease. Some wools were then blended before being carded to align the fibres, and made into loose threads known as slivers (the equivalent of cotton rovings). Worsted wool was not blended but instead was combed to remove the short fibres, which became part of other wool products. The long fibres were then made into a ball known as a top, ready for spinning.

By the late medieval period wool was a highly developed industry in England; this was also the heyday of the trade guilds who protected their members' interests, regulated entry into the trade, trained new members through apprenticeships, and maintained standards of production. By the sixteenth century the English wool trade had become a heavily regulated business, to the point where further expansion was threatened. At a time when urban populations were booming and the demand for cloth was growing vastly, the guilds became obstacles to the wider interests of the trade. The traditional medieval trade, centred on guild-controlled towns like Exeter, Honiton, Norwich and Beverley, began to lose out to places where the trade was dispersed in semi-rural communities where there were fewer restrictions. As regulation lost out to cut-throat competition, the chief beneficiary was the West Riding of Yorkshire, an area of wool-making without a large historic centre.

England's role as a principal woollen cloth-maker was confirmed by the prohibition of the export of raw wool by James I in 1614 – which stayed in place until 1824. For two centuries all wool clipped in England was processed in England too. Today we understand that the processing of raw materials creates and distributes wealth much more effectively than selling commodities; the wool trade was an early example of this 'enrichment through making'. The trade had always worked through a combination of town guilds and rural artisans working in their homes. From the sixteenth century the latter were increasingly controlled by clothiers who organised the making and distribution of cloth, and merchants, who made fortunes buying and selling it across Britain and Europe. Though the clothiers worked a system of putting-out, using home workers and paying on piece rates, there were also a few wool factories. In the 1590s the poet Thomas Deloney wrote a fictional account of the life of the legendary Jack of Newbury, who has been identified as the clothier John Winchcombe II who died in 1557. Deloney's narrative poem makes no claim to literary greatness, but it includes the following description:

> Within one room being large and long
> There stood two hundred Looms full strong:
> Two hundred men the truth is so
> Wrought in these looms all in a row.

Allow for the possibility of exaggeration, but Winchcombe was a wealthy and influential man who certainly ran some kind of wool factory, and he is unlikely to have been alone in this.

Wool cloth was not only used for clothing and bedding but also for furnishings and wall-coverings. In 1577 William Harrison wrote: 'in the houses of knights and gentlemen, merchantmen and some other wealthy citizens, it is not so gerson [uncommon] to behold generally their great provision of tapestry, turkey work . . . and fine linen . . . many farmers and skilled tradesmen garnish their joined beds with tapestrie and silk hangings, and their tables with carpets and fine naperies whereby the wealth of the country doth infinitely appear'.[4]

Note how wool was combined with linen and silk, both industries that were becoming established in England. The diaries of Samuel Pepys show him buying fashionable fabrics and clothes made of wool, leather, linen and silk, and sometimes Indian calicoes or cottons; in 1663 he bought his wife 'a chinte . . . that is a painted calico for her to line her new study which is very preetie,' having two years earlier bought an 'Indian gown for myself'.[5]

Wool production was beneficial for a wide range of people. In 1675 the author of The Weaver's Pocketbook, published in Dundee, pointed out the advantages of the prevailing system:

It is the advantage of this above many other trades, that a man may be dealing in it with a little stock, and from it get a little livelihood. It is the disadvantage of many other employments, that nothing can be done in them without several hundreds of pounds going: 'tis otherwise with this [weaving], my self have known many who came to considerable estates, who have told me they begun with ten pound; they passed but with a staff over Jordan, and at their coming back had great droves . . . It is a trade infinitely useful as to the poor. Females both women and children are imployed in preparing their yarn: children from their infancy almost, in winding their pipes, men in weaving at the loom.[6]

From the sixteenth century the West Riding of Yorkshire, stretching into east Lancashire, became the leading centre of wool production.[7] The Pennine hills and climate were unsuitable for arable but ideal for sheep farming and the soft waters lent themselves to washing and dyeing wool. Existing towns like Leeds, Bradford, Wakefield, Halifax and Huddersfield soon expanded and villages grew into small towns, spreading as far as the western slopes of the Pennines in Lancashire.

In 1724 Daniel Defoe saw woollen cloth being made throughout West Yorkshire, where 'at almost every house there was a tenter and almost on every tenter a piece of cloth, or kersey or shalloon'.[8]

An efficient system developed where the independent clothier went to market and bought the wool; his wife and children carded and spun it; the clothier then dyed the wool, wove it and took it to the fulling mill before transporting it to his stall on the market. The family could make a good living by making one or two pieces a week and farming a holding of between three and fifteen acres of land. The famous Piece Hall in Halifax was built in 1779 to accommodate these independent traders, but they were soon overtaken by big merchants who handled the buying and selling, and paid the spinners and weavers a piece rate for their work. This putting-out system drove efficiencies in the production of cloth while feeding an ever-growing and ever-diversifying market. In 1700 the textile trade accounted for 70 per cent of English exports, and of a total production worth £5 million, £1 million was earned in the West Riding. By the middle decades of the eighteenth century the area had even overtaken Norwich in its specialist field as producer of worsted fabrics and was making more than half of Britain's textile exports.

Wool made England rich and gave her a well-developed manufacturing infrastructure, but another product is also crucial to our story. Flax grown in Ulster and Scotland had been processed into linen cloth *in situ* and imported into north-west England for centuries, but when with the rising population the demand for linens for clothing and bedding increased, a spinning and weaving industry grew up in Lancashire to go alongside its indigenous wool trade. With linen being fashionable and within economic reach of even maids and servants, by 1756 consumption reached 80 million yards and by 1770 – before the cotton boom cut into the linen trade – it had increased to 103 million yards.[9] By now the linen and wool trades were concentrated in a region encompassing the West Riding of Yorkshire, south-east Lancashire and part of north Derbyshire and Nottingham.

Cotton production, in comparison, was a latecomer to England. Cotton fabrics had been imported into Europe from India and other eastern regions for centuries. In the fourteenth century raw cotton was sold by Venetian traders in Flanders, particularly Antwerp, which became the centre of a small cotton-spinning and weaving industry.[10] The Dutch wars of independence that saw the sack of the city in 1585 by Spanish troops resulted in many textile workers emigrating to England. By then Lancashire already had a small but well-established wool and linen industry, and it seems that here some Flemish weavers began experimenting with mixing fabrics, weaving linen with wool and with cotton to produce fustian. In his 1641 work The Treasure of Trafficke, Lewes Roberts provides the first record of the Manchester cotton trade:

The towne of Manchester in Lancashire, must be also herein remembered, and worthily, for their encouragement commended, who buy the Yarne of the Irish, in great quantity, and weaving it returne the same againe in Linen, into Ireland to sell; neither doth the industry rest here, for they buy Cotten wooll, in London, that comes first from Cyprus, and Smyrna, and at home worke the same, and perfit it into Fustians, Vermilions, Dymities, and other such Stuffes; and then returne it to London, where the same is vented and sold, and not seldome sent into forraigne parts, who have meanes at far easier termes, to provide them-selves of the said first materials.'[11]

But cotton manufacture remained a small industry in England, its output negligible in size in comparison to the high-quality, cheap and brightly coloured cotton fabrics brought from India by the East India Company. Increasingly European traders found it best to import white calicoes from India and to print the required patterns where they were being sold. So well was calico printing established in Britain by the end of the seventeenth century that calicoes presented a serious threat to the home textile industry; a petition presented in 1696 argued that calico printing in Bristol alone had risen from sixty to 1,000 pounds of cloth per week, while William Sherwin, the holder of a patent for printing calicoes, was employing 600 people at his various works. These may have been exaggerations but they show the level of concern among wool-makers in particular. A law was therefore passed in 1701 that made illegal the use and wearing of Indian or Chinese silks, and of Indian printed or painted calicoes, and striped or checked cottons.[12] But as the law was aimed at imports of printed cloth, it had the effect of boosting the home calico-printing industry to such an extent that it undermined its own purpose. Cottons, made principally by printing on white Indian cloth, in fact became more popular than ever: by 1711 around a million yards were being printed in Britain annually, mostly on cheap Indian calico bought at 16d to 20d a yard, with printing costing around 2d to 3d. This severely undercut the price of wool cloth and when the wool industry protested, in 1711 duties of 3d a yard on calico and 1½d on printed linen were brought in; both were doubled in 1714.

The economic downturn caused by the bursting of the South Sea Bubble in 1720 forced Parliament to act once more to protect the wool trade: in 1721 an Act extended the prohibition to all Indian cotton cloth printed or stitched in any way, excepting only muslins which would not compete with wool cloth. 'It is most evident,' the Act stated, 'that the weaving and using of printed, painted, stained and dyed calicoes in apparel, household stuff, furniture and otherwise, does manifestly tend to the great detriment of the woollen and silk manufactures of this Kingdom.'

So, a product that was popular among the British people was now effectively banned. The consumers' first instinct was naturally to carry on acquiring cotton through illicit means, but they were also looking for any maker who could produce a reasonable imitation of Indian cotton, even if coarse in comparison. Manchester had a head start through its existing cotton and linen industries; by 1700 the region was already importing 500,000 kg of raw cotton from Smyrna via London.[13] The 1736 Manchester Act was an implicit recognition that Britain was now becoming a cotton, as well as a wool, producer; it repealed some of the more draconian restrictions in the 1721 Act, including the bans on wearing certain cotton garments, and thereby gave the Lancashire industry a boost. By now cotton was also being cultivated in the West Indies and the colonies of North America, from where it could be shipped direct to Liverpool. In addition the damp, temperate atmosphere of south Lancashire gave perfect conditions for spinning fine thread.

The Lancashire cotton spinners made use of the same spindles and wheels that were used the world over, but they could not compete with the ultra-fine threads produced by the extraordinarily skilful hand-spinners of Bengal, and their threads were either coarse or would break too easily. So the Lancashire makers, probably following the lead given by Flemish immigrants, combined strong linen warp threads with cotton threads as the weft to produce fustian. When printed up these were popular substitutes for the banned Indian imports, and became the basis of a steadily growing Lancashire industry.

No duties were levied on fustian under the 1721 law, since it was not a calico. In fact the strict interpretation of that law, and whether it should be used to stop native production of cotton, was never fully tested; people wanted cotton and so long as the correct duty was paid on printed cloth (which depended on whether local excise men were assiduous) then home-made fustian was allowed. Some were willing to flout the restrictions on imported cotton; the actor David Garrick ordered a 'chintz bed and curtains' from India, which was impounded by customs in 1775. He used his influence to liberate his goods, and the bed is now in the V&A Museum in London.

The development of the cotton industry in Lancashire was dictated by the changing technology that we will examine in the next chapters, but it was growing demand in Britain, Europe and North America that led to its expansion. The effect on Lancashire itself can be seen in the family histories of the time. When Samuel Bamford (1788–1872) traced his ancestry he discovered that:

> It would be about . . . the year 1716, that my father's grandfather, James Bamford, lived in Hools Wood, in Thornham, keeping a small farm, and making cane reeds for weavers of flannel and of course cotton . . . My grandfather was Daniel Bamford . . . He came to reside at Middleton, and was a small farmer and weaver . . . My father was a weaver of muslin, at that time considered a fine course of work, and requiring a superior hand; whilst my mother found plenty of employment in occasional weaving, in winding bobbins or pins for my father, and in looking after the house and children.[14]

In three generations the Bamfords had gone from farmers making reeds for weavers to first part-time and then full-time weavers.

During that time the villages of Thornham and Middleton became part of the growing Manchester conurbation and cotton weaving moved from the cottage to the factory. Early factories were not pleasant workplaces but if weaving in cottages sounds idyllic, in reality it was a hard life. Country cottages were little more than hovels with earth floors, tiny windows and little enough space, much of it taken up by the loom. The family home might in addition have to accommodate a simple carding device, a spinning wheel and some tubs for washing the cotton. As one loom could handle four spinning wheels, several families sometimes worked together in large sheds where banks of looms and spinning wheels were run. Some weavers became master artisans, training apprentices and putting out work to spinners.

The putting-out system developed to a high degree of efficiency in the wool industry in West Yorkshire, but it was more effective still in south Lancashire. Merchants knew where to come to for good-quality cloth, while clothiers knew how to get the best deals, how to adapt to changing needs and how to keep their workers supplied with materials. The cotton industry grew steadily if unspectacularly until the 1770s. Lancashire had the advantage of a port, and mechanical expertise in the watchmaking industry; it was also a stronghold of Nonconformists embracing industrial and commercial enterprise. When mechanisation came, Lancashire was ready to adopt it at speed. But the first great technological advance was actually a false dawn, or more properly a delayed take-off.

In 1733 John Kay, a weaver from Bury, patented the flying shuttle. Kay had already invented an improved metal reed (the large comb-like device for keeping warp threads separated on a loom) and patented a cording and twisting machine for use in the worsted trade. He was clearly a gifted inventor and his flying shuttle was a stroke of genius. By mechanically 'throwing' the shuttle, which carried the weft thread, across the loom, it saved the weaver from stopping at every pass to manhandle the device. It also removed limitations on the width of cloth, which had previously been dictated by how far one or two men could stretch across to pass the shuttle back and forth. In hindsight it seems astonishing that the device was invented at such an early date, forty years or so before mechanisation really began to take hold. But while this reveals that small improvements to spinning and weaving were taking place in the Lancashire industry from the 1720s, the initial fact of Kay's invention shows that the external conditions were still not quite right for the flying shuttle to have an overwhelming impact; there were still obstacles to change.

Kay had problems convincing weavers of the reliability of his device, while those who took it up often reneged on the royalty payments of fifteen shillings per shuttle. Kay took some to court but his awards were less than the costs of the lawsuits – in fact a 'shuttle club' was formed to defend users against Kay's actions. Some weavers, fearful of losing their jobs because of the greater efficiency of his machines, attacked the devices, while others petitioned king and Parliament to have them banned. It was only in the 1760s that the flying shuttle became widely used in the Lancashire cotton industry, with weavers and clothiers keen to produce cloth more quickly for a growing market.

Once the flying shuttle spread through the industry, it became clear that spinning with traditional wheels could no longer keep pace with looms running at two, three or four times the previous speeds. By the end of the 1760s both Hargreaves's spinning jenny (invented around 1765), and Arkwright's frame (patented in 1769) had solved the problem, followed in the next decade by Crompton's mule – all three invented in Lancashire. These devices could all be driven from external power sources, meaning that the laborious tasks of turning and drawing the thread were no longer carried out by human hands. The logical development was for the machines now to be grouped together in buildings with central power sources – first waterwheels then steam engines – and it was Richard Arkwright who took the first crucial steps.

But the cotton mill was only the culmination of a wider process that transformed every Lancashire town and village, as William Radcliffe looking back on the 1780s described:

> The mule-twist now coming into vogue, for the warp as well as the weft, added to the water-twist [Arkwright's machine] and common jenny yarns, with an increasing demand for every fabric the loom could produce, put all hands in request, or every age and description. The fabrics made from wool or linen vanished, while the old loom-shops being insufficient, every lumber-room, even old barns, cart-houses, and outbuildings of any description were repaired, windows broke through the old blank walls, and all fitted up for loom-shops.[15]

By the end of the century, in the eastern part of Lancashire and adjacent parts of Cheshire and Yorkshire, there were close to 300 towns and villages whose principal income came from producing cotton in factories.

Mechanising spinning was like taking a cork out of a bottle. In the 1770s Arkwright lobbied successfully for the repeal of the 1721 Act, since cotton production was now a British industry, exporting to every part of the world. The figures are startling: in the 1750s cotton exports were worth an annual average of £86,000; by the 1770s that had increased to £248,000, and by the 1780s to £756,000. In eight years from 1775 production of British calicoes rose from 57,000 to 3.5 million yards.

But that was just the beginning. As more mills were built, the cotton gin (invented in 1793) and the powered loom (which became effective around 1800) increased productivity such that by the 1820s British cotton exports were worth £28.8 million, comprising an astonishing 62 per cent of all the country's exports. By the 1840s the world had been turned on its head and India was now the biggest export market for Lancashire cotton cloth. (Cotton remained the country's most valuable export until the 1920s when its export value reached £192 million per annum.) Imports of raw cotton which was processed by the British cotton industry rose from an average of 2.8 million pounds in the 1750s, to 173 million in the 1820s; at its height just before the First World War the figure reached 1.8 billion pounds per year. [16]

Cotton made fortunes for some. In 1837 Leonard Horner, a factory inspector, described a meeting with a cotton baron:

> On Friday I went to Hyde, a large and densely populated village, and visited a very large mill belonging to a Mr Horsfield, a man nearly 70 years of age, who is said to be worth at least £300,000 and can hardly write his own name . . . He told me that at 18 he had not five shillings in the world beyond his weekly wages of fifteen shillings. Out of his wages he saved £28, bought a spinning jenny and made £30 the first year. In 1831 he made £24,000 of profit. He employs 1,200 people. He is not a solitary case; there are many not unlike him in this part of the country.[17]

In the eighteenth century raw cotton was brought in from India, the Ottoman Empire and from new plantations in the Caribbean and the colonies of North America. But the first half of the nineteenth century saw a significant change in supply. The coastal colonies of Virginia and North and South Carolina had grown wealthy on a mix of tobacco, coffee, rice and cotton. Most was produced on family plantations worked with slave labour. Pioneers of the newly independent United States pushed west towards the Mississippi, establishing settlements in Kentucky and Tennessee. In 1803 Thomas Jefferson completed the Louisiana Purchase of a vast swathe of territory west of the Mississippi, opening the way for the settlement of the Deep South and the establishment of new states on both sides of the river. Settlers soon discovered that the conditions in Georgia, Alabama and Mississippi were ideal for the cultivation of cotton, which became the 'wonder crop' of the American South. While the Atlantic slave trade was abolished in 1807 by Britain and the United States, this period saw the beginning of the biggest forced transportation of slaves in history. From 1810 to 1860 more than a million slaves were officially recorded as crossing state boundaries, with millions more moving within states to work on cotton plantations. In 1802 the United States exported $5 million worth of raw cotton; by 1830 this had risen to $30 million and by 1860 to $192 million, by which time the nation was producing 75 per cent of the world's raw cotton – with most of the crop going to the mills of Lancashire.[18]

The British cotton industry also benefitted from the trade networks opened up by the global dominance of the Royal Navy and the nation's mercantile fleet. Lancashire cotton was cheaper and better than any produced elsewhere in the world, including the Americas and Europe, where populations were growing exponentially. Improved shipping meant that global markets could be reached more reliably and more cheaply.

The prodigious and sustained growth in the British cotton industry both relied on and fostered continual technological innovation. As the market continued to grow, faster production, better quality and labour-saving all brought rewards. And the innovations spun out into surrounding industries – Manchester became the world centre of engineering and machine-tool manufacture and its chemical industry worked on new methods of dyeing, starching, sizing and printing cloth. The cotton trade encouraged innovations in ventilation systems for factories, transport technology and cleaning products, while rapid turnover of fashions in clothing and furnishings meant that textile design was at the heart of British industry.

Cotton was the first globally traded commodity and British industry benefitted from a growing market combined with technical ingenuity. But the opportunities for expansion did not diminish the difficulties faced by innovators. Men like John Kay, Thomas Highs, Richard Arkwright, Samuel Crompton and Edmund Cartwright had to overcome problems that had defeated everyone else; they had to be inspired, then turn their ideas into working machines, and finally make them reliable and profitable. We might believe that building a machine to spin cotton would be a simple affair, but a deeper understanding of the process gives us a further insight into the technical ingenuity, commercial competitiveness and individual determination that characterised the Industrial Revolution.

11. Spinning and Weaving

Spinning yarn out of cotton, wool, flax, hemp or silk is among the oldest human skills: yarn is known to have been spun in Egypt as early as 7,000 BC. The process involves two distinct movements: twisting and drawing. The raw material, usually in the form of fibres, has to be twisted to give strength and cohesion, and then pulled out or drawn to give length and fineness.

For most of human history spinners used either a drop spindle or a spindle and distaff. Using a drop spindle the spinner allows the spindle to drop down, drawing out the yarn with its weight, while at the same time rolling it between the fingers to give the thread the necessary twist. Alternatively the unspun yarn is held on a distaff and the spindle is drawn away with one hand. Once a length has been drawn out, the spinner picks up the spindle and winds the length on to the reel of spun yarn. Then the cycle starts again.[1] The drawback with these methods is their slowness; the advantages are that the devices are completely portable, and at the highest levels of skill spinners could produce threads that were both extremely fine and sufficiently strong.

The first major change in spinning technology came with the development of the spinning wheel, which appeared in Mesopotamia and China around the eleventh century AD and in India and Europe in the thirteenth century. In the traditional wheel the spindle is mounted at an angle and is turned by a so-called great wheel, which allows the spinner a free hand to feed the unspun yarn on to the spindle. The yarn is given its twist by being held at a slight angle to the spindle and continuously slipped over the end of the spindle as it turns. As with the spindle and distaff, the spinner draws out the thread while it is being twisted. Once a full length is drawn out, a section of the thread is coiled out towards the end of the spindle. This needs to be uncoiled and recoiled on to the main reel of thread, together with the drawn-out section. The spindle is therefore put into reverse spin, until all the unreeled thread is drawn out, then put back into 'forward' motion so that all the twisted and drawn thread can be reeled on to the main reel at the bottom of the spindle – it is crucial to keep in mind this last part of the operation. The wheel is obviously less portable and more expensive to set up than the simple drop spindle, but it produces thread up to ten times faster.

Using wheels and spindles, skilled hand-spinners were able to produce cotton threads of extraordinary fineness for weaving into cotton cloths and muslins. The Bengal region of India became particularly renowned for the fineness and high quality of its cotton thread and cloth. The measure of fineness was indicated by the number of hanks to a pound: in the 1740s twelve-thread (coarse thread at twelve hanks to the pound) sold at 1s 6d a pound, while

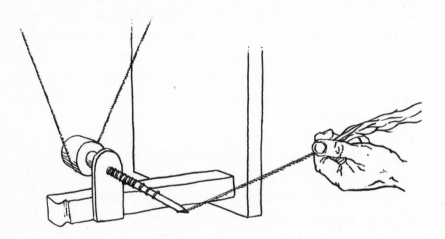

Spinning wheel spindle: The spindle is turned via the so-called great wheel, which is turned by hand or a foot treadle. The spinner simultaneously draws out the thread and imparts a twist by slipping the thread continuously over the end of the spindle.

sixty-thread was 14s and eighty-thread was 20s 6d. Indian thread was usually around sixty, but could be as high as eighty. To reach this level of strength and fineness required great dexterity from the spinner: they had to use their fingers to even out the thread as it was being drawn, while feeding just enough to give the finest thread. Imitating this delicate manual skill was the biggest challenge for anyone seeking to mechanise the spinning process.

During the sixteenth and seventeenth centuries adaptations were made to the basic spinning wheel. A foot treadle for turning the great wheel gave better speeds and freed both the spinner's hands. More intriguingly a new device called a 'flyer' was developed – this was described by Leonardo da Vinci in 1519, although we don't known how much influence he had in its development. Certainly by the 1550s it was in widespread use in a device known as the Saxony wheel.

The flyer is a U-shaped device that turns around the spindle (now more correctly a bobbin for simply reeling the thread). Both devices rotate, which gives a twist to the yarn which is being fed through a hole in the axis of the flyer, but the flyer turns slightly faster than the bobbin, thereby reeling the cotton on to the bobbin as they both turn. This ingenious system allows the yarn to be twisted and reeled at the same time. This was a considerable

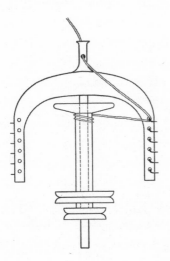

Flyer and spindle: The thread is fed onto the flyer from the top. The flyer turns at a slightly different speed to the spindle or bobbin, and this gives the thread a twist as it is wound on.

advance, instantly overcoming the need to reverse the turn of the spindle in order to re-reel the thread. However, getting the right tension in the thread was difficult and the flyer system was used mainly for spinning coarse thread.

The relative complexity of the spinning cycle explains why its mechanisation was such a difficult task. In fact, before the eighteenth century there was no real need for mechanisation. In most countries a craft economy had developed where one or two spinners in a household could supply enough thread to keep a loom busy. In India there was no shortage of labour to produce enough cotton thread to keep weavers supplied, while in Europe the cotton market was small and only slowly growing, compared to that for wool and linen, where 'traditional' methods were well established and jealously guarded from change.

Two things happened to alter this. Firstly the popularity of cotton cloth, combined with restrictions on imports, fostered a growing domestic spinning industry. Secondly John Kay's 1733 invention of the flying shuttle made weaving, particularly cotton weaving, much faster. Once this new shuttle became widely adopted in the 1760s one loom could devour thread from at least half a dozen spinning wheels. Weavers needed more yarn than they could get hold of and created an urgent need for a faster method of spinning.

The first attempts to mechanise spinning focussed, naturally enough, on the flyer system.[2] With the Saxon wheel the final stage of spinning the thread while maintaining tension was achieved by the flyer and bobbin system; but the drawing out of the unspun thread, known as the roving (or the sliver in the wool mills of Yorkshire), was done by hand. The major challenge was to devise a system that would allow the roving to be drawn out to give a consistent fineness while maintaining the correct tension in the thread. In the same decade that Kay patented the flying shuttle, John Wyatt from Lichfield devised a system for drawing out the roving using a series of pairs of rollers through which the unspun yarn would pass, with each pair running at a slightly different speed. This was a simple though ingenious idea but it was too complex to get it to work satisfactorily. Nevertheless by 1738 Wyatt's partner Lewis Paul had taken out a patent 'for the spinning of wool and cotton in a manner entirely new'. Their patent application stated: 'As the prepared mass, rope, thread or sliver passes regularly through or betwixt these rowlers, cillinders or cones, a succession of other rowlers, cillinders or cones, moving proportionately faster than the first, draws the rope, thread or sliver in any degree of fineness which may be required.'

In 1741 the pair opened the world's first mechanical spinning mill in Birmingham. Their machinery was powered by two donkeys and lasted only two years but they had no problem raising money to set up a water-powered mill in Northampton in 1743. This had five spinning frames, each of fifty spindles and each making an impressive six pounds of fifteen-grade cotton thread a day. However, the coarseness of the thread betrays the enduring problem of the roller system: stretching the yarn between two sets of rollers will increase its length, but it will not stretch the yarn evenly. In fact, once a yarn has begun to stretch the thinner points will become thinner still, while the thick parts stay thick – the more stretch, the more unevenness. Therefore Paul and Wyatt could achieve only coarse threads. In the traditional spinning cycle this problem of compounding existing unevenness in the thread is overcome by drawing and twisting the thread at the same time.

There is frustratingly little information about Paul and Wyatt's Northamptonshire venture. The mill was sold with all the machinery intact in 1764, but it appears that no one else copied their example or used their technology by paying them for a licence. As well as the coarseness of the thread, the partners' machinery was not robust enough and needed constant repair. Interestingly, in view of Arkwright's later success, another possible reason for the failure of their venture was the inability to manage the workers, with many failing to turn up for work. Matthew Boulton, who saw the Birmingham mill when he was a boy of thirteen, later described it to James Watt as 'a good Cotton spinning Mill . . . that would have got money had it been in good hands'.[3]

Instead the idea of using rollers was to be taken up in the 1760s by Richard Arkwright, although his water-frame (so-called because it was driven by water power) was probably conceived independently of Paul and Wyatt's work.

We will come to Arkwright later, but before his frame appeared, the real breakthrough into mechanisation came by abandoning the flyer and going back to the first principles of the 'twist and draw' spinning cycle. James Hargreaves was born into the Lancashire textile trade in 1720. By the time he was a young weaver, the flying shuttle was making the local demand for extra cotton yarn more urgent. His work on a mechanical device for spinning went on for some years and he probably built a working example of the spinning jenny in the late 1750s; by the mid-1760s friends and relatives were using the jenny in the Blackburn area. Hostility

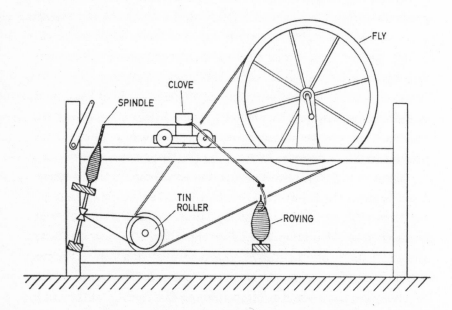

Spinning jenny: The rovings are fed on to the spindle via a gripping device known as the clove. The jenny achieves the drawing effect by pulling the clove away from the spindle to give tension, and imparts twist by slipping the thread over the end of the spindle (which is turned via the fly). The threads are pushed down on to the spindle once in every cycle.

among hand-spinners, culminating in riots and machine-breaking, led to him leaving the area for Nottingham in 1768 where he set up a workshop-cum-mill. He belatedly took out a patent for his device in 1770.

The jenny effectively copies the spinning method of the old distaff and spindle and the original spinning wheels. A row of turning spindles are placed at an angle and thread is twisted by continually slipping it over the ends of the spindles. At the same time the roving is drawn out by a small gripper, known as a clove, which moves steadily away from the spindle. Once the thread is drawn and twisted the jenny then reverses the spin to unwind the thread around the top end of the spindle (a process known as backing-off). In the final part of the cycle a wire, known as the faller, comes down on to the thread, as the spindle goes into forward motion and the clove comes back towards the spindle. All this allows the twisted and drawn thread to be reeled on to the lower part of the spindle – known as laying-on. The cycle is then repeated.

The key facet of the jenny, and its advantage over the rollers employed by Paul and Wyatt, is that careful adjustment of the spinning speed of the spindles relative to the rate of drawing back of the clove, gives a remarkably even thread. While rollers, as we have seen, tend to exaggerate the variations in thickness already extant in the roving, the jenny can even them out, giving a fine thread from an uneven roving. This had previously been achieved by the spinner's fingers; it was an extraordinary achievement for Hargreaves to replicate this intricate process with a machine. Legend has it that Hargreaves saw his daughter's spinning wheel tipped over on its side, which gave him the idea of a horizontal great wheel – but this was the least of the innovations of the jenny, which was a complex and sophisticated answer to the problem of automated spinning.

The early jenny ran eight spindles off one great wheel, using just one operator, but the number of spindles on one machine was, in theory, limitless. In 1783 the Society for the Encouragement of the Arts, Manufactures and Commerce reported: 'The construction of this kind of machine, called a Spinning jenny, has since been much improved, and is now at so high a degree of perfection, that one woman is thereby enabled with ease to spin a hundred threads of cotton at a time.'[4] At a stroke the device had unblocked the logjam caused by the inability of spinners to keep pace with the flying shuttle, thereby paving the way for the exponential expansion of the textile industry. Nevertheless, while the jenny laid the foundation for a revolution in the textile industry, it still could not produce the very fine threads made by hand-spinners. Thread from the jenny was therefore used mainly for warp, while hand-spun thread continued to be used for the weft.

While James Hargreaves had gone back to the old spinning cycle in the search for mechanisation, Richard Arkwright followed on

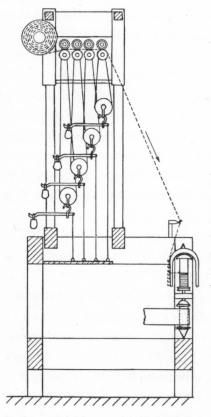

Arkwright frame: The yarn passes through a number of pairs of rollers before being fed on to a flyer which spins around a spindle or bobbin. The tension in the thread is carefully controlled by turning the pairs of rollers at different speeds, controlled via weights and pulleys.

from Paul and Wyatt by using rollers and a flyer. He patented his spinning frame in 1769. The origins of Arkwright's invention are mired in myth and controversy (see p. 192); but however he came by the original idea, it was Arkwright who turned a mechanical principle into a consistently productive industrial machine.

Arkwright's frame sent the cotton roving through a series of rollers and around weighted pulleys that gradually drew out the yarn; this seems to have been the crucial difference from Paul and Wyatt's earlier device. Through months of adjustment and experimentation in his new mill at Cromford, Arkwright was eventually able to produce even thread from uneven rovings and then to twist it by using the U-shaped flyer. He wrote to his partner Jedediah Strutt in 1772: 'Yours yesterday cam to hand together with a bill from Mr Need value 60 lb. I have sent a little cotton spun on the one spindle & find no difficulty in getting it from the Bobbin and dubled and twistd in the maner you see it at one opration. One hand I think will do 40 or 50 lb of it in one day from the bobins it is spun upon, that is in the new whay.'[5]

As the moving parts in the machine required water power, Arkwright conceived the machine and the factory system together – his spinning frame was revolutionary because of its application *and* its setting. He also developed the mechanisation of carding – his carding engine, though not the first, was granted a patent in 1775 – and the preparation of rovings, allowing a continuous flow of work through his factories. Arkwright's machine therefore brought about the mechanisation of the spinning industry, and mills with his frames were built all over Lancashire, Derbyshire and in Scotland.

The final breakthrough in the mechanisation of spinning was to have the longest and deepest legacy. Samuel Crompton was born in 1753 and when his father died in 1758 the family, like many others in Lancashire, supported themselves through cotton spinning. From early childhood Crompton used a spinning wheel, but then changed to the spinning jenny when the device became available in the late 1760s. Crompton was fortunate enough to live in an old manor house called Hall'i'th'Wood near Bolton (his family had been wealthy but fallen on hard times), where he was able to use the empty rooms to experiment with making a machine that would improve on the jenny and produce the strong fine thread that the growing industry needed. Crompton was a skilled musician, mathematician and craftsman who had gained an education at night school; he felt confident he could solve the problem. It took him seven years to perfect the machine, during which time he is said to have supported himself by spinning, weaving and by playing the violin at the Bolton theatre. Crompton later wrote about his invention: 'About the year 1772 I Began to Endeavour to find out if possible a better Method of making Cotton Yarn than was then in Generall Use, being Grieved at the bad yarn I had to Weave. But, to be short, it took me Six years, that is until 1778, before I could make up my mind what plan to Adopt that would be equal to the task I hoped it would perform. It took from 1778 to 1779 to finish it.'[6]

Crompton's Mule, so named because of its combination of the jenny and the frame, was completed in the year in which riots broke out in Lancashire over the introduction of mechanised spinning based on the jenny and Arkwright's frame. Crompton therefore initially kept his invention secret, using it to produce his own cotton thread, but news soon leaked out, attracting both interest and opposition. Crompton did not patent the device, partly because of the hostility, but also for fear of breaching Arkwright's patent. But others took up the invention and it soon overtook the jenny and the frame as the main device for mechanised spinning. It retained that position until well into the twentieth century.

So, how does it work? The mule is a complex and ingenious device that uses a series of drafting rollers to draw out and flatten the roving, which is then twisted by a spindle while being drawn out further, before being reeled on to the same spindle. Unlike the jenny, the second stage of drawing is done by mounting the spindle on a wheeled carriage, which moves away from and back towards the drawing rollers during each cycle. Others too had thought of combining the drawing rollers of Paul and Arkwright with the spinning cycle of the jenny but here, once again, the basic idea was only a small step; to build a working machine required endless determination and an ability to isolate and solve particular problems. While the process of effectively drawing out the thread twice gave the potential for fineness and strength that Crompton was looking for, the chief difficulty was precisely to coordinate the back and forth movement of the rapidly turning spindles with the finely regulated turning of the pairs of rollers. In the earliest models the operator helped fine-tune this process by holding up the movement of the carriage with one knee to increase tension, or by using a spare hand to push it faster in order to reduce tension – a process that was later made automatic. Crompton's mule was therefore able to spin the finest threads, while preserving their strength. When he had finally got the result he needed, Crompton knew what it had cost him: 'I . . . at length succeeded to my utmost desire, at the expense of every shilling I had in the world.'[7]

Crompton, like most other inventors, was hoping to reap rich rewards from his device, but he was to be disappointed. His fear of having his machines destroyed and of breaching Arkwright's patent meant that his invention was open to copying by any mill-owner with the means to build an imitation, and the strength to resist any protests. The fact that many did can be gauged from a survey conducted by Crompton himself when he sought recompense for his efforts. In 1811 he visited about 650 cotton mills in the area around Bolton to gather evidence for a petition to Parliament. He estimated that of the spindles in use, 155,880 were on a Hargreaves jenny, 310,516 on an Arkwright water-frame, and 4,600,000 were on his mule. This shows not only the dominance of his invention but also the vast expansion of the industry. By that time around 80 per cent of the cotton goods made in Lancashire were woven from cotton originally spun on mules and around 700,000 people were directly or indirectly dependent on Crompton's invention for their livelihood. In support of the inventor's petition James Watt testified that two-thirds of the Boulton & Watt engines installed in spinning mills were used for running mules. Parliament awarded Crompton

£5,000, although he had been hoping for ten times as much. The bleach works he set up with the money failed and he died in 1827 with just £25 to his name. Only after his death did his home town of Bolton see fit to honour him.

Over the next decades further innovations improved every part of the processing of cotton from its raw state to being wound on to spindles or bobbins ready for the loom, allowing most of the process to take place within a single powered mill. Carding machines for teasing out the raw cotton, washing, making rovings, winding on, spinning, packing and transportation were all improved so that the Lancashire industry could remain in front of its competitors. The Roberts Self-Acting Mule – which did away with the need for an operator to guide each cycle – was patented in 1825 and 1830, and in 1843 the ban on exports of textile machinery was lifted, giving a boost to sales of British mules and looms across the world. Technology speeded production and reduced costs to such a degree that there was a tenfold reduction in the price of fine (hundred-grade) cotton yarn between 1785 and 1795. Nowhere else in the world could compete with the Lancashire cotton industry.

Like spinning, weaving threads into cloth is an ancient human skill. Early looms used either two rods pegged to the ground to hold the warp thread taut, or used weights to pull the warp down from a horizontal bar. The weft was then threaded through the warp by an in-and-out motion. An early development on this basic method came with the opening up of the gap known as the shed. A broad flat piece of wood, known as the shed stick, would be pushed through alternate warp threads, and could be turned to open up a gap for the weft shuttle to pass straight through. Once the shuttle pass, or pick, was made, a sword-stick would be used to beat the weft thread to bring it tightly against the woven section of the cloth. Crude though these looms were, the weavers were capable of producing cloth of astonishing fineness – up to 120-warp threads per centimetre.

In the late part of the first millennium AD a more sophisticated method began to appear, in India and in the Arab world. Looms were built into frames with the warp running horizontally; alternate warp threads were threaded through holes in vertical rods known as heddles, and these heddles were hung from the top of the loom frame by strings. The shed could then be opened by pulling on one set of strings and then the other. Sometimes this pulling was done by a helper, usually a child, but a simple series of pulleys and pedals or stirrups enabled the weaver to pull the strings with their feet. This left the hands free to pass the shuttle through the shed. This type of loom spread with the Arab conquests of the Middle East and North Africa and was widely adopted in medieval Europe; it was also at the heart of the extraordinary Bengal cotton industry, which was able to spin and weave the finest cotton using hand-spinning and hand-weaving and which, as we have seen, dominated the world cotton trade before the Industrial Revolution.[8]

By the thirteenth century horizontal looms with foot treadles for opening the shed were well established in Britain. A typical English loom, used in urban workshops and rural cottages, was a large wooden structure – essentially a frame around two and a half metres long by two metres high, with the width dictated by the reaching through of the shuttle bearing the weft thread. The shed was opened by having each set of heddles attached to a horizontal bar above; rather than using alternate foot pedals, a simple counterbalance mechanism ensured that, as one bar was lifted, the other was lowered. The warp threads were kept separated and in parallel by the large comb-like 'reeds', originally made from wood and later from iron and then steel. Threading the warp on to the loom was obviously a time-consuming business, but weavers found ways to speed this up using specially made hand tools and techniques passed down through the trade. Different types of cloth could be produced by changing the relations between warp and weft: weaving the weft past sets of up to sixteen-warp threads at a time would give a satin weave, used mainly in silk, while changing the warp sets for each pass of the weft could give a diagonal effect to the weave, known as twill, which is common in denim cotton and in worsted wool.

In late medieval England weaving moved out of urban workshops to cottages in the countryside. Here a family would be part of a farming community with access to wool; the women and children would clean, comb and spin the wool, while the men wove the cloth and took it to the market. The development of ever finer wools led to the emergence of the so-called new draperies and, as we have seen, from the sixteenth century the supply of raw materials and the selling of cloth began to be taken over by clothiers and merchants operating a putting-out system. Where previously a farming family would have spun and woven their own wool, the new draperies called for thread made from worsted fibre, sometimes mixed with linen and cotton, which were obtainable only through clothiers and merchants who bought in bulk from shipping firms bringing cotton and flax from across the world.

The ancient hand-craft of weaving was given a mighty jolt in the 1730s with John Kay's invention of the flying shuttle. Previously the weft thread was passed back and forth through the shed by hand; this limited the width of the loom and the speed of weaving. The flying-shuttle mechanism used a pair of leather straps as slings to throw the shuttle across the shed. The left and right straps were alternately 'snapped' into action by the weaver pulling a cord; the shuttle then flew across the shed before hitting the strap at the other end. The word 'flying' is deceptive – the shuttle actually ran along a wooden track that was positioned below the warp thread – but it certainly describes the apparent speed of travel. The ends of the wooden shuttle were tipped with brass and later steel to resist the continual bashing it got at each end of its run. Once the shuttle had passed, the weft was beaten into place and the shed reversed before the shuttle was sent back in the other direction. A further development of the flying shuttle followed in 1760 when Kay's son Robert invented the drop box, which allowed any one of a set of shuttles, each loaded with a different coloured thread, to be brought into action by the weaver.

The flying shuttle increased the speed of weaving dramatically, and consequently the demand for spun yarn. Weavers were forced to spend their mornings trying to find spun wool, linen and cotton yarn for their looms. But once the spinning jenny, frame and mule started to spread from the 1770s, weavers had enough yarn to keep busy and the textile market boomed. But this was a short-lived boom for the cottage weaver. Mechanisation had increased the productivity of spinning by orders of magnitude; now inventors and manufacturers began to look for ways to mechanise weaving too.

The man who first succeeded in the mechanisation of weaving was Edmund Cartwright. As he recalled:

Happening to be at Matlock in the summer of 1784, I fell in company with some gentlemen of Manchester, when the conversation turned on Arkwright's spinning machinery. One of the company observed, that as soon as Arkwright's patent expired, so many mills would be erected, and so much cotton spun, that hands could never be found to weave it. To this observation I replied that Arkwright must then set his wits to work to invent a weaving mill. This brought on a conversation on the subject, in which the Manchester gentlemen unanimously agreed that the thing was impracticable; and, in defence of their opinion, they adduced arguments which I certainly was incompetent to answer, or even to comprehend, being totally ignorant of the subject, having never at that time seen a person weave.[9]

Cartwright had an unusual background for an eighteenth-century inventor. Following the traditional route of a son of the English gentry he was educated at Wakefield Grammar School and University College, Oxford before becoming an Anglican rector and, in 1783, a canon at Lincoln Cathedral. Although he never saw a loom before 1784 he decided that he was capable of designing and building exactly the device that the expert Manchester gentlemen said was impossible. As with the mechanisation of spinning and the Newcomen and Watt engines, mechanising weaving depended on making a device capable of endlessly repeating a complex cycle of movements that normally required a highly skilled craftsman. To get through a cycle once without human intervention was only part of the achievement: sustaining the cycle reliably was the key. Cartwright realised that he needed to turn the rotary motion used by mills into a series of motions to open the shed, throw the shuttle, beat the weft, and progress the cloth forward, each minutely coordinated with each other. To do this he set about devising a system of cranks, eccentric wheels, cams and toothed cogs. His first power loom, patented in 1785, could operate a loom but failed to maintain the cycle, so Cartwright took out five more patents; his final patent for the power loom was granted in 1787. He then felt confident enough to build a factory in Doncaster to make his machines but this venture failed, probably for managerial rather than technical reasons. But, imperfect though his machines were, Cartwright had shown that an automated loom driven from a remote power source could be made. Now other more skilful engineers piled in with technical improvements. Cartwright's loom needed the cycle to be stopped every so often for the warp thread to be sized and then dried with hot irons, but in 1803 William Radcliffe invented the dressing frame, which sized and dried the warp threads before they were wound on to the warp roller, thereby allowing the weaving to be continuous. Radcliffe also invented a ratchet that enabled the warp roller to feed the loom automatically.

Power looms were designed and built to be used in factories where a single source of power, either a waterwheel or a steam engine, could drive a large number of individual looms. Once Watt had successfully adapted his steam engines to smooth rotary motion, weaving mills with a thousand looms could be built. The increase in productivity was stark, as one inventor noted:

A very good Hand Weaver, a man twenty-five or thirty years of age, will weave two pieces of nine-eighths shirting per week, each twenty-four yards long . . . A Steam Loom Weaver, fifteen years of age, will in the same time weave seven similar pieces. A Steam Loom factory containing two hundred looms, with the assistance of one hundred persons under twenty years of age, and of twenty-five men will weave seven hundred pieces per week.[10]

At the Great Exhibition of 1851 a cotton power loom was displayed that could weave 220 passes of weft per minute.

People also looked for new ways to print and colour cloth, including weaving patterns into the cotton fabric. While this was important for the textile trade itself it also had far-reaching implications elsewhere. Plain cloth, particularly cotton, was traditionally printed using wood blocks. In 1752 Francis Nixon of Dublin began using engraved copper plates, which allowed exquisite detail to be printed on to cloth in repeat patterns; this was taken a stage further in 1783 when Thomas Bell patented the use of copper rollers for printing calico. Roller printing was eventually taken on by the traditional paper-printing industry. Vast quantities of plain cotton could now be rapidly printed into colourful cloths

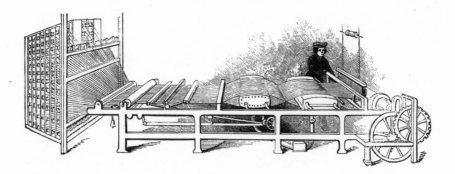

Starching: Weavers found that warp threads were easier to work if they were starched. This device heats the thread and applies starch mechanically.

that became highly fashionable. The next challenge was to mechanise the weaving of coloured patterns.

Knowledge of the Chinese draw-loom, along with the secrets
of silk production and weaving of patterned cloth, travelled along
the Silk Road in the late Middle Ages. By the fourteenth century
weavers in Florence, Lucca and Siena were using draw-looms to
produce exquisitely patterned silk and velvet. Louis XI brought
Italian weavers to France in the fifteenth century, making Lyons
the centre of European silk weaving. It was in France that the
next significant innovation was made.

In order to weave an intricate pattern into the cloth using a
draw-loom, the weaver pulls up different sets of warp threads at
each pick, or pass, of the weft thread. By doing this in a controlled
sequence, a pattern emerges in the cloth. The draw-loom operator
achieves this by pulling strings attached to the top ends of the
healds, which are rods attached to the warp threads. For plain
weaving the healds would be in two groups, and each would be
raised alternately. In pattern weaving, there will be several different

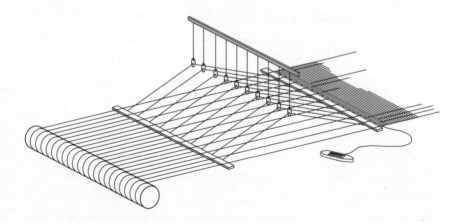

Draw-loom: One set of warp threads is drawn upwards using a series of strings
(known as healds) attached to a draw bar. This opens the shed, through which
the shuttle carrying the weft thread is passed. The weft is then beaten into
place to give the cloth a tight finish. Only one of the alternate set of healds
is shown here.

groups and they must be lifted at different points in the pattern cycle. In a complex pattern it could take around two weeks to prepare or 'tie up' the loom before weaving could begin.

In a draw-loom the lifting was done by a so-called drawboy, working under instruction from the weaver. The boy might be sitting on a beam above the loom pulling the strings upwards, or, as was more common in Europe, standing alongside the loom, pulling strings (known as 'simples' or 'tail-cords') downwards over a set of pulleys. The pulling of the simples in the correct sequence was obviously a highly complex task; making it work automatically was one of the great challenges of the age.

The first step towards the automation of pattern weaving was taken by the French weaver Basile Bouchon in 1725, building on the principle of the draw-loom. Bouchon punched a series of holes in a roll of paper in a predetermined pattern. A line of needles was pushed against the paper by a gentle spring device; when a needle came opposite a hole it passed through, and this movement pulled a string which in turn pulled on a simple, thereby lifting that heald and the warp thread. When a needle did not meet a hole, the warp thread did not lift. At each pick the roll of paper would be moved on one line of holes and the process would begin again. In 1728 Jean-Baptiste Falcon replaced Bouchon's paper with a series of stiff cards linked together on a roll, and in 1745 Jacques de Vaucason mounted Bouchon's paper device on top of a loom. In all these cases the lifting of the healds was still done by a boy. There was strong resistance to the Vaucason loom in France and it seems not to have been developed further; this was a classic case of the right machine at the wrong time and place.

Then in 1801 Joseph Marie Jacquard achieved the breakthrough into wholly automated pattern weaving. The famous Jacquard loom was granted a patent in that year in France and in England in 1820; though industrial spies had brought it to Britain before then. The Jacquard device essentially took the cards made by Falcon and used them in the way designated by Bouchon and Vaucason, so a series of punched cards rolled over a square 'roller' presenting a different set of holes at each pick. The needles pushed against the cards and either lifted warp threads or left them flat. The device did away with the need for a drawboy and because it could specify individual warp threads with ease, it enabled smoother and more intricate patterns to be made. Even better, the cards themselves could be taken off the loom at the end of a run and stored away for future use.

The dobby loom was an adaptation of the Jacquard loom, with a simpler and more robust mechanism using rods with pegs to trip the device that pulled the simples. Jacquard and dobby looms remained at the centre of the weaving industry into the twentieth century. Historians of science have long noted that the binary principle of the Jacquard was used in the punchcards of early computers, where a combination of simple on/off switches produced an operating system capable of complex tasks. The NAND gate, the basic component of the computer chip, is the modern equivalent: a simple binary device that, like the Jacquard loom, produces immensely complex results.

A *hand-weaver and a spinner*: The Jacquard cards are arranged in a continuous loop above the bed of the loom.

By the early nineteenth century, continual innovation over a period of four decades had made Britain the centre of world cotton production. The fiendishly difficult problems involved in mechanising spinning and weaving had been solved by a handful of British inventors. And these solutions had effects far beyond cotton production. They demonstrated that technical innovation could improve productivity to such a degree that jobs were gained rather than lost; and they gave a huge boost to the engineering, tool-making and machinery trades, and this in turn allowed other industries to become mechanised. The cotton trade was the crucible of the revolution that led Britain and then the world into an industrial future.

Too Much Too Soon: William Lee

Knitting of stockings, like all hand knitting, is a skilled but slow process. Stockings were standard wear for most people from medieval times to the nineteenth century (when paved walkways made trousers feasible for men) and the craft was particularly strong in the Nottingham area. The hand-knitter works by holding a series of loops, which are at the top of the knitted web, on one needle, and then transferring them one by one to another needle; as each loop is transferred the knitter adds in another loop by pushing the needle into the existing loop, twisting it and pulling it up. This action pulls in more yarn, which the knitter holds, usually twisted around their finger, from where it feeds into the loops.

As early as 1589 William Lee, a native of Calverton in Nottinghamshire, invented the stocking knitting frame. Essentially he used a series of looped needles, one for each stitch, to pull the new yarn down into the last line of the web, and then to push the yarn through holes in the web, from where it would be picked up by a separate device and pulled upwards to form the next line of the knitted web. The resulting long column of knitted material could have its sides stitched together to form the tube of a stocking. Lee's first machines had just eight needles, and so created only a coarse fabric, but he soon adapted it to twenty needles.[11]

The immediate fate of Lee's invention helps explain why the Industrial Revolution did not happen in Elizabethan England. His application for a patent was refused. The grounds are unclear, but the novelty of the device would not have counted: he would have had to demonstrate the advantages it held for the knitting trade. And if London guilds could show that it would put people out of work, the patent application was a lost cause. But Lee pushed ahead anyway. An agreement with one George Brooke dated 6 June 1600 shows that his partner was to invest £500 in return for a share of the profits, but Brooke was arrested soon afterwards and, in 1603, executed for treason.

Lee left the country and took his invention, and possibly some workers and machinery, to Rouen where he was granted a patent. There is much uncertainty as to the exact dates of Lee's life and work in France but in 1610 or 1612 he set up a partnership providing machinery to make silk and wool stockings for a local manufacturer. The last written record of Lee in 1615, describes him as an English gentleman whose occupation is 'knitter of stockings'.

Some later accounts suggest that Lee's brother James, who had gone with him to France, returned first to London and then to a village near Nottingham and reintroduced the frame. One reason for the subsequent slow spread of the frame was its cost – around £20 or £30 in the 1660s – so it was used for the high-priced end of the market while hand-knitters continued to make basic woollen goods. In 1664 there were around 400–500 frames in London, a hundred in Nottingham and fifty in Leicester. But over the next century lower rents and wages, as well as freedom from guild regulations, saw the industry move from London to the East Midlands.

Looking back to the middle of the eighteenth century William Gardiner wrote: 'The manufacture in Leicester chiefly consisted in making pink stockings for the lower orders; and, for the higher, pearl-coloured with scarlet clocks. In the dress of men the waistcoat flaps came down nearly as low as the knee; and the stockings made long enough to reach the top of the thigh, were gartered on the outside and the top rolled down as far as the leg . . . The chief [export] article was white and brown thread hose for Spain, Portugal and the West Indies.'[12] Derby, the third city of the East Midlands, became the centre of silk-stocking production.

12. Richard Arkwright: The King of Cotton

'The thirteenth child of a family steeped to the lips in poverty, [Arkwright] was turned into the world without education, which in after life he never found time to acquire. Trained to a servile handicraft, and without a shilling of capital, the position from which he raised his fortunes had not one of the advantages enjoyed by Crompton; but to compensate for this he possessed an indomitable energy of purpose which no obstacle could successfully oppose.'

Gilbert J. French, *The Life and Times of Samuel Crompton* (1859)

Was there ever a man more suited to the challenges of his time, more akin to the spirit of his age than Richard Arkwright? Arrogant, restless, dedicated, generous, convinced of his own genius and unimpressed by his social betters, Arkwright was a giant among giants; a northerner of humble origins who rose to become the world's first industrial magnate. His achievements speak for themselves: he transformed the cotton industry from a craft trade into an international powerhouse; he invented the factory system and made it pay; he was the focus of the most famous patent trials in history; acquired an immense fortune; and attracted ridicule, exasperation, admiration and adulation in equal measure. For some he embodied the greed, low-dealing, bullying and ambition that were the worst aspects of capitalist endeavour; for others he was a heroic pioneer, a rough-and-ready soul who dared to do what others would not, who put dukes in their place, treated his workers well and brought prosperity to everything he touched and to every region in which he invested. Other industrial entrepreneurs – Boulton, Wedgwood, Stephenson – combined technical ingenuity with business acumen and personal vision, but Arkwright was the king of them all. He embodied the buccaneering spirit of industrialisation and its impatience to reshape the world.

Richard Arkwright was born in 1732 in Preston in Lancashire, then a small prosperous town of around 5,000 inhabitants on the banks of the Ribble.[1] His father Thomas was a tailor who apprenticed his son to a barber at nearby Kirkham. According to family recollections Richard showed signs of mechanical ingenuity as a youth, forever fixing and making small machines. In 1750, at the age of eighteen, he moved to Bolton to work for a peruke-maker called Edward Pollit – a peruke was a gentleman's wig, and barber and wig-maker were alternative descriptions of the same trade. In 1755 Arkwright married Patience Holt, daughter of a schoolmaster with some property to his name, but his wife died a year later. He married again in 1761 and the following year took on a public house in Bolton, the Black Boy, while continuing to travel around Lancashire to build up his wig-making and barbering business.

It was around this time that Arkwright began seriously to pursue the making of a machine for spinning cotton thread. Through his travels and connections he was thoroughly immersed in the textile trade and he knew that demand for cotton was growing. He was also aware of the spread of the flying shuttle in the cotton districts: men of technical ingenuity all over Lancashire were looking for ways of spinning cotton more quickly to keep up with the growing demand from weavers.

As we have seen, the idea of drawing out cotton rovings between pairs of rollers running at slightly different speeds had been developed by Lewis Paul and his partner John Wyatt, but their machinery had proved inadequate.[2] The rollers did not do a good enough job in producing a fine even thread ready for twisting, the machinery was unreliable and the mills were poorly run. Arkwright knew the problems that rollers induced and was aware that others had lost money backing the idea. Nevertheless by 1767 he had embarked on solving the problem.

The myths surrounding Arkwright's invention of the water-frame are legion. There are claims that he was working on a perpetual-motion machine, that a sailor in his barber's shop had told him of a Chinese spinning device, and that he stole the idea from a customer who was a cabinetmaker. The central legend, however, derives from Arkwright's dealings with two local men – Thomas Highs and John Kay – and it has become the most contentious story of the Industrial Revolution.

Thomas Highs was a reed-maker based in Leigh, Lancashire, and in the 1760s he too was working on ideas for a spinning machine. He enlisted the help of his neighbour John Kay, a clock-maker (a different John Kay from the inventor of the flying shuttle) and by 1765 the two men were working on a machine using rollers. Arkwright met Kay in March 1767 and again in October in Warrington where the clockmaker lived. Kay told Arkwright about his work with Highs, and with Arkwright's input Kay was able to build a model based on the design he had developed with Highs. Arkwright took the machine to Manchester and then to Preston.

According to Arkwright's modern biographer, Robert Fitton, this is the point at which the claims of priority for Highs and Kay become secondary to the clear evidence of Arkwright's singular inventive persistence. Essentially the two mechanics had designed and built a series of rollers, in the spirit of Lewis Paul, with a fly and bobbin taken from a Saxon wheel. Arkwright's task was then to make this device fulfil its intended task of spinning fine, even, cotton thread. He had to address two problems. First, the spacing of the pairs of rollers was key to the drawing out of the thread and was related to the lengths of fibre within the cotton – too close and the internal fibres would break, too far apart and the thread would remain uneven. Second, the degree of pressure between each pair of rollers was essential to separating out the twisting of the thread, later in the process, from the earlier drawing. Arkwright understood that in the Saxony wheel the operator does this by hand, holding the roving so that the spinning action does not work its way back up into the undrawn thread; Lewis Paul's machine had not managed this and the result was uneven, lumpy thread.

In 1768 Richard Arkwright left Preston for Nottingham (coincidentally the same year as James Hargreaves arrived there), then a town of 15,000 or so inhabitants with a tradition of stocking knitting. The reasons for Arkwright's move from his native Lancashire have been hotly debated; some have argued that he went there to escape the notice of Thomas Highs, others have pointed to the potential hostility of Lancashire spinners. The pull may have been stronger than the push, though: here was a ready market for cotton yarn, as well as a few thousand workers used to working with, making and repairing complex textile machines – there were more than 1,200 knitting frames in Nottingham at that time.

Arkwright arrived in Nottingham with two relatives, John Smalley and David Thornley, with whom he immediately went into partnership as 'Joint Adventurers and Partners' in a venture to exploit his new spinning machine. Each would put in enough money for a patent to be obtained and to exploit the invention for commercial gain. Each of the three was to own three-ninths of their company, and up to £500 the profits would be divided evenly. After that, Arkwright would take 10 per cent over and above the others. This arrangement was to last for fourteen years, but early on in the development of the enterprise Thornley could no longer put in the required funds and sold part of his share to Smalley.

In July 1769 a patent was granted for Arkwright's spinning frame. The specification drawing was detailed, showing not only how the thread was to be drawn and spun, but how the bobbins could be adjusted to run faster or slower, how weights kept the rollers tight and how the power was taken off from the main factory driveshaft via a wheel and belt. Almost immediately the partners took the lease on some land in Nottingham in order to build a cotton-spinning works. The cost was £105 up front, plus £50 rent per year, and the location in the ninety-one-year lease was specified as: 'All that Messuage, Burgage and Tenement with the Outhouses Buildings Maltrooms Barn Stable Yard Garden Close or Paddock thereunto adjoining . . . in Nottingham . . . in or near two certain streets or Places there called Goosegate and Hockley.'[3] This was near to the location of Hargreaves's mill, established earlier in 1769. Soon more money was needed than Smalley could supply, and the partnership was forced to seek funds elsewhere. The Nottingham bankers Ichabod and John Wright were interested, but felt that they too had insufficient funds and passed Arkwright on to Samuel Need, an investor who had made a fortune from his investment in Jedediah Strutt's Derby rib machine. Need persuaded Arkwright to show a model of his machine to Strutt and, in January 1770, in an agreement that would have vast historical effects, Samuel Need and Strutt handed over £500 in return for a half-share in Richard Arkwright & Co. Someone who knew all three men later commented: 'Arkwright was the head, Strutt the hands and Need the sinews, for he had the purse.'[4]

Immediately the firm commissioned a builder to construct a horse-powered mill on their land in Nottingham. However, even before this mill opened, the partners, in a radically bold move, decided to build a mill powered by water at Cromford, a remote village twenty-six miles away. Water had been used for textile mills before, notably at the Lombe silk mill in Derby and Lewis Paul's Northampton mill, and it seems that Arkwright and Strutt were looking for large amounts of constant power for their machinery. The Derwent Valley was an established site for water-powered manufactories, already boasting a corn mill and a smelting mill for the local lead-mining operation. Looking back at Cromford, Arkwright described it as: 'a place affording a remarkable fine Stream of Water, And in a Country very full of inhabitants vast numbers of whom & small children are constantly Employed in the Works'.[5] The partners leased land and the rights to the waters of Bonsall Brook for £14 per year 'Together with full and free Liberty Power and Authority . . . to Erect and Build one or more Mill or Mills for Spinning Winding or Throwing Silk Worsted Linen Cotton or other Materials and also such and so many Waterwheels Warehouses Shops Smithies and other Buildings Banks and Dams Gail Shuttles and other Conveniences as they should think proper for the effectual Working of the said Mills.'[6]

They then bought Steephill Grange, a 1714 house, and used the stone to build a mill which became the template for industrial buildings across the world for the next 150 years. These buildings had little precedent in English or indeed world architecture, yet now they look as perfectly constructed as they could be. Arkwright had to work out how the power take-off from the waterwheel would operate, how the machinery would allow the work to flow without hold-ups or overstocking, how each operation would communicate physically with the others, and how the workers would best be positioned to run and repair the machines. Then he had to recruit men to build the machinery. Meanwhile he had to work out how much the mill would cost to run and how much profit he might make. All of this for a man who was trained as a wig-maker.

Fortunately Arkwright seemed to have limitless confidence in himself and his invention, as well as in the demand for cotton thread. Recruiting workers from the families of local miners and craftsmen, his advert in the *Derby Mercury* on 13 December 1771 read:

COTTON MILL, CROMFORD. 10th December 1771.
WANTED Immediately, two Journeymen Clock-Maker, or others that understands Tooth and Pinion well: Also a Smith that can forge and file. Likewise two Wood Turners that have been accustomed to Wheel-making, Spoke-turning, &c. Weavers residing in his Neighbourhood, by applying at the Mill, may have good work. There is Employment at the above Place for Women, Children, &c., and good Wages.[7]

Here we are witnessing a key factor in the Industrial Revolution: the fetching in of long-developed skills in mechanical trades and cloth trades into a unified production system. Workers such as George Hodges, whose indenture certificate survives, were hired on an eleven-year contract with weekly wages starting at ten shillings and rising to thirteen shillings for a thirteen-hour day, six-day week. Hodges was bound to the Arkwright firm for £10,000 – meaning that he could not leave before his contract was fulfilled without incurring a massive fine. This ensured that workers did not take the secrets of Arkwright's production methods elsewhere.

A long letter to his partner Jedediah Strutt, written from Cromford in March 1772, shows Arkwright in full flow: 'Sir Yours yesterday came to hand together with a bill from mr Need Value £60. I have sent a little cotton spun on the one spindle & find no Difficanty in Getting it from the Bobbin & Dubeld & Twisted in the maner you see it at one opration one hand I think will do 40 or 50lb of it in one day from the bobbins it is spun upon.' The letter continues for another 1,500 words or so, covering production, supplies, wayward workers, the possibility of spinning worsted wool on his machine, the need for a fire pump, as well as locks for the doors and a large knocker or bell in order to 'Let no persons in to Look at the works except spinning.'[8]

Once the first Cromford mill was up and running and making money for him, Arkwright began to show his unparalleled skill as a deal-maker. First he had to address a historic difficulty in the cotton industry. As we have seen the 1721 calico Act imposed duties on the sale of printed calicoes in order to protect British textiles from cheap Indian imports. While Arkwright's frame made the Act redundant – calico and other fine cotton cloth was being produced at home – frustratingly, makers were being treated inconsistently by the notoriously fickle excise men. In June 1774 Arkwright and Strutt persuaded Parliament to pass an Act that distinguished home-made from Indian cotton which continued to be restricted. British cloth would have three blue threads running in the selvage and it would be stamped 'British

Manufactory'. The result was a massive influx of investment into the British cotton industry. British calicoes continued to attract a duty of 3d per length and the increase in duty revenues – from £710 in 1775, to £14,288 in 1780 and £44,732 in 1783 – shows the rapid expansion in the trade. Arkwright had pushed open the door.

Even before the cotton boom, the barber from Bolton had become the world's first industrialist. By 1775 he had developed a new carding machine that, together with his spinning frame, effectively covered the whole production process from raw cotton wool to finished thread. When he sought a patent for his new machine he saw no reason to include his original partners in this; in fact he wanted rid of Smalley, whom he now regarded as an impediment. But Smalley would not go quietly and the legal wrangles went on until February 1777, when he agreed to take £3,202 16s 5½d from Arkwright, Need and Strutt for his share in the original patent and the partnership's mills in Nottingham and Cromford; he would also be paid £100 a month until the expiry of the original spinning-frame patent. Though he had agreed not to set up in competition, Smalley soon opened a thriving spinning mill at Holywell in Flintshire. When Samuel Need died in 1781 his executors sold his interests in the company to Arkwright and Strutt for around £20,000 – the two men were now in control of their own fortunes.

Arkwright's personal finances were cloaked in secrecy, but there can be no doubt that the Cromford mill and the licensing of his machinery to others brought huge financial success. By 1775, just three years after the opening of Cromford, Elizabeth Strutt wrote to her father Jedediah: 'Mr Arkwright came here on Wednesday night & brought his daughter a very pretty letter from her Brother – and would you think it – a very elegant little watch whitch he bought for her at Manchester – on thursday morning they sett off from here to Birmingham my sister and Miss Arkwright in genteel riding dresses . . . They talk'd of going to France & the whole Town believes they are gone there but every body thinks they will not like it.'[9]

Strutt too had become a wealthy man, as once again his daughter appreciated: 'Findern [her mother's home village] is a strange desolate place now – I used to think it very fine & have spent many a happy day there, but I think I am happier now – everyone is surprised when they consider what we are, and what we have been. I often think of it & I never think of it but my heart & eyes overflow with joy & gratitude. I can never thank you enough, nor ever repay the vast, vast debt I owe you.'[10] That phrase 'what we are, and what we have been' speaks volumes; it was now possible to rise up in society and become something different through money.

The original mill at Cromford was closest to Arkwright's heart; he built a house there, became the ostensible lord of the manor, and based his business and social interests in the village. In 1776 a second mill, 130 feet long and seven storeys high, was put up at Cromford, doubling the firm's output. Spinning work was now being done through the night and preparatory work in the day. In 1790 John Byng, the author of a series of travel diaries, wrote: 'I saw the workers issue forth at 7 o'clock, a wonderful crowd of young people, made as familiar as eternal intercourse can make them; a new set then goes in for the night, for the mills never leave off working . . . these cotton mills, seven stories high, and fill'd with inhabitants, remind me of a first rate man of war; and when they are lighted up, on a dark night, look most luminously beautiful.'[11]

In 1784 it was recorded that the Arkwright mills 'are worked night and day or at least 23 of the 24 hours one hour is allowed for examining oiling and cleaning. There is a regular relief of hands watch and watch about as in a ship.'[12]

Once the Cromford mills were a proven success, the stage was set for Arkwright to expand his industrial empire. In 1777 plans were laid for a new mill at Chorley in Arkwright's native Lancashire. Around £4,400 had already been spent on the new building when disaster struck. The American War of Independence had cut off supplies of cotton to Lancashire hand-spinners and the sight of mechanised mills taking what little there was enraged them. Josiah Wedgwood described what he saw as he travelled to Bolton through the west side of Manchester on 2 October 1779: 'In our way to this place, a little on this side of Chowbent, we met several hundred people in the road. I believe there might be about five hundred; and upon inquiring of one of them the occasion of their being together in so great a number, he told me they had been destroying some engines, and meant to serve them so through all the country.'[13]

Two days later a crowd of around 8,000 destroyed Arkwright's mill at Chorley, with rumours flying that the rioters also had his Derbyshire cotton mills in their sights. A hastily convened force of cavalry, passing through Derbyshire on its way to Manchester, calmed local fears, and the people of the Derwent Valley who had benefitted from Arkwright's mills also took steps to defend them. In the event the rioters did not get to Cromford, and the rebellion subsided.

Undeterred by his Chorley setback Arkwright immediately built a spinning mill at Harlam where he installed a steam engine to pump water. Arkwright and his son Richard also bought interests in mills across Derbyshire from Cressbrook to Wirksworth, Darley Abbey and just north of Cromford at Masson. The Masson mill, built in 1783, still stands, a timber-framed red-brick building, 150 feet long and thirty feet wide, five storeys high and topped with a fine cupola.[14] Following a fire in November 1781 Arkwright rebuilt his original mill in Nottingham and began corresponding with Boulton & Watt; but he did not take the plunge and order a steam engine to drive the mill. Finally he became convinced of the advantage of steam over water power and, in 1790, ordered an engine to drive his mill at Hockley near Nottingham.

From the mid-1770s until his death in 1792 Arkwright was a man on fire, making deals, buying and selling land, setting up new ventures with new partners and selling off others. No doubt this made him a desirable man to know, but also an exasperating man

Sir Richard Arkwright

to deal with, as James Watt confirmed in 1784: 'Some years ago he [Arkwright] applied to us at two different times for our advice which we took the trouble to give him, in one or more long letters, which he never had the manners to answer but followed his own Whims till he threw away several 1000£s and exposed his ignorance to all the world, & then in disgust gave up the scheme.'[15] Watt's frustration is understandable but, as we shall see, he later stood by Arkwright in his troubles over patents, and regarded him as a bona fide fellow inventor when others did not.

Arkwright extended his empire into Staffordshire, Manchester and, with a spectacular visit in 1784, Scotland. By then mills were already using his machines illegally at Penicuik, Rothesay and

Dovecothall in Renfrew, and through legal licence at Paisley, where Corse, Burns & Co. had built a six-storey mill. While the American war disrupted cotton imports, it devastated the tobacco firms of Glasgow, who then became eager to diversify; Arkwright, on the other hand, battled continually with the Manchester cotton spinners and saw Scotland as an ideal ground for expansion. During his visit in the autumn of 1784, he was feted in Paisley where 'for his good deeds done and to be done for the well and utility of the Burgh . . . was by the magistrates and Town Councill . . . Made and Created a free Burgess'. The *Glasgow Mercury* of 7 October 1784 went on to report: 'Mr Richard Arkwright, Esq of Cromford, Derbyshire, the ingenious manufacturer of cotton yarn, was in town, on a tour to view the Manufactures of Scotland . . . On Friday [1 October] they were entertained by the Lord Provost and magistrates in the Town-hall, and Mr Arkwright presented with the freedom of the city.'[16]

Arkwright was treated as a hero who would bring the riches of the cotton trade to Scotland. Among those who greeted him was David Dale, the owner of cotton mills at Lanark. One story suggests that Dale took Arkwright to the Clyde Falls immediately after a banquet, knowing that the site would impress his cash-rich visitor. Together they agreed to build mills at New Lanark, powered by the spectacular water flow, and spinning there began in 1786. The partnership ended soon after, however, and the mills would pass to Dale's son-in-law Robert Owen in 1810, who became famous for his principles of common ownership and philanthropy. After his visit to the Clyde Falls Arkwright travelled on to Aberdeen, where he helped to set up a mill at Woodside and offered to train local workers at Cromford, and finally to Perth where cotton works were built at Stanley on the Tay.

His own mills were only part of Arkwright's cotton empire; he also earned from licensing his spinning frame to other mill-owners. No written agreements outlining the terms have survived, and there is a strong suspicion that Arkwright came to verbal agreements in order to avoid sharing the income with his original partners, who still had a stake in the patent. He also limited the number of licensed spindles at each mill to 1,000 to disable any serious competition to his own mills. In 1780 a spinner asserted that Arkwright charged £7,000 for every 1,000 spindles, while in 1785, Robert Peel, a notable Lancashire textile-maker, claimed that Arkwright was charging £2 per spindle. At a conservative estimate of 50,000 spindles licensed to other mill-owners, this brought Arkwright an enormous annual income.

By 1782, by his own estimation, Arkwright had sold water-frames and carding machines to hopeful entrepreneurs in eight counties; he reckoned that this had engendered an industry employing 5,000 people and investments of around £200,000. This assessment was part of his evidence in support of a request to have his patent extended; it had been granted for fourteen years and was therefore due to expire in 1783. It was this attempt to extend his patent that so infuriated the spinners of Manchester, which by the 1780s had become the centre of the cotton trade. They believed that Arkwright's licence fees were too high and many of them doubted the originality of his invention. Part of their case was that Arkwright had made a fortune from his invention already. Edward Bearcroft argued during Arkwright's patent trial of 1785 (see Chapter 13) that he had earned around £100,000 from the water-frame.

As well as buying his frames, other mill-owners copied Arkwright's factory template. More important perhaps, they looked at Arkwright's wealth and power and saw that all this could come from the cotton industry. Arkwright was a rival and an enemy, but he was also an inspiration.

Arkwright's innovations extended to his workforce: he pioneered the use of apprentices in factories. Early factories became notorious for the use of pauper apprentices, taken en masse from parish workhouses and put to work often in appalling conditions. However, Arkwright's son told the 1833 parliamentary inquiry that, while children had been used, parish or pauper apprentices had never been employed at Cromford. There is evidence from an account by one of his workers, Simeon Cundy, that he had 'Entered Mr Arkwright's factory . . . as a worker in the card-room [aged six in 1782]; four years after became an apprentice for seven years, to learn the turning, filing, and fitting up of wood, brass, iron, steel, and every branch of machinery.'[17] Cundy later became a manager at William Young's mill in Bakewell. Rees's *Cyclopædia* of 1813 also declared that 'such works as Messrs Strutts' at Belper, Mr Arkwright at Cromford in Derbyshire . . . and many others, are schools for mechanics in almost every department of that science; and good ones too, as the cotton manufacturers are convinced, that it is in their interest to attend to every minutia in the construction of their machines, which may render them more durable and their operations more perfect'.[18]

Inspections of the works at Cromford when it had passed to Arkwright's son confirmed the view that the workers were treated well and the mills kept clean. In fact, Arkwright Jnr was one of the few mill-owners who welcomed the 1803 law which outlawed the employment of children under nine, and restricted the working hours of those under eighteen.

John Byng, who visited Cromford in 1789, wrote: 'Below Matlock a new creation of Sir Richard Arkwright's is started up, which has crowded the village of Cromford with cottages, supported by his three magnificent cotton mills. There is so much water, so much rock, so much population and so much wood that it looks like a Chinese town . . . This house, and village appear so clean, and so gay, as to quite revive me, after the dirt and dullness of Bakewell.'

Byng also witnessed an annual event organised by Arkwright: 'a grand assortment of prizes, from Sr R. Arkwright, to be given, at the years end, to such bakers, butchers &c, as shall have best furnish'd the market . . . They consist of beds, presses, clocks, chairs &c. and bespeak Sr Rd's prudence and cunning; for without ready provisions, his colony cou'd not prosper: so the clocks will go very well.'[19]

The working day at Cromford was shorter than in other mills, the workers better fed, and the boys given breaks for breakfast and tea; elsewhere they had to eat as they worked.

By 1780 Richard Arkwright had become wealthy enough to

present his daughter Susanna with a £15,000 dowry on her marriage to the son of an iron-making family. By then he owned a large swathe of land around Cromford, and was granted further ownership when Matlock Common was subject to an Enclosure award. The social kudos to accompany his wealth and fame came when, on 22 December 1786, he was knighted. The honour was provoked by Arkwright's presentation of a Loyal Address to celebrate George III's escape from assassination at the hands of Margaret Nicholson that August, but it did not prevent the British aristocracy from ridiculing his attempts at aggrandisement. On his way to receive his knighthood Arkwright visited Sir Joseph Banks; and a noble acquaintance of Banks gave the following account of the day's events:

> . . . the Great Mr Arkwright who came to Sir Josephs in a black wig, brown frock, woosted stockings & Boots to ask him to go with him . . . Sir Jos. too good-natured to refuse agreed but asked him about his dress. Mr Ark— proposed going as he was, for he was not afraid they were but Men and so was He – however it was agreed he should take off his boots & return with good shoes at the proper hour[.] Our friends . . . were not a little surprised to see little fatty appear a beau with a smart powdered bag wig so tight that coming over his ears it made him deaf; a handsome striped satin waist coat & proper coat with a sword, which he held in his hand . . . What a pity you happened not to be there [at the ceremony] as the scene was excellent, the little great Man had no idea of kneeling but crimpt himself up in a very odd posture which I suppose His Majesty took for an easy one so never took the trouble to bid him rise.[20]

Those with a distaste for snobbery will find the next account more agreeable: 'During his stay in London, he was in company with some noblemen, one of whom, possessing more pride than parts, asked him whether he had not once been a barber. "Sir," replied Arkwright, with a spirit truly noble, "I was once a barber, and am apt to conclude, had your lordship been a barber, you must have continued a barber still.'"[21]

Arkwright continued his social ascent when he was made high sheriff of Derbyshire in 1787. Arriving at Derby for his official duties he was accompanied by at least thirty gentlemen decked out in the most gorgeous dark blue and gold livery, his coach painted and swathed in sumptuous fabrics and, for the duration of the assizes, he 'provided a plentiful Table, with the choicest Wines &c. for such Gentlemen as pleased to partake of the noble Banquet'.[22]

In 1782 he bought the manor of Willersley and four years later began building his mansion Willersley Castle, a Gothic-revival pile of seven bays complete with battlements on the slopes of Wild Cat Tor. His later years show him still wheeling and dealing, in particular trying to set up cotton plantations in West Africa to supplement the supply from the West Indies. In 1789 Arkwright had his portrait painted by Joseph Wright of Derby, who had already painted his daughter Susanna and son-in-law; Arkwright's portrait was also painted by Mather Brown.

Arkwright fell ill in July 1792 and died the following month. His funeral at Matlock was attended by over 2,000 mourners and he was buried in the chapel he had built at Cromford. A report in the *Gentleman's Magazine* described the cortège passing Wild Cat Tor: 'The road was now nearly impassable from the crowds of people and carriages; for, Sir Richard Arkwright's funeral passed the Torr for Matlock church . . . The ceremony was conducted with much pomp and, as nearly as I can remember, was thus: a coach and four with the clergy; another with the pall-bearers; the hearse . . . followed . . . and about fifteen or twenty carriages, closed the procession, which was perhaps half a mile in length.'[23]

The magazine also stated that Sir Richard 'died immensely rich, and has left manufactories the income of which is greater than that of most German principalities [derived from circumstances] that promote the prosperity of a country. His real and personal property is estimated at little short of half a million.'[24]

*

Victorian aesthetes liked to say that the portraits of Arkwright showed a vulgar and ruthless man, and it seems that Britain has never quite known what to make of its first industrialist. Arkwright was a new kind of man; the first industrial magnate with nation-wide ambitions, and the first commoner to have become ennobled through industrial entrepreneurship. He invented and perfected machinery that he then turned into an economic tool; he devised the factory system and made it work; he built an unprecedented commercial empire through a combination of skill, confidence, grand vision and meticulous attention to detail; and he turned the cotton industry of northern England and Scotland from a minnow into an international economic powerhouse. But in a society dominated by those born into money and social standing, the transformation of a tailor's son from Preston into a national symbol of industrial and commercial power had been hard to take.

13. Arkwright on Trial

The most sensational patent trial in history took place in June 1785, at the King's Bench in London. The buccaneering figure of Richard Arkwright, the king of cotton, was under attack. His attempts to extend his patents had roused his competitors to fury; now the very foundations of those patents, on which Arkwright had built his fortune, were being called into question. By 1785 Arkwright had already undergone three patent trials to defend his inventions and to prosecute illegal users; the result so far was 2–1 to Arkwright. But at each trial the stakes had been raised higher, and now the whole of Arkwright's intellectual property was in the balance. The world watched and waited.[1]

In 1769 Arkwright had been awarded a fourteen-year patent for the invention of a spinning frame; in 1775 he was awarded a further patent for a carding engine – it also included other processes such as preparing rovings – which stood until 1799. By the early 1780s Arkwright's devices were being used under licence in cotton mills across Derbyshire, Lancashire and Scotland. While most mill-owners paid up, some used the machines without permission hoping either to keep their use secret or to be able to face down any threats from the patent-holder. As we have seen, enforcing patents was the task of the inventor, not the patent office, and no one going to court to protect or overturn a patent could be sure of the outcome.

In February 1781 Richard Arkwright threatened legal action against spinners for infringing his 1775 patent. Three mill-owners immediately came to an agreement with the inventor but the

Manchester mill-owners decided to resist; in March they met 'to consider the most effectual Means of obtaining the Free and general Use of Engines and Inventions for the Manufacturing of Cotton, and of opposing any Attempts that may be made by any Person or Persons at obtaining a Monopoly of the Use thereof'.[2] In response Arkwright took legal action against nine Manchester firms. The battle lines were drawn.

Submissions made by lawyers reveal the industrial secrecy that infected the cotton trade. Arkwright claimed he had been barred from gathering evidence due to 'the Extraordinary Caution observed at Most of the Works to conceal their machines – at many they made every Person who entered the buildings take an Oath not to disclose what they saw & at almost all Strangers & every body but approved Friends were excluded . . . it was with the utmost difficulty and Personal Danger that the Plts servants could get to make the observations they did.'[3]

On 17 July 1781 the case came before Lord Mansfield in Westminster Hall. The first defendant was Colonel Mordaunt. His counsel, Edward Bearcroft MP, had spotted a weakness in the plaintiff's case. As he later recorded: 'it was this; that if this was a new invention, Mr Arkwright had not fairly communicated it by his specification, but had absolutely contrived to hide it'.[4] This sudden introduction of the specification as a crucial element came as a shock to Arkwright. Patent specifications reflected the reluctance of inventors to show their hand and were kept deliberately vague – once the judge ruled that the specification must be clear, Arkwright was stymied. The jury found the patent invalid and Arkwright withdrew his prosecution of the other cases.

The Manchester spinners were naturally delighted but a much bigger threat loomed as Arkwright sought an Act of Parliament to extend his 1769 spinning patent. He argued that a huge amount of work had gone into perfecting his machine after the patent was obtained; but what weighed against him was the amount of money he had earned from the invention. (This was in contrast to the James Watt patent; when that was extended by twenty-five years

Death Threat

Richard Arkwright's attempt to extend his 1769 patent provoked fury from the Manchester mill-owners. When he received a death threat via his Manchester solicitor's office on 28 November 1782, he published it in the *Manchester Mercury* to expose his competitors' unscrupulous methods:

'Sir

'I am very sorry to hear that you will do all you can to distress the trade of Manchester: after you had lost the Cause in London this town thought you would then have been easy [seeing] the remainder of your time in the patent out. But you still keep doing all you can, and not only that but you have been heard to say that you was determin'd to ruin every person that enter'd into that Business. The purpose of this is to advise you that if you do not withdraw all your prosecutions before December is out I am determin'd to lay in wait for you either in this town, Nottingham or wherever I most likely find you. I will as sure shoot you as your name is that which it is, dam you. Do you think the town must be ruled by such a barber as you. Take notice if you are in town on Saturday next I will make an end of you [should I] meet you wherever I can.

'I am not yours, but a friend to the town of Manchester.'[5]

in 1775, not a single engine had yet been sold.) Arkwright's competitors lobbied hard against him and, in late 1782, one even threatened his life. Arkwright's publication of the anonymous letter in the *Manchester Mercury* was intended to expose the villainy of his opponents, but to no avail – Parliament refused to act on his petition.

In response Arkwright threw himself into pursuing those spinners who had infringed his 1769 patent, which now had just months to run. Singling out Thomas James of Nottingham as a test case, and paying minute attention to the specifications, in December 1783 Arkwright persuaded the Court of Common Pleas to find in his favour. Arkwright and Strutt were awarded only nominal damages and did not pursue the defendant for compensation, but the victory made Arkwright determined to overturn the loss of his 1775 carding patent. Once again he focussed on a single miscreant, his neighbour Peter Nightingale, and this time he ensured that his legal team was prepared for every eventuality, including objections to the all-important specification.

Legal preparations went on through 1784 before the case was heard at the Court of Common Pleas by Lord Loughborough in February 1785. Arkwright's counsel argued that the specification only made sense when viewed in conjunction with earlier machines, of which this was an improvement. Three models were presented to the court, showing different stages of development of the carding machine, including the improved patented model. The Arkwright side had also gathered celebrity witnesses. Erasmus Darwin encouraged James Watt to come to the aid of Arkwright: 'I think you should defend each other from the ingratitude of mankind.'[6] Watt, Darwin and other witnesses stated that they would have no trouble building a machine from the carding-engine specification, if they also had the previous machine in front of them. But Edward Bearcroft for the other side argued that the patent application did not make any mention of a previous machine and was therefore invalid. The judge disagreed.

The most persuasive evidence came not from distinguished experts, but from five men who had actually built the machine from the specification. Thomas Wood testified that he built carding machines in 1782 although he had never visited Cromford and therefore received no other instruction; the same story came from Samuel Wise, John Stead and two others. The defence counsel pressed Stead to describe the machine, but Lord Loughborough asserted that his inability to do so was not material; if he could build the machine he did not need to be able to describe its workings. The five witnesses impressed the judge, who cited their evidence in his summing-up. Having started at 11 a.m., the case finished at 9 p.m. with the jury declaring for Arkwright. Having spent £1,000 on the case, he was awarded the one shilling in damages he had requested.

Arkwright and his solicitors returned immediately to Derbyshire, visiting mills at Matlock, Burton and Ashbourne to give their owners notice to cease operations. They also went on to Peter Nightingale's mill at Cromford, where Arkwright graciously offered his defeated rival the chance to continue his business by paying the rate of five shillings per spindle per annum for day work, and a further five shillings for night work.

While the Mordaunt verdict in 1781 had been a blow to Arkwright, the reinstatement of his carding patent in February 1785 was potentially a dagger at the heart of the industry. The patent was drawn so widely that, if upheld, every cotton spinner in England would have to pay a royalty to Arkwright. Since the 1781 trial, cotton spinners had invested huge sums of money in new mills and machinery on the understanding that it was free to use; the expansion of the industry was now at risk. The Manchester mill-owners therefore immediately applied for a writ of *scire facias* which would require Arkwright to defend the basis of his patent before a judge and jury. The writ was granted by the Crown and the case of *Rex* vs *Arkwright* was set for June 1785.

While the early trials had left room for further actions, both sides knew that this would be the deciding case. Edward Bearcroft once again appeared for Arkwright's opponents. He first argued that Arkwright's 1775 carding patent repeated much of the earlier 1769 spinning patent, including the crucial use of rollers, and was therefore an attempt to extend his earlier patent beyond its legal term. He then examined the ten elements of the 1775 patent specification, arguing that none of them were truly original and several were in fact superfluous to the working of the machine. In any case, he declared, the original spinning patent of 1769 had been wrongly awarded, as Arkwright had stolen the machine from Thomas Highs.

Highs and John Kay appeared in person to testify to Arkwright's dishonesty in stealing Highs's original idea. In his evidence, Highs reported that he had met with Arkwright in Manchester in 1771, two years after the patent had been granted:

> We were in some discourse about the rollers: I told him, he would never have known them but for me; and he put his hand in this manner, I remember very well in this manner, to his knee, and that was the answer he gave; also he told me, when I told him it was my invention, Suppose it was, he says, if it was, he says, if any man has found a thing, and begun a thing, and does not go forwards, he lays it aside, and any other man has a right in so many weeks or months . . . to take it up and get a patent for it.[7]

John Kay told the court of his association with Highs. He reported that he had passed on to Arkwright what he had learned about the machine from Highs, and that Arkwright had asked him to make a model of Highs's roller frame. By the time of the summing-up the case had drifted away from Arkwright. Justice Buller gave the jury three questions to answer for each of the two patents. Was the invention new? If so, was it invented by the defendant? And finally, was it sufficiently described in the specification? This last point particularly exercised the judge, who saw it as crucial to the development and implementation of patent law. The specification must enable the public to understand the invention in detail: 'This I take to be clear law, as far as respects the specifications; for the patent is the reward, which, under an Act of Parliament, is held out for a discovery, and therefore, unless the discovery be true and fair, the patent is void. – If the specification, in any part of it, be materially false or defective, the patent is against the law, and cannot be supported.'[8] A patent application must reveal the idea to the world and in return expect protection. The judge further stated – and this was surely fatal to Arkwright's case – that if any elements within the patent were not relevant to the invention but were added merely to puzzle or confuse, then on that ground alone the patent would be void. Not surprisingly the jury did not even feel the need to leave the courtroom but immediately brought in a verdict against Arkwright.

When Arkwright's solicitors tried to apply for a new trial in the Court of the King's Bench or in the Court of Chancery, Justice Buller told them that 'the defendant had not a leg to stand on'. The Lord Chief Justice, Lord Mansfield, also refused the application and on 14 November 1785 Arkwright's patents were cancelled.

The court's verdict caused rejoicing in Manchester, where a special broadsheet announced: 'to the great joy of thousands, the old fox is at last caught by his overgrown beard in his own trap . . . it is hoped, the dose that has now been administered to him, will entirely purge him from all his hatefulness and tyranny, and from his every justifiable claim and demand, whereby he has amassed such an immoderate sum of money'.[9]

But others were not so sure that the verdict was a good outcome. On 13 August 1785 James Watt wrote to Matthew Boulton: 'I am tired of making improvements which by some quirk or wresting of the law may be taken from us, as I think has been done in the case of Arkwright, who has been condemned merely because he did not specify quite clearly. This was injustice, because it is plain he has given this trade a being – has brought his invention into use and made it of great public utility.'

While Watt feared for his own patents, Boulton believed Arkwright had lost because he was essentially in the wrong. He wrote to Watt after the 1785 trial: 'Surely you cannot think it just that any tyrant should tyrannise over so large a manufactory by false pretences. He had no shadow of right and the whole court were unanimous that no mention was made in his specification of the thing or principle that was there in dispute.'

The Arkwright case was a landmark. It sent a clear signal to inventors that if they did not supply accurate, original and usable specifications they could lose the rights in their inventions, whatever patents they were awarded. Arkwright, in this at least, proved an unwilling pioneer.

14. Manchester:
The First Industrial City

Manchester is *the* city of the Industrial Revolution. Its prodigious growth from a market town in the early eighteenth century to an industrial metropolis of world importance a hundred years later is well documented. The factories, slums and terrible living conditions that ensued are part of industrial folklore, as described by the French writer Alexis de Tocqueville in 1820: 'Crowds are ever hurrying this way and that in the Manchester streets . . . From this foul drain the greatest stream of human industry flows out to fertilise the whole world.'[1] But Manchester was also the wonder of the modern world, a nexus of innovation, vision and commerce; a place that drew engineers, inventors, merchants, workers, social commentators, politicians, writers and visitors from all over the world. This was the world's first industrial city.[2]

Manchester was fascinating because everything about the place was new; it grew from a small town to a world city in a few decades – from 10,000 inhabitants in 1720 to 70,000 in 1800 and 140,000 in 1830 – and all on the basis of the industrial production and trading of one commodity: cotton. Or so it seemed; while cotton was the commercial driving force, Manchester was from the very beginnings a multifaceted city showing innovations in education, politics and social arrangements. And while Manchester was an industrial city, it combined production and trading in a mutually supportive process – there were always more warehouses than factories – and rapidly built the social infrastructure of a modern city to support its astonishingly successful commerce.[3]

For some, Manchester was full of robber barons making money without concern for the poor amongst whom they lived. But this belied the other side of the city, for while the cotton industry provided the money it also drove new social forces into being. Manchester became a seedbed of Chartism, trade unionism and socialism, and it provided a radical alternative voice in the country against the established powers of the capital; at the same time the city's merchants and middle classes formed an influential force, leading the campaign for the repeal of the Corn Laws and in favour of free trade, while opposing imperialist adventurism, thereby expressing a brand of liberalism that became known as the Manchester School.[4]

So how did Manchester become not only the first industrial city but the prototype modern city? In 1795 the physician and editor John Aikin wrote: 'the cotton manufacture; a branch of commerce, the rapid and prodigious increase of which is, perhaps, absolutely unparalleled in the annals of trading nations. Manchester is, as it were, the heart of this vast system, the circulating branches of which spread all around it, though to different distances . . . its influence is spread, more or less, over the greatest part of Lancashire, and the north-eastern portion of Cheshire.'[5]

Aikin pointed to an important fact: Manchester was not an isolated city but the centre of a web of connections. It was a kind of super-economy within the industrial economy of south Lancashire, which was itself the focus of British industrialisation. The Industrial Revolution saw the concentration of productive activity, previously spread widely across the country, into particular areas: in 1831 an astonishing 70 per cent of industrial jobs were in Lancashire and the neighbouring West Riding of Yorkshire.[6] Birmingham, Derby, Nottingham, Coalbrookdale, Cromford, Sheffield, Halifax, Leeds, Bradford and even Camborne and Merthyr Tydfil are all important places in our story; but Lancashire was undoubtedly special.

In 1835 Edward Baines, author of *History of the Cotton Manufacture in Great Britain*, first outlined the region's natural geographical advantages: rivers to provide water power, coal for steam engines, connection to the port of Liverpool, soft water, a damp atmosphere ideal for spinning fine cotton, and easy access to sources of iron and chemicals. Lancashire had a tradition of cotton production dating back to 1600, and the cotton industry had remained relatively free of regulation.

In the fifteenth and sixteenth centuries certain English towns were designated wool towns and production outside those towns, within their counties, was prohibited. However, four northern counties which were known for their coarse cloth were allowed to produce in rural districts with few restrictions on the number of looms. In the 1530s, in an attempt to boost linen production, the state ruled that every landowner with more than sixty acres in tillage must give over a quarter of an acre to flax or hemp. Lancashire certainly took advantage of these measures and became known for coarse woollen cloth and for fustians produced in villages and cottages throughout the county. By the time of Defoe's travels to the region in the 1720s, cotton was being made in Manchester, Bolton, Bury, Blackburn, Middleton, Chadderton and Hollinwood near Oldham.

By the 1740s and 50s, according to parish registers, over half the adult males in Lancashire derived most of their income from textiles. The upland areas of Lancashire and West Yorkshire were traditional sheep-rearing country and the poor soil encouraged textile production to supplement farming income; in Rossendale there were as many weavers as farmers before industrialisation. By the mid-eighteenth century, putting-out had become a highly developed system in south Lancashire; spinners and weavers knew how to operate, manage, repair and often build their looms, water-wheels, spinning wheels and hoists.

The region also had a highly developed watchmaking trade, which was supplemented by a strong tradition of clockmaking, hinge-, nail- and lock-making in and around the Warrington area; this tradition of skilled engineering was crucial to Lancashire's later development. In addition south Lancashire and Cheshire were already beginning to develop the chemical industry that was to grow so prodigiously around Widnes, Runcorn and the Mersey

Valley. As chemicals were essential to textile production, the industry boomed on the coat-tails of the cotton phenomenon.

So south Lancashire was a small self-contained industrial economy, and at a time when land transport was cumbersome, John Aikin found a good system of turnpike roads, enabling horses, carriages and wagons to travel at speed, allowing more goods to be carried more quickly. The Bridgewater canal had opened in 1761, and further extensions had linked the heart of Manchester to the Mersey and the canal to the Mersey–Trent system, thus allowing access both to the seaport of Liverpool and the industrial areas of the Midlands. The Leeds to Liverpool canal began carrying traffic in 1774, passing through Lancashire's industrial heartlands. Primarily built to transport coal from Worsley to Manchester, by 1791 the Bridgewater canal was carrying around £20,000 worth of coal and £30,000 of other goods, as well as accruing £3,800 in passenger fares. Traffic through Liverpool also increased dramatically: 1,317 vessels paid duties of roughly £2,300 in 1757; by 1770 the number of ships had risen to 2,100 and duties paid to £4,150; by 1800 this had risen again, with 4,700 vessels paying a total of £23,400.[7]

The improved transport infrastructure in this small region enabled people to travel easily in search of work, business partners, premises, materials and markets. As we have seen, Richard Arkwright regularly travelled from his base in Bolton for his original business of wig-making and made crucial contacts in Warrington, Leigh and Preston. But better transport also allowed the evolution of a sophisticated and changing relationship between Manchester and the nearby towns. In the putting-out system merchants based themselves in the market towns, with individual spinners and weavers working in the surrounding countryside – 3,000 in the Blackburn area, for example. With the introduction of new workplaces, either fully powered mills or joint working in converted buildings, production moved from the countryside into the market towns and even to the edges of Manchester town centre – in Ancoats and along Oxford Road – where the merchants now also based themselves as almost every clothier was now within reach of the Manchester market. The satellite towns of south Lancashire thus became production bases rather than independent markets, and while Rochdale, Bolton, Blackburn and Burnley were factory or mill towns, with the majority of their workers and investments going into cotton production, Manchester was predominantly a trading city.

By the 1780s, when the first factories began to appear on the fringes of the town centre, Manchester's major streets were already lined with warehouses, and over the next decades they spread outwards to form the commercial heart of the city, from St Anne's Square to Market Street and along Mosley Street to Princess Street. On Cannon Street in 1815 there were fifty-seven warehouses containing premises for 106 firms trading and producing cotton. Over the same period the number of steam-powered spinning mills in Manchester and Salford increased from just one (owned by Richard Arkwright at Shudehill) to eighty-six. The factories were concentrated to the east of the centre in Ancoats, where the enormous mills of the Murray brothers and McConnel & Kennedy sat among densely packed jerry-built housing, with more on the western fringe of the city along Oxford Road. This industrial zone was expanded outwards to the east and north and through Salford in the following decades while the city centre remained a commercial trading zone.[8]

The warehouses in the heart of the city were not simply used for bulk storage, but for displaying wares – by the early nineteenth century the whole world came to Manchester to buy its cloth, including Nathan Rothschild, who established a textile business there before moving to London.[9] Samuel Bamford worked as a warehouse assistant on Cannon Street around 1810 and his job was to carry cloth pieces up to the first-floor salesroom where they would be spread out on the floor on a white cloth. As he recalled: 'A scramble then commenced among the buyers, which should get the most pieces; sometime they have met me at the sale door and tore them off my back; and many a good coat have I seen slit up, or left with the laps dangling, after a struggle of that sort.'[10] While

the warehouses brought in money through sales, the cotton factories provided work for the tens of thousands who flocked to the
city: by 1815 the city's factories employed 11,500 workers and by
1841 nearly 20,000. McConnel & Kennedy, established in 1797,
moved to a new eight-storey mill in Ancoats in 1818; the mill
employed 1,545 people and was the wonder of the age.

However, while cotton was its lifeblood, any image of a city
stuffed with smoky factories and little else would be misguided.
In fact this ultra-modern city was in some ways a reinvention of
the great mercantile centres of old: for the wharves of Venice,
Smyrna and Amsterdam, read the warehouses of Cannon Street
and Mosley Street; for the craft workshops of Lyons, Leipzig,
Florence and Toledo, read the great mills of Ancoats but also the
small makers of the Medlock district. This heady mix of the
mercantile and the industrial, the commercial and the manufacturing, needed a vast array of people to service its needs, from
street cleaners to doctors, publicans to judges, and engineers to
waggoners. In 1841, for example, only 18 per cent of the town's
workforce was directly employed in cotton production and sale,
compared to 50 per cent in Ashton and 40 per cent in Oldham
and Blackburn. The city's growth and wealth was driven by the
cotton industry, and by the promise of work that it held out to
any who cared to go and find it, but Manchester also showed the
world how a modern city had to develop a supporting infrastructure in order to function effectively.

The physical network of south Lancashire also produced a
series of social networks. In their travels around the region and
within, Manchester traders, merchants, entrepreneurs and inventors were liable to get to know one another and develop common
interests. Textile workers with an eye to furthering their prospects
could see every aspect of the industry all around them; many were
quick to learn and to set up their own workshops or small manufactories, perhaps specialising in machine repair or a particular
kind of finishing or dyeing. At the same time the proximity of so
many producing centres provided the right combination

of solidarity and competition – mill-owners knew they had to innovate to keep ahead of their rivals, or at least keep up with the latest devices and processes.

The great textile inventions originated in Lancashire because the skills in spinning, weaving and machine-making were there, and because the inventions were rapidly adopted (sometimes unscrupulously) by the Lancashire industry. The jenny and the mule were both quickly taken on and continuously improved: when James Hargreaves fled to Nottingham his jenny stayed in Lancashire and flourished, while in Derbyshire Richard Arkwright was a sole innovator whose work was assiduously exploited in his native county. (Lewis Paul's spinning mills in Birmingham and Northampton were left to wither: had he set up in Manchester or Bolton, the story may well have been quite different.) Then when Arkwright's patents were overturned in 1785, the way was open for all cotton spinners to make spinning frames and mules; and Lancashire engineers piled in with improvements, culminating in the 1825 self-acting mule made by Richard Roberts, a Welsh engineer who had set up business in Manchester.

Manchester's singular political history contributed to the peculiar combination of commercial free-for-all and radicalism that came to characterise the city. Before it became a municipal borough in 1838 Manchester was run as a medieval manor with a Court Leet, complete with a reeve and two constables – all voluntary – and a paid deputy constable. The parishes within the old manor looked after the roads, collected rates and gave out poor relief. An Act of 1792 established Police and Improvement commissioners who looked after night policing, street paving and lighting, cleaning and refuse collection.

By the early nineteenth century the local aristocratic families had mostly left the region, with the Mosleys of Manchester Manor selling up and moving to Staffordshire. This left Manchester as a town with virtually no aristocratic involvement in its governance, or indeed its political, social or cultural life. The Tory Anglican establishment was instead made up of middle-class merchants and mill-owners like Robert Peel and the three Birley brothers, John, Hugh Hornby and Joseph, who all became Lord-Lieutenants of Lancashire. They were generally ex-pupils of Manchester Grammar School and sat on the Court Leet.

However, many of the early Manchester mill-owners were Nonconformists and therefore barred from the traditional roles in government; so instead this liberal faction built an impressive social and commercial and eventually political network. The Unitarian community, centred on the Cross Street and Mosley Street chapels and including families such as the Heywoods, Hibberts, Gregs, Percivals, Philipses and Potters, was particularly powerful. And as well as developing networks in industry and commerce Lancashire's Nonconformists fostered a culture of technical training and education that sustained the region for several generations. Most famous of these was the Warrington Academy, founded in 1756, which was maintained by public subscription and which educated some of the most important Lancashire industrialists. Founders of the Manchester Literary and Philosophical Society – set up in 1781 and, besides the Royal Society, England's oldest scientific society – were predominantly from the Warrington Academy, and provided informal education through lectures, discussion groups, libraries and the like.

Tensions between the two political and religious traditions grew more intense after the French Revolution of 1789, with the radicals under Thomas Walker forming the Manchester Constitutional Society and the *Manchester Herald* beginning to press for reform. The Tories responded by organising riots in which the paper's offices were attacked and, once war with France was declared, they had Walker jailed for sedition. This bitter divide was the background to the infamous Peterloo massacre in 1819, when a public open-air meeting in favour of parliamentary reform was brutally suppressed. Fifteen people were killed and several hundred injured by troops wielding sabres.

Nevertheless the Manchester men had much in common. In

the 1780s more than 64 per cent of Lancashire mill-owners were middle-class men, most of whom had previously run textile work-shops of different kinds.[11] They were small-scale businessmen, technically and commercially astute, and powered mechanisation gave them the chance to go up in scale. James McConnel and John Kennedy, founders of one of the biggest mills, were both sons of farmers from the south of Scotland, and James Halliwell began as a porter in the Peel family warehouse before becoming a mill-owner on his own account. More common were those like Peter Drinkwater who opened a steam-driven factory in 1789, after owning a fustian business complete with warehouse. And Samuel Oldknow was already a maker of muslins when he opened his two huge mills at Stockport and Mellor in the early 1790s.

The Lancashire cotton industry had shown itself eager to take on innovation, to adopt new ways of working that built on its existing expertise and structures. But once the first jennies, frames, mules and improved looms had been installed the demand for more machines became insatiable. The men who built the mills needed men who could build machines and they often went into partner-ship with them. Engineering began to migrate from the Warrington area into Manchester itself, and while trade directories from 1772 and 1773 show no engineers in the city, by 1781 there were iron-mongers, brass-founders, and wire- and pin-makers, as well as two loom-makers, two shuttle-makers and a dozen makers of reeds.[12] Later in the 1780s a plethora of specialist makers of spinning equipment appear – and in the 1790s they began to call themselves engineers. Aikin noted that:

> To the ironmongers shops, which are greatly increased of late, are generally annexed smithies, where many articles are made . . . The tin-plate workers have found additional employment in furnishing many articles for spinning machines; as have also braziers in casting wheels for the motion-work of the rollers used in them; and the clock-makers in cutting them. Harness-makers

have been much employed in making bands for carding engines, and large wheels for the first operation of drawing out the cardings, whereby the consumption of strong curried leather has been much increased.[13]

Of water-frames, Aikin wrote: 'These machines exhibit in their construction an aggregate of clockmaker's work and machinery most wonderful to behold.'[14] The demand for these skills soon outstripped the capacity of Lancashire; metalworkers of all kinds came from across the country, earning high wages in the new boom town of Manchester.

Once Watt's steam-engine patent expired in 1800 the demand for engine-builders also increased. The firm of Bateman and Sherrard was an early manufacturer in Salford; Aikin described their foundry 'in which are cast most of the articles wanted in Manchester and its neighbourhood, consisting largely of large cast wheels for the cotton machines; cylinders, boilers, and pipes for steam engines; cast ovens and grates of all sizes'.[15] The company had already begun building steam engines before 1800, and afterwards was able to expand.

More readily available iron meant that the early machinery made of wood and brass was replaced with cast and worked components. This was a difficult process – everything, we must remember, was being done for the first time in human history – but was well under way by 1820, by which time Manchester had replaced Birmingham as the centre of British engineering. Here there was continual demand for engineering skills and here there was money to be made – wages in some trades were double in Manchester compared to the Midlands.

The rapid growth of cotton and its industrial spin-offs made Manchester a magnet for engineers, inventors, entrepreneurs, artisans and labourers. The towns of Lancashire and north Cheshire grew steadily in population: the market towns of Wigan, Warrington, Preston, Stockport, Blackburn, Bolton and Rochdale reached around 5,000 by 1770, Liverpool 34,000 and Manchester combined with Salford 30,000. By 1800 the population of Manchester and Salford had more than trebled to 100,000 and by 1830 had doubled again. While this inevitably put strains on the provision of housing, sanitation, and health care, Manchester was at the forefront of dealing with these problems (see Chapters 23 and 24).

Manchester's subsequent history has also reflected a key element of the Industrial Revolution, for the city has retained a culture of continuous innovation; far from being a museum piece, Manchester has entered the so-called post-industrial age with its spirit of practical ingenuity intact. It has remained a commercial city with manufacturing the servant rather than the master of its industrial power.[16]

V. Iron

'We had a visit today from a Mr Cort of Gosport who says he has a forge there and has found some grand secret in the making of Iron.'

JAMES WATT TO MATTHEW BOULTON,
14 DECEMBER 1782

15. Abraham Darby's Blast Furnace

The ability to produce cheap and plentiful iron was a key component of the industrial economy. The earliest powered machinery, including steam engines, was made of iron and soon iron was needed for girders and rail tracks, rivets and ships' hulls, tappets and locomotives. It is for this reason that Ironbridge in Shropshire has acquired world fame as a birthplace of the Industrial Revolution. It was at Ironbridge, then called Coalbrookdale, that Abraham Darby first managed to produce cast iron in a blast furnace using coal rather than charcoal. This breakthrough occurred in 1709, some sixty years before the classic period of the Industrial Revolution began, and sixty-seven years before his grandson built the bridge, made entirely of cast-iron girders, that now gives the town its name. Abraham Darby and Coalbrookdale deserve their place in history, for the production of cast iron was a vital step in the conversion to a productive economy based on coal. The effects were to be profound.

Iron is the most useful of all metals. Ever since people first learned how to smelt iron around 3,500 years ago it has provided the tools and weapons with which human society has developed. Smelted iron is known from Asia Minor from around 2000 BC and by the eighth century BC large-scale production was evidently possible: 160 tons of iron bars were found in the palace of the Assyrian king Sargon II at Khorsabad in modern Iraq. From the eighth to the sixth centuries BC an iron-based culture known as Hallstatt became the dominant culture of central Europe with smelting and metalworking techniques spreading north and west, reaching Britain by 500 BC.[1] Useful though it is, iron does present difficulties to the would-be tool-maker. The melting point of pure iron is around 1,540°C, an impossible temperature to reach in any pre-industrial furnace. This forced iron-makers to adopt a range of strategies to induce the metal to separate from its ore and form a useful compound that could be worked at a lower temperature. Being an ironmaster was therefore not unlike being a master chef, knowing from skill and experience how to manage a complex process to achieve the right result. The most common iron ore is haematite, which is essentially the chemical compound ferric oxide; the task of the smelter is to separate the haematite from its surrounding rock, and to remove the oxygen from haematite while replacing it with a small amount of carbon.

From the earliest times there were two distinct processes – bloomeries and blast furnaces – that produced two different types of iron. Bloomeries used a bed of hot charcoal in a pit or dome of clay or stone, with pipes laid in the bottom to allow air to circulate or be pumped in by bellows. Once the furnace is fired, pieces of iron ore and more charcoal are added in through the top. This induces a chemical process that frees the iron from its ore without reaching the melting point of pure iron. In bloomeries the temperatures reached around 1,200°C with clods or 'blooms' of iron containing solid iron, slag and unburnt charcoal coalescing inside the furnace. The ironworkers then pulled out the blooms using tongs or rakes and hammered them to separate the iron from the slag. The main product of the bloomery was workable wrought iron, though some ironmasters made small amounts of cast iron and even steel through the bloomery process. All the iron produced in Europe in the pre-Roman Iron Age was made using bloomeries.

The alternative method of producing iron was the blast furnace, which has today replaced the bloomery in almost all cultures. Here again a chemical process is used to get round the difficulty of attaining a high enough temperature to melt the iron. Blast furnaces are sophisticated devices; they are known to have existed in China as early as the fifth century BC but reached Europe

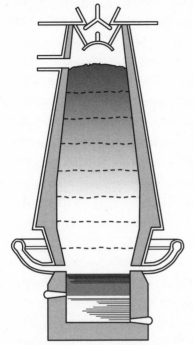

Blast furnace: Iron ore, coke and lime are fed into the top of the furnace, which burns continually. Air is 'blasted' into the bottom and, when the conditions are right, the tap at the foot of the furnace is opened to allow iron to flow out into moulds.

only after AD 1000; the Sussex Weald was probably the first area in Britain to adopt the blast furnace, sometime around 1500. Blast furnaces produce cast iron or pig iron which is high in carbon and strong but brittle; it is ideal for use in cannons, and the development of artillery may have been the main incentive for the development of blast furnaces in Europe.

Unlike the bloomery, which has a definite cycle of production, the blast furnace works continuously. Fuel and iron ore are tipped into the top of the tall furnace, while air is introduced by blowing in from the bottom. Gases escape through the top and phases of slag and iron are tapped out from the bottom. Ironmakers found that iron ores with high lime content produced slag that flowed more easily, so rather than rely on the natural content, they began to add lime powder to the furnace. In order to make cast iron a blast furnace needed to reach 1,300°C, a temperature that was achievable with charcoal. Making the furnace taller saved fuel, as did leaving the mix to cook longer. With a constant water supply to operate the bellows, once the furnace had been 'blown in' its 'campaign' could continue until the fuel ran out or the furnace lining wore out. In practice, until the late eighteenth century, most European blast furnaces ran through the winter and were refurbished in the summer.

Cast iron or pig iron produced by blast furnaces contains around 3 to 4 per cent carbon, 1 to 2 per cent silicon and manganese, 0.5 per cent phosphorous and less than 0.1 per cent sulphur. The relatively high carbon content gives structural strength but cast iron is unsuitable for working in a forge; this requires bar iron or wrought iron which has a carbon content of less than 0.5 per cent, as well as reduced silicon. The conversion from cast iron to bar iron was achieved through a separate smelting process known as a finery. The forges themselves (sometimes known as chaferies) could use coal for heat, but the blast furnace and the finery required charcoal in order to avoid contaminating the iron.

As blast furnaces got bigger, making bar iron by this two-stage process became much more economical than using bloomeries; the output from a blast furnace reached around four tons of cast iron per six days (known as a founday) by the late seventeenth century. As almost every county in Britain has some source of iron ore, ironmaking was therefore widespread, although there were areas of special significance: the River Severn became an important artery for the iron trade linking the iron- and coal-rich areas of Shropshire and Staffordshire with the Forest of Dean coal mines and the trading and manufacturing centre of Bristol. By the late seventeenth century a huge variety of iron goods was being sold at fairs across England. As Thomas Baskerville reported from Stourbridge fair near Cambridge in 1677–8: 'For here you shall see large streets and shops full of all the variety of wares that are to be sold in London, and great quantities of iron brought from several parts of the nation and elsewhere.'[2]

The fuel to ore ratio in a blast furnace was 1:1, so while the iron content of good ore was around 20 per cent, five tons of charcoal were needed to produce one ton of cast iron; bar iron needed almost as much fuel again. As both the capacity of blast furnaces and the demand for iron increased during the seventeenth century, people tried to substitute coal for charcoal as the furnace fuel. However, because the coal had to be mixed with the ore and therefore became part of the chemical reaction, it introduced impurities, particularly sulphur, which rendered the iron useless. But there was a pressing need to replace charcoal; and while there were concerns over the consumption of wood, coal was available and cheap. The solution of the problem was Abraham Darby's smelting method, the first great technological breakthrough of the eighteenth century.

Darby was born in 1678 on a farm near Dudley in the West Midlands. Forty years later Daniel Defoe described the area: 'Every Farm has one Forge or more; so that the Farmers carry on two very different Businesses, working at their Forges as Smiths, when they are not employed in the Fields as Farmers. And all their work they bring to market, where the great Tradesmen buy it up and send to London ... We cannot travel far in any direction out of the sound of the hammer.'[3]

Even in Darby's childhood ironmaking was a well-developed business. Some cast iron was produced locally in blast furnaces but most was brought from furnaces in the Forest of Dean up to forges in the upper Severn and West Midlands, where there were good supplies of charcoal and water power. Large-scale finery forges made bar iron and rods which they sold on to farmers who ran small forges as a sideline. Farmer-smiths made everything from nails to firebacks which they sold to merchants with warehouses along the Severn in Stourport, Welshpool and Bridgnorth. From there the finished products would be shipped on to Bristol and London.

Abraham Darby gained first-hand knowledge of metalworking in his father's forge. The family were Quakers and John Darby sent his son away to Birmingham – a free, non-corporate town with a large established Society of Friends – for his apprenticeship. He was apprenticed to Jonathan Freeth, described as a 'weighty Friend' (i.e. one who spoke with authority at meetings), who was a maker of malt mills for the brewing trade and therefore a skilled pre-industrial engineer. At the end of his apprenticeship in 1699 Darby moved to Bristol and set up in the same business.[4] Bristol was then the second city in England with many Quaker families engaged in the metal trades. From the beginning Darby showed an interest in innovation. In 1702 he founded the Bristol brass-wire company with a group of Quaker partners; in 1704 he travelled to Holland to discover how to cast brass pots in sand, and with his assistant John Thomas (another Quaker) invented the technique, patented in 1707, of using a similar method to cast pots in iron.

Soon afterwards, Darby made the move that was to give him and his family immortal fame. It seems his business partners did not want to expand the Brass Works in Bristol so Darby sold them his share and used the money to buy the lease on an old blast furnace at Coalbrookdale on the River Severn in Shropshire. On the face of it this is a strange move, but it seems likely that Darby bought the site with a very clear purpose in mind.

His achievement becomes clearer if we look briefly at previous attempts to replace charcoal with coal in blast furnaces. Patents for using coal to smelt iron granted to Sturtevant (1611), Ravenson (1613) and Dud Dudley (1622) had all been unsuccessful. In 1665 Dudley published *Metallum Martis* in which he claimed to have perfected the method, but later examinations of the slag from his furnaces revealed this to be untrue. While Dudley had made some progress, his patent was not extended and it seems that his ideas were not taken up elsewhere. Abraham Darby was related to Dudley through his mother's side of the family and is likely to have known his work, but just as important for his breakthrough were two other developments.

The first was the technique of making coke from coal, suggested in 1603 by Hugh Plat as a process similar to making charcoal from wood. Coke is produced by baking coal in sealed ovens to drive off water, volatile liquids in the form of tar, and coal gas; the solid remnant is high in carbon. From the 1640s coke was used in roasting malt, to get round the problem of fumes from coal affecting the taste, a process described by Robert Plot in his 1686 work *The Natural History of Staffordshire*: 'they have a way of charring it [coal] in all particulars as they do wood, whence the coal is freed from the noxious steams that would give malt an ill odour. The coal thus prepared they call coke which conceives a heat almost as strong as charcoal itself, and is as fair for most uses, but for melting, fineing and refining of iron, which it cannot be brought to do, though attempted by the most skilful and curious artists.'[5]

Plot reported an attempt by an ironmaker called Blewston to smelt iron with coke at Wednesbury in 1677, but 'experience, that great baffler of speculation, shewed it would not be'.[6] Another contemporary writer lamented, 'Oh if this coal could be so charked as to make iron melt out of the stone, as it maketh it in smiths' forges to be wrought into bars.'[7] By the late 1600s, coke was being used in smelting lead and copper and in the glass industry, but the great problem remained: how to get it to work in smelting iron without imparting impurities into the finished product.

Abraham Darby was well placed to make the crucial leap as he had experience of both the brewing and the metalworking industries. The crucial element in the process was sulphur. Coking does not reduce the sulphur in coal, so using coke in a blast furnace produced sulphur-rich iron which was of no use. Darby must have known about the low sulphur content of Shropshire coal (around 0.5 per cent). As one historian of the industry has noted: 'This was unusual in Britain; some coals have high sulphur, some make good but unreactive coke, but some of the Shropshire seams produced good coke with high reactivity and low sulphur.'[8]

At Coalbrookdale, where the Severn and Coalbrook both cut deep gorges through the Middle Coal Measures, as well as the overlying ironstone, there had been extensive mining since the earliest times. In addition, the Severn was the industrial waterway of the iron, coal and wheat trades, and crucially the river gave access to water power to drive the blast-furnace bellows. All in all, if Darby was looking to develop coke as a fuel for blast furnaces, then Coalbrookdale must have looked a very good prospect.

According to the following letter, Darby moved there in 1709, but he actually fired up the blast furnace using coke in January of that year, so it is likely he moved in 1708 or earlier; by 1711 he had certainly given up all his interests in Bristol and focussed on his Shropshire operation. This account written in 1753 by his daughter-in-law Abiah Darby reveals the inventor's persistence:

> It was my husband's father, whose name he bore [Abraham Darby I] who was the first that set foot on the Brass Works at or near Bristol that attempted to mould and cast Iron pots etc., in sand instead of Loam . . . in which he succeeded. The first attempt was tryed at an Air Furnace in Bristol. About the year 1709 he came to Shropshire at Coalbrookdale, and with other partners took a lease of the works which consisted of an old Blast Furnace and some Forges. He here cast Iron Goods in sand out of the Blast Furnace that Blow'd with wood charcoal . . . Sometime after he suggested the thought that it might be practicable to smelt the Iron from the ore in the Blast Furnace with it Col; Upon this he try'd with raw coal as it came out of the mines, but it did not answer. He . . . had the Coal coak'd into Cynder as is done for drying Malt and then it succeeded to his satisfaction. But he found only one sort of Pit Coal would best suit . . . He then erected another Blast Furnace and enlarged the works.[9]

Darby's aim was to produce iron that would be good for casting in sand but not too hard for the forgers to work into bar iron. The coke achieved a higher temperature than the charcoal, giving a fluid iron good for casting thin hard metal but also suitable for thicker pieces to be worked. Its sulphur content has been estimated at 0.1 per cent but the presence of manganese meant that this was taken up as the innocuous manganese sulphide and therefore caused no harm to the iron.[10] The silicon content increased sharply over charcoal iron, giving a softer grey cast iron that was better for working directly but difficult to process in a finery.

As well as providing a much cheaper and more plentiful fuel, and reaching higher temperatures than charcoal, coke had other advantages. A blast furnace usually operated from twenty to thirty weeks, with the rest of the year spent gathering charcoal for the next blast. This downtime was usually in the summer when river levels were lower and water power for the bellows reduced. With the use of coke the break in the production cycle was much shorter; ironmakers just needed to remake the hearth, recondition the furnace and repair the bellows. Darby and other ironmasters shortened the downtime further by laying out ponds and weirs to store water for dry periods.

Darby's technique was revolutionary but it did not spread rapidly, partly because it was a method that had to be learned, rather than a device. We must also allow for the possibility that, while in general terms the invention was a real breakthrough, for individual ironmasters with established chains of fuel supply, it may not have been of much interest. We should also remember that, before the Industrial Revolution of the late eighteenth century created a set of conditions in which innovations could thrive, inventors were relatively isolated.

Nevertheless Darby taught the technique to his employees and the firm expanded out of Coalbrookdale, taking on furnaces in Cheshire and at Dolgellau. To begin with, the ironmasters who most successfully made the change to coke were within striking distance of the Shropshire coalfield with its low-sulphur coal. Once Darby had shown that using coked coal in a blast furnace was possible, any ironmaster could adopt the technique, using his own ingenuity to make it work. Darby died in 1717 but he founded a dynasty of ironworkers, and the Coalbrookdale Company, run by his son and then grandson (Abraham Darby II and III) continued at the forefront of innovations in this crucial industry.

Coke technology transformed the production of cast iron. In 1720 20,500 tons of pig iron and 14,900 tons of bar iron were produced in England and Wales by charcoal furnaces, with only 400 tons of cast iron produced by coke furnaces; by 1788 the ratio had been reversed, as 76,000 tons of cast and bar iron were produced in coke furnaces, while only 2,500 tons of cast iron were produced using charcoal; by 1806 there were just eleven blast furnaces using charcoal while 162 used coke.[11]

Cast iron was needed for the making of cannon, particularly during the Seven Years War (1756–63), a conflict that cemented Britain's place at the centre of a global trading network. Along with the Darbys, the best-known ironmaker of the eighteenth century was John Wilkinson, who built furnaces at Bersham and Broseley. Both the Darbys and the Wilkinsons began to make high-quality cast iron by taking the iron from the blast furnace and smelting it again in a reverberatory or air furnace. This is a device that separates the fuel from the iron mix (either ore or roughly made cast iron) rather than heating both together. The chemical reaction that produces the right composition of iron is brought about by letting the heat and fumes from the fuel pass through the iron mix.

The ability to make plentiful cast iron helped to feed the boom in machinery that came with the inventions of Hargreaves, Crompton and Watt in the late eighteenth century. Abraham Darby II was the first to make cast-iron cylinders for Newcomen engines, which were much bigger and stronger than the previous brass cylinders. In the next generation John Wilkinson took this a stage further by making a device for boring out cylinders with extreme accuracy, rather than casting them. This not only improved the performance of artillery; it also, crucially, enabled James Watt to build steam engines to his desired high specification. For many years Boulton & Watt pressed their customers to use only John Wilkinson cylinders in their engines.

The improvement of Newcomen engines by Smeaton and others, together with the new Watt engines, gave a further impetus to the ironmasters as the iron and steam industries fell into a productive symbiosis. As early as 1742 Abraham Darby II brought a Newcomen engine to Coalbrookdale to pump water to keep the blast-furnace bellows working at all times. Then, in 1768, John Smeaton patented an engine that drove blowing cylinders, which could produce a blast of air direct from a steam engine without need of waterwheel or bellows. Wilkinson built working blowers which were installed at Broseley and at Dowlais in 1776; they became so effective that by the early 1800s some ironmakers were able to use coal instead of coke. These changes enabled the production of cast iron in Britain to increase from about 20,000 tons in 1720 to 250,000 tons in 1800.

The cast-iron bridge which Abraham Darby III, grandson of the original Abraham, built over the Severn at Coalbrookdale in 1779 is one of the wonders of the modern world and remains a symbol of Coalbrookdale's place at the heart of the Industrial Revolution.

16. Henry Cort and Cheap Iron

While subsequent generations of Darbys and others improved on Abraham Darby's innovation, one more major obstacle stood in the way of cheap, plentiful iron. While coke could be used to produce cast iron, making wrought iron or bar iron of the kind that could be worked in a chafery forge still needed large quantities of charcoal. In fact, the finery-forging process used more fuel than the smelting – to make one ton of bar iron required 1.5 tons of pig iron and around 1.2 tons of charcoal. In the most common process the cast iron was heated over charcoal and then beaten with hammers (some worked by water power in the bigger forges). Charcoal remained the only option because heating and hammering iron over coal would introduce impurities that degraded the iron.

So while sufficient cast iron could be produced in Britain, bar iron had to be imported in great quantities from Sweden and Russia.[1] A long list of patents in the mid-eighteenth century shows how anxious British ironworkers were to make the leap from charcoal to coal or coke, but most were vague in their specifications and probably did not achieve much. Nevertheless it seems that some substitution of coal for charcoal had become possible. In 1737 the agent for Lord Foley – owner of vast estates in Worcestershire – told a House of Commons committee: 'In some places along the River Stower in Worcestershire they sometimes use Wood only to draw it into Coop and Anchonies, which take up Four Cord only, and from thence they draw it into Bar with Stone Coal; but the greatest Part of Iron is drawn by Charcoal.'[2]

In 1766 Richard Whitworth reported that the forge in Upton

consumed eight tons of charcoal and five of pit coal per week, and that twelve forges in Shropshire and Cheshire produced fifty-two tons of bar iron using fifty-nine tons of charcoal and thirty-seven of pit coal.[3] They were probably using a two-stage process with a reverberatory furnace (in which the fuel is kept separate from the iron) converting cast iron to bar iron, which could then be worked on a chafery forge. In one process, patented by the Carnage brothers at Coalbrookdale and Bridgnorth, grey iron of the type made by Darby was converted in a furnace where the flame was deflected by bricks. This was widely taken up and the resulting iron was good for making nails. As Richard Reynolds wrote in 1784: 'The nail trade would have been lost to this country had it not been found practicable to make nails with iron made with pit coal. We have now another process to attempt, and that is to make *bar iron* with pit coal.'[4]

By the time Reynolds was writing, Henry Cort, an iron-forger from Fareham in Hampshire, had just taken out a patent that described the solution to the problem. Cort was born in Lancaster in 1741, the son of a builder. In the 1760s he was working for the Royal Navy where his duties included finding reliable sources of high-quality wrought iron at a time when this was in short supply.[5] In 1774 he inherited from his wife's uncle an ironworks at Funtley near Gosport, along with contracts to supply iron goods to the navy. With a secure order book Cort was in a position to experiment with ways of making wrought iron using coal.

Henry Cort's first patent, granted in January 1783, was for a rolling machine for making bars and bolts; his second, taken out the following year, covers the crucial process of puddling. The patent reveals how much the processing of iron depended on a close understanding of the practicalities of each step. First, the forger needed to melt pig iron in a reverberatory furnace (or bring it molten from the blast furnace). Holes in the furnace walls allowed workmen to stir the melt with iron rods, which is the technique known as puddling:

After the metal has been for some time in a dissolved state, an ebullition, effervescence, or such like intestine motion takes place, during the continuance of which a blueish flame or vapour is emitted; and during the remainder of the process the operation is continued (as occasion may require) of raking, separating, stirring, and spreading the whole about the furnace till it loses its fusibility, and is flourished or brought into nature. As soon as the iron is sufficiently in nature, it is to be collected together in lumps, called loops, of sizes suited to the intended uses.[6]

Instead of being heated again and hammered in the finery forge, these loops were then – under the terms of his first patent – put between rollers at welding heat. Rolling at this stage, rather than at the end, pressed out all the impurities, leaving high-quality bar iron. As one of Cort's friends described the process: 'As the stirring of cream, instead of mixing and uniting the whole together, separates like particles to like, so it is with the Iron: what was at first melted comes out of the furnace in clotted lumps, about as soft as welding heat, with metallic parts and dross mixed together but not incorporated.'[7] The rolling had the effect of pressing the 'dross' out of the iron.

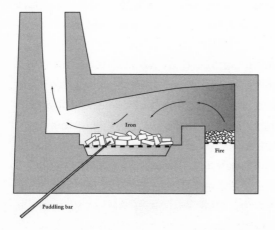

Puddling furnace: In this version the fuel is separated from the iron ore. The rods are used to stir the liquefying ore so that clods of iron are formed. The clods are then run between rollers, which squeeze out the remaining slag.

This process used techniques that were already in use – rollers had been used for making rods or bars for decades and puddling had also been tried elsewhere. But Cort's combination of puddling and rolling produced high-quality iron far more efficiently than other methods. His iron was as good as the Swedish *oregrund* and, while the old method of using steam-operated hammers to drive out impurities produced a ton of iron in twelve hours, Cort could produce fifteen tons in the same time by rolling.

Cort's ironworks were run in financial partnership with Admiral Adam Jellicoe, whose son Samuel was a working partner. Once Cort's process was established, Jellicoe Snr got the Navy Board to declare that they would only purchase iron made in this way and, over a number of years, the Jellicoes invested £50,000 into the business. Unknown to Cort, however, much of this money had come from public funds through the admiral's position as Deputy Paymaster of Seamen's Wages. Cort had given Jellicoe the rights to his patents as security and, when the fraud was uncovered, Cort's patents were confiscated by the government and he was made bankrupt.

It may well have been difficult for Cort to enforce his patents in any case; his was a new process, not a new machine, and iron-masters could claim that each part of the process had been in use before. However, as the importance of his discovery became apparent, other ironmakers lobbied on his behalf and he was paid a state pension of £200 from 1794 until his death in 1800.

Cort showed a remarkable faith in his own ability to solve the problem of producing bar iron with coke. In 1779, a full five years before his second patent, he had consulted Matthew Boulton about a steam engine, probably to pump water to drive his forge and slitting mills, and in 1782 he visited James Watt. As Watt wrote to Boulton on 14 December:

> We had a visit today from a Mr Cort of Gosport who says he has
> a forge there and has found some grand secret in the making of

Iron, by which he can make double the quantity at the same expense and in the same time as usual. He says he wants some kind of Engine but could not tell what, wants some of us to call on him, and says he has some correspondence with you on the subject. He seems a simple good-natured man but not very knowing.

Cort wrote to Watt six months later, by which time he had secured his first patent and was no doubt working on the process on his patent:

When I did myself the pleasure to call on You at Soho – We had some conversation on the Subject of Iron – I intimated I had solicited a Patent for my invention of Manufactg Iron – on an improved method – wch have obtained and You were kind enough to say You would mention me to Mr Wilkinson. I have therefore taken the liberty of enclosing a Lre to that Gent and I will be obliged to You to forward him – amongt other things I profess to make Ordinary Iron – Tough – by a short and simple process.

When you can say anything of the forge to be worked with Steam – I will thank you to communicate the same to me – excuse this trouble – I will do as much or more for You.

In contrast to the slow spread of Darby's technique, iron-makers immediately latched on to Cort's new method. Iron-making in South Wales in particular was fuelled by the process with Richard Crawshay, one of Wales' biggest iron-makers, increasing capacity from 500 tons of bar iron in 1787 to 10,000 tons by 1812. The huge expansion in iron production brought a matching demand for power to run rollers, furnaces, forges and mills, which was supplied by steam engines with rotary power. Better steam engines also enabled deeper mining for iron ore and coal. Faster production of bar iron using Cort's process drove up demand for cast iron, which was its raw material: output of cast iron rose from 68,000 tons in 1788 to 250,000 tons in 1806. The ready availability of good quality iron meant that machines of all kinds could be produced more easily, further boosting industrial production in textile factories, for instance.

Last but not least, freed from the need for wood and water, which had dispersed the industry and separated the furnaces from the forges, iron-making could now be integrated on single sites on coalfields and iron fields. Huge investments were made in plants where furnaces, forges and rolling and slitting mills all worked in line. Parts for mules, looms and carding machines, hoists, bridges, buildings and eventually railways were now churned out in their millions. British iron-making took a central role in the revolution that was to take over the world.

Henry Cort in The Times

The following article appeared in *The Times* on 29 July 1856, in support of a petition to Parliament to provide the family of Henry Cort with a pension:

'Now with reference to the case which we are about to bring under the notice of our readers, and which is the subject of an advertisement in our columns today, we would begin by disclaiming the faintest shadow of responsibility. We have not investigated the truth of the allegations to which we are about to advert, nor, indeed as they refer to scientific matters, and to secret passages of the scandalous history of England 60 years ago, do we esteem ourselves competent to conduct an inquiry of that description. We wish merely that others should know, as we know, the story of Henry Cort, the father of the British Iron Trade: that is, that they should cast a glance over this brief abstract of a petition which his destitute family have presented to the House of Commons. This petition has been forwarded to us, and the allegations it contains are so completely of a national character that, for once, we violate a general and necessary rule, and have determined to give to them all the publicity in our power. Time was, some 70 years ago, that England was dependent upon Sweden and Russia for her supply of wrought iron. Henry Cort, of Gosport in the county of Southampton, an iron manufacturer, invented, and secured by patent, in the years 1783-4, two processes which relieved us from this commercial servitude, and liberated for the use of English manufacturers the supplies of iron which are stored up so profusely under the surface of these islands. "The first process effected the cheap manufacture of wrought iron by the use of pit coal in the puddling furnace; the second process, which was rolling this cheap wrought iron through grooved rollers, enabled the manufacturer to produce 20 tons of bar iron in the same time and with the same labour previously required to manipulate one ton of an inferior quality by the tedious operation of forging under the hammer."

'This allegation is given in the words of the petition. Before the year 1785, when iron was, comparatively speaking, but slightly used for commercial, maritime, or social purposes, we paid annually to Sweden something like £1,500,000 for wrought iron. Then came the war, came commercial embarrassment, depreciated paper, foreign prohibitions, and an overpowering and increasing demand for more and more iron. The inventions of Henry Cort carried us easily through this period of sharp trial, and, as his descendants allege, were the principal cause of our success. It would indeed be impossible to exaggerate the advantages resulting from an unlimited supply of "the precious metal". The only points for consideration in this case are whether, first, to Henry Cort, and to him alone, the credit is due of enabling us to draw upon Vulcan at sight; and, secondly, whether he did not obtain all the remuneration to which he was fairly entitled by receipts from his patents, and so forth.

'Now, upon the first point, we are bound to declare that Mr Cort's son has succeeded in obtaining the signatures of the most eminent engineers and ironmasters in England to the petition in which he sets forth his father's claims to be considered as the exclusive author of the improvements in the manufacture of iron. The point is one upon which hostile criticism is very desirable, but until such very powerful attestation as we see incorporated in this petition is disproved there is no doubt a very violent presumption that Henry Cort, of Gosport, is entitled to be considered as the Tubal Cain of our century and of our country.

'Let anyone think of our iron fleet, iron gunboats, iron mercantile marine, iron railways, iron engines, iron cotton mills, iron suspension and tubular bridges, iron batteries, iron palaces, etc., and then ask himself what should be the measure of public gratitude to the descendants of a man who endowed his country with such an amount of wealth and power. While others have, upon the strength of Henry Cort's discoveries, been raised to the position of millionaires, his children are almost starving. We should be ashamed for the honour of England to mention the amount of the pension which has been conceded to them by the Crown and Parliament. It is about equal in amount to the wages of a domestic servant of the humblest description, and even this has been made subject to deductions. For the sake of our national credit, it behoves all persons of influence in the country to give the case of Henry Cort's children their immediate consideration. In bringing the subject under their notice our duty is discharged.'

By the time of this article a son, Richard, and a daughter, Louisa, survived. Louisa died in 1859, questions were raised over Richard's character, and the matter was never satisfactorily resolved.

17. Crucible Steel

The production of steel was vital to the industrial economy; its workability, strength and durability made it an essential material. From medieval times steel had been used sparingly for the production of blades for swords, knives and scythes, where the material retained its strength even when made extremely thin. This property later became crucial in the precision engineering of components for instruments, clocks and watches. And in the Industrial Revolution its strength and suppleness were employed in rails, locomotives and wagons for the railway system.

Steel is essentially iron with around 1.5 per cent carbon and with other additives like nickel giving it particular properties.[1] Once the Bessemer process was invented in Britain in the 1850s steel became relatively simple to make, but before then it was an extremely laborious, skilled and time-consuming process. The key component was the controlled introduction of carbon into bar iron, a process known as carburisation; too much carbon would make the steel brittle like cast iron, too little would fail to impart the necessary strength and suppleness. Until the eighteenth century it was thought near-impossible to make steel from English iron, in which the high phosphorus content made the take-up of carbon difficult. Steel was instead imported from Sweden and Russia at a price around three times that of bar or wrought iron.

The alternative was to produce steel in Britain from imported Swedish iron and it seems this process was first begun in the areas around Newcastle and Sheffield, although we can't be sure when it started. Sheffield was known for its knife-making from as early as the fourteenth century, but this was a small craft industry.

There were small centres of steel-making in other parts of the country, such as Robertsbridge in Sussex. More significantly, a German colony of steelworkers and sword-makers settled at Shotley Bridge in County Durham in the 1690s, probably bringing new techniques with them. By the early eighteenth century, however, Sheffield had become a centre of steel-making when Samuel Shore, for example, is known to have owned several steel furnaces in the city.[2]

Making steel was arduous. Bar iron was heated with charcoal for six to seven days to produce high-carbon 'blister steel' which was then reworked in specialist forges. But the process tended to give an inconsistent composition because bars could have carbon at the surface but not the centre. To produce high-quality steel for sword blades and the like, a master forger needed to beat and fold the steel over and over to give high strength at the required thinness of blade. Some forgers collected bars of blister steel in bundles and heated and hammered them to produce shear steel. This was used for products like clock parts, razor blades and needles, as well as the knives and swords for which Sheffield became famous.

The different production processes all involved a huge amount of fuel and skilled labour. Forgers were understandably keen to find a way of making steel directly in a furnace in the same way as cast iron, but here again it proved impossible to reach the required temperature of 1,600°C with charcoal, and using coke would cause unacceptable impurities. The breakthrough came in Sheffield through the work of Benjamin Huntsman, who devised a way of separating the steel melt from the fuel; the Huntsman process revolutionised the industrial production of steel.

Like Darby, Benjamin Huntsman was a Quaker, born in Barton on Humber in 1704 to German or Dutch parents. By 1730 he was established as a clockmaker in Doncaster, where he began to experiment with making a more suitable steel for the springs and pendulums. Sometime around 1742, apparently dissatisfied with the steel from his suppliers, Huntsman moved to the Handsworth district of Sheffield to work on a new process.[3] Handsworth was the centre of a glass industry that operated furnaces at high temperatures; glass-makers also used particular clays that could withstand the heat. Huntsman now put pieces of roughly made blister steel and shear steel in a clay crucible and heated them to very high temperatures. The crucibles – each nine to eleven inches high – were an important part of the process. Huntsman searched for a material that would withstand the extraordinary heat, eventually settling on clay from Stourbridge mixed with local Sheffield earth. The fuel was kept separate from the metal so coke could be used instead of charcoal without corrupting the product. The metal was heated for five hours, when a special secret flux (probably ground glass) was added. The intense heat freed the metal from the silicate slag; the crucible was then lifted and the molten steel poured into moulds. High-quality steel was now available to forgers in whatever form they needed.

This sounds simple but, as with Darby and Cort's work on iron smelting, the key was to manage the process, the ingredients and the equipment precisely in order to get exactly the right composition of steel. Huntsman used some locally made blister and shear steel as his raw material, but mostly imported iron from Sweden. He did not patent his method, however, preferring to keep it secret. There is an old myth that the Doncaster iron-maker Samuel Walker disguised himself as a beggar and was allowed into the Huntsman works to warm himself, where he proceeded to memorise the process; there is certainly evidence in Walker's journal that he had a clay crucible for steel-making by November 1749.

By 1774 three steel refiners are mentioned in the Sheffield Directory: Huntsman, Bolsover and Marshall; by 1787 there were twenty firms listed as Steel Convertors and Refiners, with at least seven using the crucible process. Though these firms were copying his process, Huntsman's steel was for a long time regarded as the best, and the company supplied not only steel but also tools and cutlery. At first Sheffield cutlers did not like the new Huntsman steel, considering it too hard to forge and work, but Huntsman built up an impressive order book of foreign customers, supplying cutlers in Paris, Berlin, Geneva and St Petersburg, and the Sheffield cutlers learned how to use it too. Its uses spread well beyond the cutlery trade: by 1794 Jedediah Strutt had an account with the firm, using Huntsman steel in his spinning machines; John Wilkinson's Low Moor Ironworks bought small amounts and may well have used the steel for cutting tools for the boring of engine cylinders; and Matthew Boulton too was buying cast steel from Huntsman from 1793, sometimes as blanks for the dies he used in his mint at Soho. Huntsman was partly paid in coins struck in the mint – on 14 August 1798 Boulton sent him £100 in pennies.

Sheffield had been a centre of steel-making before Huntsman, but afterwards it became a world powerhouse, with Charles Cammell and James Marsh building forges and rolling mills on Brightside and across the city.[4] It was the coming of the railways in the 1840s that brought the greatest boom: Sheffield's steel output rose from 200 tons per year in 1840 to 20,000 tons in 1860, by which time the city was producing 40 per cent of Europe's total. Then in 1861 John Brown & Co. brought to Sheffield the Bessemer process, which uses a blast of hot air to burn away impurities, enabling the mass production of low-priced steel. Steel-making spread out from Sheffield to other iron districts but the city remained the centre of the cutlery trade; at one point in the nineteenth century it was estimated that 80 per cent of the world's cutlery was made in Sheffield. By that time steel was also an essential component of powered industrialisation – without a cheap and efficient process for making steel the pace of early industrialisation would have been severely curtailed.

Industrial Dynasties: The Walker Family

The Walkers were iron-makers in South Yorkshire; the progress of this family firm of Congregationalists echoes the technological innovations of the eighteenth century.[5]

1730   Joseph Walker is a small farmer with a profitable sideline in nail-making and cutlery, including knives, sickles and scythes. He is helped by his three sons Jonathan, Samuel and Aaron.

1740   Following Joseph's death Jonathan takes on the farm, Aaron the forge and Samuel becomes master of the village school while making sundials.

1741   Aaron builds a small foundry behind the forge in which he casts iron goods.

1746   The three brothers move their forge and buy a farm on the banks of the Don, Samuel writing in his diary 'I thought myself so well settled [but] I began to see the disadvantage of being so far from a navigable river.'

1762   The works are being driven by four waterwheels, which attracts a writ from the owners of water rights on the Don.

1764   They build four new houses at the works together with one large and three small extra workshops. They are now employing clerks, masons, carpenters and wheelwrights.

1767   The Walkers install a blast furnace fuelled, for the first time, by coke. They also install a tinplate shed and enlarge the boring house.

1768   Traveller and chronicler Arthur Young visits the Walker plant and the surrounding area:

Rotherham is famous for its ironworks . . . Near the town are two collieries out of which iron is dug, as well as coals to work it with: these collieries and works employ together near 500 hands. The ore here is worked into metal and then into bar iron, and the bars sent into Sheffield to be worked and to all parts of the country: this is one branch of their business. Another is the foundry, in which they run the ore into metal pigs and then cast it into all sorts of boilers, pans, ploughshares etc.[6]

1775   The American War of Independence brings demand for cannon made from cast iron. The Walkers install a Newcomen engine to pump water to keep their waterwheels turning.

1776   Production of iron cannon increases from forty tons to 450 tons; over the next five years the total cannon produced per year at the works reaches 1,220 tons. A third blast furnace is built along with a new boring house.

1781   The Walkers install a new Boulton & Watt engine and another waterwheel.

1793   War with France brings more demand for cannon; the Walkers are now producing 26,000 tons of cannon per year.

1820   The end of the French wars brings a slump in the iron market and, with supplies of ore around Rotherham depleted, the Walkers move their operation to Staffordshire.

VI. Transport

'We are credibly informed that there is a Steam Engine now preparing to run against any mare, horse or gelding that may now be produced at the next October meeting at Newmarket.'

THE TIMES, 8 JULY 1808

18. Rivers and Roads

The industrialisation of Britain was marked by a series of symbiotic relationships between different industries, between agriculture and manufacturing, between innovation and economic expansion, all feeding off each other. There is, though, another important element: an effective transport system was essential to all the processes we have looked at. Moving coal and iron ore, corn and copper, cotton and salt and myriad other goods through the manufacturing process and into the hands of the end user was crucially important.

Coal was arguably the most important cargo. As early as the 1670s around 2 million tons a year were being moved in Britain: 1 million tons by sea, around a quarter of a million tons by inland rivers, and the remainder by road. Land transport was the most difficult as roads were easily turned into rutted bogs by wheeled vehicles and quickly became impassable. Before 1700 hauliers came to collieries with horses and carts to collect coal, some as long-haul merchants, some as regional distributors, others as local householders. It would take around ten pack-horses or a substantial cart to carry a ton of coal, so even a modest colliery producing a few thousand tons a year would create a huge amount of traffic, often along unmade tracks. When bad weather made these tracks impassable coal was left piled at collieries.[1]

Colliery owners began to get round the problem by building tramways or trackways using wooden rails to take coal from the pithead to the nearest navigable water. They found that running horse-drawn wagons along the rails made them faster and kept the roadways in good condition; although the rails needed frequent repair, this was easier to manage than the upkeep of roads. The wooden rails were sometimes topped with a strip of iron, with full cast-iron rails first used at Coalbrookdale in 1767.

The earliest documented English railway tracks were built in 1603–4 on Sir Francis Willoughby's estate at Wollaton running to the River Trent; another running from Broseley to the Severn was opened in 1605. The crossings, points, inclines, loading methods and wagons that were developed for trackways provided a template for the powered railways that followed 200 years later. Trackways required a good deal of upfront investment – in 1700 the tracks cost around £200 per mile, with rolling stock, equipment and horses on top. Maintenance could be expensive too, but the increase in capacity made it worthwhile: a wagon could take double the load of a cart and a haulier with a wagon could shift between five and eight times as much freight on a tramway as on an average road. At Gibside colliery near Gateshead a new track built to Dunston staithe on the Tyne in 1701 enabled annual production to increase from 20,000 to over 70,000 tons in just two years.[2]

Before the nineteenth century roads remained poor and travel a hazardous, time-consuming and exhausting business. While materials could be moved by trackway, barge and ship, roads were the essential medium of most passenger transport. The wealthy could go by carriage or ride their own horse; for those with moderate means it was possible to hire a horse for a long journey, or buy one in one place and sell it in another; the poor simply walked. From Tudor times parish authorities had been made responsible for the upkeep of roads but by the late seventeenth century increased traffic made local arrangements inadequate for major routes. In 1663 Parliament permitted the parishes along the Great North Road to collect tolls in return for maintaining the road, and in 1696 the first formal Turnpike Trust was set up in Surrey, which allowed a group of trustees to erect toll gates on public roads at which they could collect money to be used for maintenance. Parliament dictated a maximum toll for each kind of vehicle passing along the road and a toll-keeper sat in an isolated spot, perhaps with a physical barrier, perhaps with a blunderbuss: William Pitt the Elder was once shot at by a toll-keeper when his party went through a gate without paying. By the 1780s there were 15,000 miles of turnpike roads in Britain.[3]

Despite the proliferation of tolls and turnpikes, roads were not always kept in good condition. Travelling any distance remained an arduous affair and it was clear that to carry wagons and carriages effectively better roads would need to be built. One of the pioneers of road construction was the extraordinary figure of Jack Metcalf from Knaresborough in Yorkshire.[4] Blind from the age of six, Metcalf already had a colourful career as a fiddle-player, soldier, gambler and trader before setting up in the 1740s as a haulier of goods from Leeds to Manchester and Knaresborough to York. He had developed a stagecoach line in the north of England when a turnpike trust was set up in his area in 1765; the trust commissioned Metcalf to build a series of roads that were able to carry heavy wagons and withstand wet weather. His innovation was to build strong foundations under the road surface, and to use a convex surface to enhance drainage, with gutters running down either side. Metcalf used rafts to build roads across bogs and was an astute surveyor, able to calculate materials and costs accurately. He went on building roads across the north of England, giving manufacturers and commercial travellers easier access to markets and canals and ports. When Metcalf died in 1810 aged ninety-three he was a hero in his hometown, if little known outside Yorkshire. Others followed in his footsteps including Thomas Telford and the Scottish engineer John McAdam, who developed new methods when working on the Bristol Turnpike from 1816. McAdam managed to do away with massive foundations by creating a tough, well-draining 'crust' made of small stones lying on a bed of larger stones. But while road-making improved, the upkeep of roads often fell behind. As Arthur Young noted in 1770: 'Rotherham to Sheffield excruciably bad, very stony and excessively full of holes . . . To Lancaster (turnpike) and to Preston (turnpike) and again to Wigan (turnpike) very bad with ruts which measured 4 foot deep and floating with mud only from a wet summer.'[5]

Turnpikes in 1740 (above) and 1770 (opposite): In the thirty years from 1740 road-building extended turnpikes from occasional highways to a system linking almost all the major towns and cities of England and Wales.

Nevertheless coach transport began to improve. While in 1700 the trip from Norwich to London took fifty hours, by 1800 the journey had been reduced to nineteen hours; over the same period the coach journey from Manchester to London was reduced from ninety hours to thirty hours. As well as shorter journey times, comfort was improved as leather strap suspension was replaced by metal springs in 1706, followed by superior axles and wheel

bearings. Horse-breeding produced the Cleveland Bay, the classic carriage horse that could maintain a steady and rapid pace for the twenty miles between staging posts. Mail coaches were introduced in 1784 that could travel the 120 miles from Bristol to London, for example, in sixteen hours.[6] By 1800 every town and village east of the Severn and south of the Trent was within a day's journey of the capital. The mail coaches provided regular services for passengers and also marked the beginning of a reliable national postal service, which gave a further boost to trade and commerce.

*

For most of human history travel by water has been far easier, quicker and a lot more comfortable than journeys overland. The coast of Britain is dotted with inlets and estuaries that offer shelter to coastal shipping as well as loading and embarkation points, while its rivers reach deep into the heart of the island. Great efforts were made in the seventeenth and early eighteenth centuries to make rivers navigable and by 1725 few people in Britain lived more than fifteen miles from a waterway that carried some kind of transport. While passenger traffic was important, the main function of waterways was to carry goods, with inland ports thriving as centres of trade. Gainsborough in Lincolnshire, for example, was an important shipping point on the River Trent, where coastal carriers offloaded goods to be taken on to Lincoln and Derby by smaller craft or by road. A good example of improvement in river transport came in 1740 with the clearing of the Medway in Kent. Before then iron and iron products like cannon from the smelting district of the Weald had been taken down to the ports on the Kent coast and then shipped up to merchants in London; after 1740 goods could be sent straight north along the Medway to the Thames.

But of all the rivers in Britain the most important for the industrialisation of the country was the Severn. In 1766 Richard Whitworth wrote: 'There is no river that has such a length of navigation as the Severn; you may navigate a vessel of fifty tons, and not a lock the whole way, two hundred miles up to Welch Pool, except in an excessive drought.'[7] In the eighteenth century half the ironworks in Britain were within the Severn drainage basin, using the river as their trading highway. On the Severn and the lower reaches of the Thames barges and frigates could carry twenty to forty tons, while flat-bottomed trows carried eighty tons. These used sails when possible and horses or men to tow them when there was no wind.

In 1779 Dr T. Nash described Wribbenhall, the old centre of the iron industry near the confluence of the Severn and Stour, on the edge of the Wyre Forest:

Navigable waterways in England and Wales, 1750: Before the age of canals, rivers had been improved to provide inland waterways into the heart of the island of Britain.

Wribbenhall, from its excellent quays and vicinity to Bewdley was long the prinicipal port of Worcestershire. From Manchester, Stourbridge, Dudley and the ironworks of the Stour, innumerable pack-horses came laden with the manufactures of these places to be put on board the barges and sent to their various destinations . . . At a spring tide I have been told 400 pack horses have been for several nights quartered in this neighbourhood, and in consequence Bewdley was a rich and very trading town.'[8]

Iron bought here was taken to the slitting forges and nail-makers of the Stour region and their products brought back. Bewdley was then such an important trading centre that 'Bewdley prices' were quoted by ironmasters all over the country. Why, then, is Bewdley not a major town today? In 1766 the Duke of Bridgewater

planned the Wolverhampton canal to have a basin at Bewdley but
the townspeople objected and instead it was built at Stourbridge,
which then thrived as the main centre for trade from the Black
Country. Birmingham rather than Bewdley then became the fashionable residence for many ironmasters: Richard Baddley, Richard
Parkes, John Fidoe, William Hunt and Samuel Garbett all took
up residence in the Old Square in Birmingham.

In the other major centre of iron and steel production, South
Yorkshire, the problem was that communication between
Sheffield and Hull, the major east coast port, was impossible
by water. Boats made it as far as Bawtry via the Trent and the
Idle, and goods such as Swedish iron were then hauled overland.
In 1726 and 1727 plans were laid before Parliament to improve
the Don, allowing traffic as far as Tinsley, three miles from
Sheffield, and by 1739 most of the traffic had been deflected
from Bawtry on to the new route. But it wasn't until 1819 that
a canal from Tinsley to Sheffield gave the city a direct route to
the sea at Hull.

While the Severn was the centre of the iron trade, it was the
Tyne that was the main artery for Britain's coal trade, with 1,400
or so colliers plying the trade from Newcastle to London in 1700.
The capacities of the colliers had quadrupled from fifty to 210 tons
from 1574 and imports of coal into London increased from around
50,000 tons in 1587 to around 500,000 tons in 1700.[9] Ports all along
the east coast benefitted from the trade. In 1724 Daniel Defoe
described Ipswich as:

> the greatest town in England for large colliers or coal-ships,
> employed between New Castle and London. They built also there
> so prodigious strong, that it was an ordinary thing for an Ipswich
> collier, if no disaster happened to him, to reign (as seamen call
> it) forty or fifty years, and more. In the town of Ipswich the
> masters of these ships generally dwelt, and there were, as they
> then told me, above a hundred sail of them, belonging to the
> town at one time, the least of which carried . . . 300 chaldron of

coals; this was about the year 1668 (when I first knew the place). This made the town be at that time so populous, for those masters, as they had good ships at sea, so they had large families, who lived plentifully, and in very good houses in the town, and several streets were inhabited by such.[10]

The development of the Tyne also showed that improving waterways for industrial traffic was far from simple. A thirteenth-century bridge across the river at Newcastle was washed away by floods in 1771 and its replacement was soon shown to be inadequate. The river was narrow with sandbanks and had been further restricted by tons of debris dumped from quays, staithes and salt pans. This became critical as the colliers that took coal from Newcastle down the east coast, returned with ballast which they dumped in the river. They could not dock directly on to the jetties and staithes, and had to be loaded from keels; now the low stone arches of the new bridge put a limit on how far colliers could go upstream and even the keels needed removable masts to make it upstream. As a result the coal-shipping trade moved downstream when colliers started mooring at North and South Shields and insisted that the coal be brought to them there.

Parliamentary Acts to improve harbours and to make rivers navigable – for example, the Mersey and Irwell in 1720, and the Douglas in 1757 – were mostly sponsored by coal owners while the mineral trade also supported the building of harbours. But all these improvements were quickly overtaken by the increasing amount of goods that needed to be moved. The demand for coal, in particular, continued to grow and it was the ever-increasing need to move it that impelled a double revolution in transport – first the building of canals and then the construction of railways.

19. Canals and Locomotives

Up until the 1750s improvements to rivers and harbours, as well as the building of trackways, helped to improve the movement of bulk goods including, most crucially, coal. The rate of improvements increased as trade picked up but the real revolution in transport began in 1759. Two years previously the Duke of Bridgewater, then only twenty-one, returned from a tour of Europe where he saw the famous Canal du Midi which, since 1680, had joined the Atlantic to the Mediterranean via the Garonne River and the Étang du Thau. Inspired by this extraordinary piece of engineering – and by the canalisation of Sankey Brook near his home – he decided to build a new canal to connect his coal mines at Worsley with Manchester. This was a massive undertaking involving huge engineering works and financial commitment (the debts on the Canal du Midi were still outstanding eighty years after its completion). But there was money to be made too: the duke's initial proposal to Parliament was supported by merchants in Manchester on condition that the price of coal delivered to them would drop to 4d per hundredweight.

The bill was approved in March 1759 and work began. James Brindley was brought in as engineer and proposed that the canal should cross the Irwell River on an aqueduct. The idea was ridiculed at the time but gave birth to one of the great wonders of industrial engineering. The route to Stretford was completed by 1761 and the connection with Manchester made the following year, with a tunnel carrying the coal into Deansgate in the heart of the city. At the other end the canal entered the mine itself, as described by the writer and industrial enthusiast Samuel Smiles:

It is at Worsley basin that the canal enters the bottom of the hill by a subterranean channel which extends to a great distance – connecting the different workings of the mine – so that the coals can be readily transported in boats to their place of sale . . . In Brindley's time this subterranean canal, hewn out of the rock, was only about a mile in length, but now extends to nearly forty miles underground in all directions. Where the tunnel passed through earth or coal, the arching was of brickwork; but where it passed through rock, it was simply hewn out. This tunnel acts not only as a drain and water-feeder for the canal itself, but as a means of carrying the facilities of the navigation through the very heart of the collieries; and it will readily be seen of how great a value it must have proved in the economical working of the navigation, as well as of the mines, as far as the traffic in coals was concerned.[1]

The duke immediately began work on taking his canal in the other direction to link it with the Mersey. Though beset with difficulties this branch, which connected Manchester to Liverpool and the sea, was opened in 1776. The Bridgewater canal was an instant success – though the duke himself had to wait decades for a return on his huge investments, the price of coal in Manchester dropped by two-thirds while people came from across the country to admire the aqueduct and tunnels. Other industrialists immediately saw the benefits of building canals and there was a scramble to get routes approved by Parliament, accelerated by fierce competition between rival groups of investors. Josiah Wedgwood had built up a huge pottery business in Stoke and became the chief sponsor of a scheme to build a canal linking the Mersey to the Trent, which would run past his works; his chief concern was that a rival project would leave his business isolated. Typical of the entrepreneurs of the period, Wedgwood knew that he needed to go beyond the bounds of his business in order to create the necessary infrastructure: 'I scarcely know without a good deal of recollection whether I am a Landed gentleman, an Engineer or a Potter, for indeed I am all three by turns, pray heaven I may settle to something earnest at last.'[2]

The Trent and Mersey canal was begun on 26 July 1766 when Wedgwood ceremonially dug out the first sod of earth and James Brindley carried it away in a wheelbarrow. Groups of wealthy men lobbied hard for their own routes, but if their plans were approved by Parliament they had to spend a lot of capital before they saw any returns. The Trent and Mersey canal consumed £130,000 up front, with two further injections of £70,000. Shares for £200 were issued, the money being recouped through tolls set at 1½d per mile (freight costs by road were typically 10d a mile). The route included the Harecastle Tunnel which, at over a mile and a half long (2,880 yards), was more than double the length of any other tunnel in the world. British industrialists were showing enormous ambition undaunted by costs.

In 1793–4 alone, thirty new canal projects were launched and canal fever saw Midlands towns like Tipton criss-crossed by canals run by different companies. However, of the 165 canal Acts passed between 1758 and 1801, ninety had coal carriage as their main interest. In Birmingham in 1800 the transport of coal by road cost thirteen shillings a ton; once the Wednesbury canal opened this was reduced to 6s 8d, and by the early nineteenth century 1,500 collieries and ironworks faced on to Birmingham's system of canals, where 68,000 long boats transported over 2 million tons of coal per year.[3] Production of the famous anthracite or steam coal from Wales was boosted by the building of a canal to the Neath Valley and beyond, opening up the western coalfield. And the portion of the Yorkshire coalfield between Sheffield and Barnsley, which had suffered from being away from a navigable river, benefitted from the Dearne and Dove canal, which was built in 1793 specifically to serve the needs of the South Yorkshire collieries.[4]

Britain's canals were built by squads of mobile labourers, known as navigators or navvies, working their way across the countryside and bringing an entirely new world to previously isolated communities. Using just picks and shovels they dug trenches four feet deep and fifteen feet wide (to allow two boats to pass). Tunnels and occasional cuttings were made with the help of gunpowder, making canal work dangerous as well as physically hard. Every canal was lined with clay, which was then puddled into a hard non-porous layer by cattle or barefoot labourers.

It was colliery owners and iron-makers who drove the canal-building boom in order to get their goods to market, but there were profound effects on the social and commercial cohesion of the country. In his 1779 account, *The Journey From Chester to London*, Thomas Pennant describes the difference a canal could make to all aspects of life:

> The cottage, instead of being covered with miserable thatch, is now secured with a substantial covering of tiles or slates, brought from the distant hills of Wales or Cumberland. The fields, which before were barren, are now drained, and, by the assistance of manure, conveyed on the canal toll-free, are cloathed with a

Canals and waterways, 1810: By the end of the canal boom, every major industrial centre in England was connected to the system.

William Smith: Reading the Rocks

One of the best canal surveyors was an Oxfordshire man called William Smith.[5] Born in 1769, Smith gained a reputation in Somerset for surveying areas with potential coal seams, and giving sound advice to landowners. His eye for the land led him to draw up plans for water supplies and drainage. In the 1790s he was taken on by the Somerset Coal Canal Company as a surveyor and in his work Smith noticed more and more evidence of a regular order within the layers of rock. The cuttings and tunnels opened by the canal builders exposed the bands or strata of rock and Smith was the first to understand that the different rock types were not random occurrences but followed a regular pattern that was repeated across the country. He drew charts of rock layers, but then he began to notice that particular types of fossils were regularly found in particular layers, so that the fossil type rather than the physical character of the rock was the surest guide to the position of the strata within the overall scheme.

A journey across England from Somerset to the Midlands, Yorkshire and the north-east, made at the behest of the canal company, confirmed Smith in his beliefs; he understood that England was underlain by a regular pattern of rock types and he was able to draw some of the earliest geological maps to illustrate his ideas.

William Smith was a professional artisan, a working tradesman from the same stock as Darby, Trevithick and Arkwright. He was interested in patterns of rock strata because they told him where to find coal for his clients. Smith did not submit his findings to the journal of the Royal Society: he kept his trade secrets to himself. He finally published his maps only when he found the support of wealthy sponsors.

beautiful verdure. Places which rarely knew the use of coal are plentifully supplied with that essential article upon reasonable terms.'[6]

Building canals not only connected Britain's industry to its customers, it also trained a generation of brilliant engineers in techniques to overcome the challenges of the British landscape. Staircases of locks, such as thirty locks rising sixty-seven metres on the Worcester and Birmingham canal at Tardebigge, carried the canals over difficult terrain, while tunnels like the Harecastle on the Trent and Mersey canal and the 5,500-yard Standedge Tunnel on the Huddersfield canal, which took sixteen years to complete, took boats through seemingly impossible obstacles. This was engineering on an heroic scale. But as well as training engineers and surveyors and, in the process, giving birth to the practical science of geology, canals brought the Industrial Revolution to all parts of the country. Gangs of workers, new technologies and economic benefits introduced British people to the beginning of a new era.

The network of canals linking the major cities and the major centres of industrial production was largely completed by the early nineteenth century. Coal, iron, limestone, cotton and all kinds of goods were brought to canal wharves either by seagoing vessels or via roads and trackways, or tramways as they became known. Canal owners stood to gain from more traffic, so they now took over from coal owners as the builders of tramways. These were effective but the major limitation on the amount of traffic came from the need for a separate wagon for every horse or team of horses and the ensuing congestion clogged up the tramways. What was required was a locomotive with the power to pull a chain of wagons.

This was the background to the famous trial of Richard Trevithick's locomotive in 1804 at the Pen-y-darren ironworks in Merthyr Tydfil, where iron-makers needed to move bulk goods to a canal ten miles away. The crucial factor here was that the ironworks already had a tramway which comprised most of the essential elements of a railway – a parallel set of wooden rails, running at a reasonably even level, along which horses drew loaded wagons. Trevithick's steam-powered locomotive managed a good pace of around five miles per hour, but it was the power of the engine that mattered more than its speed of travel – its ability to pull a train of ten wagons along rails was the real beginning of the revolution in steam transport. Richard Trevithick was a serial inventor building stationary high-pressure engines, as well as loco-motives and a host of other devices; he was impatient with the immense practical difficulties that stood between a few prototype engines and a fully-fledged transport system and moved on to other applications of steam. Fortunately, other engineers imme-diately saw the benefits of his locomotive.

One of the earliest developers of steam railways for coal mines was John Blenkinsop, a Yorkshire estate manager who worked in concert with the Leeds engine builder Matthew Murray; the two men were the first to turn steam locomotion into a profitable enter-prise.[7] Born in County Durham in 1783 the son of a stonemason, Blenkinsop was apprenticed to his cousin Thomas Barnes, a Northumberland mine manager. In 1808 he became an agent on the Middleton estate near Leeds, which contained several coal mines and, crucially, was the site of a tramway running from the collieries into Leeds. As at Pen-y-darren, this proto-railway used horses to draw wagons running along wooden rails; built in 1758 and running over land outside the Middleton estate, it was the first railway authorised through an Act of Parliament to cross other people's land.

When Blenkinsop joined the estate, Trevithick's demonstra-tion at Pen-y-darren had already inspired other colliery owners to look at steam. At the Wylam colliery in Northumberland Christopher Blackett commissioned local engineers including Timothy Hackett to build a locomotive to run on his tramway; in 1811 a one-cylinder locomotive was tried but, while the necessary steam power could be generated, the problems now switched to the strength of the rails and the adhesion of the wheels to the tracks. It soon became clear that wooden, and even iron-topped, rails would be inadequate, as a locomotive pulling a large number of wagons would fail to gain purchase on the slightest incline.

John Blenkinsop had the advantage that the Middleton railway had iron 'edge-rails' laid in 1807; these were L-shaped rails where the edges gripped the even wheels of the wagons (as opposed to the usual system of having flanged wheels to grip the flat rails). In 1812 Blenkinsop commissioned Matthew Murray to build a locomotive for the Middleton railway. The result was the *Salamanca*, a twin-cylinder locomotive that was so successful that Blenkinsop immediately ordered three more, all of which ran successfully for twenty years. While Trevithick's locomotive used a single cylinder, with a heavy flywheel employed to even out the drive cycle, Murray used two cylinders to achieve the same effect, giving extra power and reducing the locomotive's weight. At the same time Blenkinsop overcame the problem of wheel slippage by laying a toothed rail alongside the weight-bearing rails; the *Salamanca* engine drove a wheel with cogs that fitted into this rail. The system, known as rack and pinion, was successful and was used in other places until the mid-nineteenth century, but it created problems at high speeds and laying the extra rail incurred considerable expense; by mid-century it was found unnecessary as the problem of slippage could be solved through improved weight distribution.

Once the Middleton colliery started running locomotives to the River Aire in the 1810s it triggered interest across the country. Here is the response of John Walton, a partner in the colliery, to the Duke of Portland's agent in Ayrshire:

Willington, Newcastle on Tyne

11 October 1813

Dear Sir

In reply to your favour of the 6th instant I shall at all times have great pleasure in affording his Grace the Duke of Portland . . . every information in my power respecting the new mode of leading our Coals by Steam Engines instead of Horses.

The Engine which is used is considered of four horses Power, of Trevithick's invention, being the most powerful we have in use at present and is made by Fenton, Murray and Wood of Leeds . . . and costs £380 including £30 paid to Trevithick for his patent right.

The Engine is so constituted that by the operating power of Cranks which turn a Cogged wheel working in Metal Coggs cast upon one side of the Rail laid and used as the Railway.

At Leeds they have been daily at work for some time back leading their Coals in this way and as their Road is perfectly level their Engines take with great ease 24, twenty Boll wagons loaded at a time – each weighs with its contents about 3½ tons, making an aggregate weight of 84 tons. When the Machine is lightly loaded it can be propelled at a rate of 10 Miles an hour; but when properly loaded it is calculated to go at the rate from 3½ to 4 Miles an hour upon a level way . . .

Should the length of the lead from his Lordship's concern in Ayrshire be considerable I have no doubt that an immense saving will be made by the adoption of Mr Blenkinsop's new method.

Yours most respectfully

John Walton[8]

While the use of steam locomotives on colliery railways was spreading, another innovation took place in Swansea. A group of investors involved in mining and quarrying at Mumbles on the western end of Swansea Bay needed to move rock and ore to Swansea docks five miles away. Boat cargo across the bay was dangerous and cumbersome and a canal was impractical. The solution was to build a tramway all the way around the bay in the flat area between the town and the beach; it opened in 1806, with horse-drawn wagons carrying bulk cargo. Benjamin French, one of the original investors, immediately saw the potential for passenger transport and agreed to pay the other partners £20 a year for the right to run a passenger service. On 25 March 1807 the world's first passenger railway (albeit horse-drawn) opened for business.[9] Two years later Elizabeth Isabella Spence wrote: 'I have never spent an afternoon with more delight than the one exploring the romantic scenery at Oystermouth (Mumbles). I was conveyed there in a carriage of singular construction built for the conveniency of parties who go hence to Oystermouth to spend the day. This car contains twelve persons and is constructed chiefly of iron, its four wheels run on an iron railway by the aid of one horse, and the whole carriage is an easy and light vehicle.'[10]

Steam locomotives were the product of collieries, where there was a need for their power, fuel to run them and engineers to build them. Not surprisingly, the man who was to take the steam locomotive out of the pits and across Britain and the world was himself a colliery worker. George Stephenson was born in the village of Wylam near Newcastle in 1781.[11] His father worked at the local colliery and the family had no money for schooling or an apprenticeship. But once George started work in nearby Newburn colliery, as a hand on the winding gear, the illiterate young man paid for night school where he learned to read and write. However, life remained a struggle. In 1804 Stephenson moved to Killingworth where his daughter died in infancy and his wife died of tuberculosis. He left his young son Robert in the care of relatives and went to Scotland in search of better-paid work but he was forced to return when his father was blinded in a mining accident.

In 1811 Stephenson's situation began to improve as he was given the chance to show his engineering skills. The stationary engine at Killingworth High Pit needed repair and Stephenson offered to help; his successful work won him the position of engineer for Killingworth and he began to be recognised as an expert on steam engines. Within three years he had built a steam locomotive in the colliery's workshop, which was used for hauling coal. It used flanged wheels rather than an edge-rail track and did away with Blenkinsop's toothed rack rail, relying on the adhesion between the wheels and the rails; it managed to pull thirty tons of coal at around 4 mph. Stephenson went on to build another eleven locomotives at Killingworth, some for use on the Hetton colliery railway. Opened in 1822, this was the first railway built from scratch by Stephenson and the first line specifically designed for steam locomotives. While Stephenson was a brilliant builder of locomotives, his greatest contribution was to bring engines and railways together. He improved the tracks, which were still liable to buckle or break even if they were made of cast iron, and worked to distribute the weight of the engines through more axles.

In 1818 Edward Pease, a wealthy merchant from Darlington, began to lay plans for a railway connecting Darlington to Stockton, a port on the Tees. This would enable the collieries of south Durham access to river transport, but there were objections from local landowners including one Matthew Cully:

5th February 1819

A set of Merchants and Speculators are endeavouring to obtain an Act of Parliament to enable them to make a Railway from Stockton to Darlington . . . The said Speculators being a few individuals who hope to be benifitted at the expense of the country, as the measure is not for the general benefit, and will . . . prove disastrous to those concerned. The said projected Railway will very materially injure the highly cultivated district through which it is proposed to carry it and cut up and intersect the enclosures which are now laid out at much expense . . . for the purpose of agriculture and good management as besides the Darlington line, which passes for nearly two miles through my property, a Branch is intended to go to Piercebridge . . . through the best part of my property. It is well known that the damage done, in making roads . . . besides the depridations . . . committed upon the crops and other property of Landowners, by the trespassing of Cattle and people employed in the traffic of the said railway. And it does not meet with the concurrence of the Landed Proprietors over whose property it is proposed to carry it, on the contrary it is almost universally opposed by them.[12]

Nevertheless, Pease got his way and in 1821 Parliament passed a bill enabling the building of the twenty-five-mile railway. The company Pease formed was responsible for the track and would hire out the line to anyone who wished to use it. Pease first envisaged pulling wagons along a track by horse, but was persuaded by George Stephenson to invest in building steam locomotives – an early indication of Stephenson's persuasive powers and his ability to get powerful people to support him. Together they set up Robert Stephenson and Company to build engines, with Stephenson's son Robert as managing director. The company's first notable engine was *Locomotion*, which ran on the Stockton & Darlington Railway on its opening day on 27 September 1825. Though originally planned as a colliery line, it was in fact the world's first public railway, with passenger cars as well as coal wagons. While locomotives and tramways had been around for decades, this marrying together of the two was a great landmark. Five years later the *Observer* was still in awe: 'The adaption of rail-ways to speed was never, we believe, thought of till the opening, in September, 1825, of the celebrated Stockton & Darlington rail-road, a work which will for ever reflect honour on its authors, for the new and striking manner in which it practically demonstrated all the advantages of the invention.'[13]

Stephenson had become a national figure; the railway was there to stay. The Stockton & Darlington line taught Stephenson that gradients were a real problem to locomotives, using up disproportionate amounts of their power; railways had to be kept as level as possible. He had wrought-iron rails made for the new railway, which were longer and tougher than cast iron but they were expensive; he needed to find makers who could offer better value. Meanwhile the cotton industry had expanded so rapidly that even the new canal system could not keep up with the amount of goods to be shipped from the industrial centres to the nearest port. The industrialists of south Lancashire now wanted their own railway.

A company was formed by Liverpool and Manchester merchants, and an enabling Act passed through Parliament in 1826; George Stephenson was commissioned to survey possible routes from Manchester to Liverpool and was appointed chief engineer for the building of the railway. The thirty-five-mile line included the

Wapping Tunnel beneath Liverpool (the first tunnel under a city) and crossed the near-bottomless Chat Moss using brush floats (a technique learned from Jack Metcalf's road-building). It had a total of sixty-four bridges and viaducts, crossing rivers, canals and streets, as well as cuttings and embankments to keep the track as level as possible.

Despite the example of the Stockton & Darlington line, the steam locomotive had not yet become the obvious choice of transit power. There was much support for stationary engines pulling wagons through drums and cables, while other competitors such as Goldsworthy Gurney were intent on building steam road vehicles to make the journey. It was therefore decided to hold a series of trials at Rainhill to determine not just which locomotives should run on the line, but whether locomotives were suitable for the task at all. The trials that took place in October 1829 give a fascinating snapshot of the state of steam locomotion at the time. It was clear that the examples of Trevithick, Murray and Stephenson had inspired a raft of engineers to try their hand at designing and building high-pressure steam engines with the capability of driving a wheeled engine, and that any lingering thoughts of road-based vehicles were being rapidly overtaken by rail-based transport.

The trials came down to five locomotives. Each engine was to make ten return trips along a one-and-three-quarter-mile track, making thirty-five miles in total, the length of the Liverpool & Manchester Railway. The average speed was to be ten miles an hour, the steam pressure 50 psi at the outset, and all the fuel and water necessary for the journey had to be carried on board. Two competitors dropped out before the start of the trials proper, leaving just three. The *Sans Pareil* built by Timothy Hackworth, a former colleague of Stephenson, nearly completed the arduous trials before cracking a cylinder; although it didn't win the competition it would be used on the Liverpool & Manchester Railway for several years. The *Novelty* built by Ericsson and Braithwaite reached 28 mph, but on the second day of the trials suffered a pipe fracture that damaged the engine. The surviving entry was

Rocket designed by George and Robert Stephenson, which pulled thirteen tons at an average speed of 12 mph and a top speed of 30 mph. The Stephensons were given the contract to produce the locomotives for the world's first fully functioning inter-city railway.

The astonishing speed of the *Rocket*, its ability to carry its own fuel and water, and its awesome power proved beyond doubt that a steam railway locomotive outperformed any alternative technology. George Stephenson's genius, demonstrated so well at Rainhill, was to produce a device that was both technically innovative and a consistent and reliable performer; his experience as engineer in the collieries of the north-east had shown him the waste of time and money brought on by unreliable machines. In addition he understood that good locomotives needed good tracks, and he was able to provide both.

The Liverpool & Manchester Railway was opened with great fanfare on 15 September 1830 when around 800 people, including the Duke of Wellington, boarded the first train from Liverpool, while another train set off in the opposite direction. Frances Ann Kemble was one of the first people to give an account of travelling at speed: 'Enormous masses of densely packed people lined the road, shouting and waving hats and handkerchiefs as we flew by them. What with the sight and sound of these cheering multitudes and the tremendous velocity with which we were borne past them, my spirits rose to the true champagne height, and I never enjoyed anything so much as that first hour of our progress.'[14]

That first journey became famous for another reason. When the train stopped at a halfway point to take on water, the prominent politician William Huskisson got down from his carriage and stepped on to the parallel track where he was hit by a locomotive travelling in the opposite direction. He died later that day. Huskisson was the world's first railway fatality, and a warning of the power of the new technology.

George Stephenson went on to build engines and railways that formed the foundation of the railway age. Eager railroad builders bought the first engines to be used in the United States from the Stephenson works, while his railway building focussed on the industrial areas of the north of England. Other engineers like Joseph Locke and Isambard Brunel took on the baton, sometimes in competition and occasionally in partnership with Stephenson. His influence established his preferred gauge as the industry standard, while Brunel used a wider gauge on the Great Western Railway, believing his tracks would never be joined to others. When railways in different parts of the country were joined into a national network a commission decided on the narrower Stephenson gauge (4 ft 8.5 in) for all railways.

Stephenson had shown the way by taking railways out of the collieries and ironworks and into the world of passenger transport. Soon railway travel itself became an enjoyable pastime. One of the first railway excursions was run in 1841 from Sheffield to Derby with fares of 7s for first class, 5s for second class, and 4s for third class who travelled in open wagons. Some 2,000 people embarked on the great adventure with five engines pulling a total of forty-five carriages and wagons. Several hats were lost along the way but the only casualty was a worthy gentleman who in his excitement at arriving at Wicker station stood up and fell overboard.[15]

Railways quickly went from private ventures into being the basic infrastructure for the nation's transport. As they were built and run by individual companies at their own risk, the result was a fairly haphazard network, including many duplications of routes and multiple stations in the same town serving different lines; Rotherham, for example, by the mid-nineteenth century a town of around 40,000, had three railway stations. But while private companies put up the money, the government took an interest from the beginning. In 1838 Parliament decreed that railways should carry the mail and when the telegraph was invented the following year, telegraph wires ran alongside railway tracks. But it was the Railway Act of 1844 that created a national transport system. Parliament obliged every railway company to run at least one train per day with carriages available for third-class passengers.

The train should run over the whole of their track in both directions and travel at a minimum of 12 mph; the carriages should have seats and be protected from the weather; and the lowest fares charged should not exceed 1d per mile.

While the coal industry drove the early development of railways, it was to be the steam railways that drove the expansion of the coal industry through the nineteenth century, consuming huge quantities of fuel and transporting coal easily to other customers. In 1869 railways were using around 2 million tons of coal per annum; by 1900 that had risen to 12 million tons. The number of passengers carried increased from 5.5 million in 1838 to 30 million in 1845 and to 111 million in 1855. The number of miles of railway grew from 500 miles in 1838 to 5,000 miles in 1848 and 10,000 miles in 1860, by which time the basic network of British railways was complete. In 1846, when railway speculation reached its peak, 272 Acts of Parliament giving permission for the forming of railway companies were passed.[16]

While railways had begun as carriers of bulk cargo over short distances, long-distance rail now moved coal throughout the country. The figures speak for themselves:

1834   2,100,000 tons came to London by sea; 2,000 tons by canal.
1846   3,400,000 by sea; 60,000 tons by canal; 8,000 tons by rail.
1880   3,700,000 tons by sea; 6,200,000 tons by rail.

The development of a rail network made it easy to get coal to London from any of Britain's coalfields; the monopoly enjoyed by the north-east and the east coast shippers was severely eroded. But shipping was the next mode of transport to benefit from the application of steam power – something that had been tried with little success by different inventors in the eighteenth century. The age of ocean-going steamships arrived in 1838 with the launch of Brunel's *Great Western* and by the 1870s the screw propellor and high-efficiency compound engines made ocean travel affordable and safe, transporting millions of migrants from Europe to the

Americas over the next decades. Steamships also became military weapons of great strategic value.[17]

Some have argued that the heroic age of British engineering came to a halt in the 1860s. Isambard Kingdom Brunel and Robert Stephenson died in 1859, and the latter was given one of the grandest state funerals of the age. By that time other countries were catching up with British industrialisation, while the nation was beginning to suffer from the 'English disease' whereby men who make money from industry and commerce educate their sons to become gentlemen who abhor endeavour, and look down on the artisan skills that enabled their forefathers to shake the world. Few such afflictions hampered German or American engineers, who became expert at the skill that had driven the original Industrial Revolution – the ability to turn ideas about making things into commercial industrial machines and processes.

VII. Money

'The desire of food is limited in every man by the narrow capacity of the human stomach, but the desire of the conveniences and ornaments of building, dress, equipage, and household furniture, seems to have no limit or certain boundary.'

ADAM SMITH, 1776

20. Producers and Consumers

The Industrial Revolution was driven not just by ingenuity, it was also powered by money. Money created demand for goods, it allowed investment in commerce and industry and it changed the ways that people thought about their lives and their work. Since the Renaissance certain parts of Europe – particularly northern Italy and Flanders – had led Europe from a medieval mindset based on faith and tradition towards a commercial culture based on finance, trade and wealth. But it was Britain that was to make the most of this new world, emerging as the richest nation and using its wealth to transform the fate of humanity. We will first see why Britons became the wealthiest people in the world, before examining how they spent their money, and the profound effects that brought about.

The early modern period had seen a remarkable divergence in the fortunes of European citizens. In 1525 average wages for unskilled workers in London, Amsterdam, Vienna and Florence were roughly equal at around 3 g of silver per day. A century later London and Amsterdam wages had grown to 7 g, while wages in Vienna and Florence stood at 4.5 g. By 1725, the gap between southern and northern Europe had widened further, with London workers averaging around 11.5 g and Amsterdam 9 g while in Vienna and Florence wages had decreased to just 3.5 g per day. In fact, by the eighteenth century workers in southern Europe barely earned a subsistence wage, while in England many workers could expect three to four times the cost of their basic needs.[1]

We have seen how this wealth had been created by the English wool trade, the divergence into craft manufacturing and the historic decline of the Mediterranean in favour of the Atlantic as the trading highway of Europe. Investment in a powerful navy, the success of the North American colonies and trading ties with India, combined with military victories over her Dutch and French rivals, had seen Britain dominate Atlantic and Indian Ocean trade.

While global trade opened up markets and gave access to raw materials, Britain's existing prosperity, built on the solid economic foundations of the wool industry, saw work, wages and profits distributed throughout its population. And while international commerce enabled Britain to expand its trading base, its economic foundations remained in wool and craft manufacturing. The spread of wealth across the country and through the population gave purchasing power to a large number of people and in the process created a new kind of society and economy. Well, nearly new. In fact, the Dutch had led the way, creating a society with a large middle-class element in the seventeenth century. The population of the Netherlands was much smaller than Britain's in the following century, but the Dutch example provides striking evidence of a new kind of consumption and a new kind of 'luxury'. In the seventeenth century ordinary Dutch citizens could buy goods like Delft tiles, cabinets, tables and chairs, as well as tobacco pipes, watches, silverware, tapestries and ceramics which had all been produced by local craftsmen. This was not rabid consumerism nor a narrow search for social status; people chose to acquire items of quality from an indigenous craft tradition in order to create a sense of domestic well-being. The burghers of the Dutch Republic were sober Calvinists with a strong puritanical streak, but they had built the first consumer society – albeit in a refined way: they were aware of the dangers of avarice and personal ambition and tended to buy with an eye to the purpose and quality of goods.[2]

The British 'middling classes' came to consumerism about a hundred years after the Dutch, and their views of what should be bought and why were remarkably similar, at least to begin with. British reflections on luxury were framed by the strong sense of disdain for the immediate past, in particular for the court of Charles II. As the economist Thomas Mun wrote in 1664: 'The general leprosie of our piping, potting, feasting, fashion, and the mis-spending of our time in idleness and pleasure . . . hath made us effeminate in our bodies, weak in our knowledge, poor in our treasure, declined in our valour, unfortunate in our enterprises, and condemned by our enemies.'[3]

Historians therefore talk of the Old Luxury of the Restoration and the New Luxury of the eighteenth century.[4] As well as the search for exquisite refinement and status, the key element of the Old Luxury was that it could not be replicated by the lower orders. This followed an age-old pattern in which elites distinguished themselves by acquiring foreign materials and goods that the rest of society could not afford or gain access to. The New Luxury that began to emerge around 1700 was different: this was a leap to a new state of consuming, born out of the wider availability of disposable income. Old Luxury was dictated by the court, New Luxury was generated by urban society, and because the new consumerism aimed to give affordable comfort and pleasure, rather than simply social status, it multiplied and diffused throughout society.

In the course of the eighteenth century the ability to buy household goods and fashionable clothes spread out from the middle class to all except the poorest in society: shopkeepers, traders, small manufacturers and workers had the means to buy items beyond their most basic needs. By the early decades of the eighteenth century the average unskilled British worker could afford a diet that included bread, meat, eggs and cheese, as well as beans, peas and beer. He or she regularly bought other essentials like fuel for cooking and heating, candles, linen cloth, lamp oil and soap, still leaving enough over for occasional luxury items such as tea, sugar, coffee, chocolate and tobacco.[5] Studies of household inventories from 1675 to 1725 show that workers possessed basic items such as tables, benches, cooking pots and pewter vessels, while many also had books, clocks and looking-glasses, curtains, china, and utensils for making and drinking tea.[6] At the same time new types of furniture emerged: court and press cupboards, chests of drawers, cabinets, as well as new styles of tables and chairs.[7]

Contemporary writers noted the thirst for more goods and luxuries, but belonging to the better classes they often misjudged the motives of those below them and assumed that the poor wished simply to emulate the rich. In 1726 Daniel Defoe declared that 'The poor will be like the rich and the rich like the great . . . and so the world runs onto a kind of distraction at this time.'[8] While in 1714 the philosopher Bernard Mandeville wrote: 'We all look above ourselves and fast as we can, strive to imitate those that some way or other are superior to us.'[9]

Sir James Steuart writing in 1767 hints at other motives: 'Let any man make an experiment of this nature upon himself by entering into the first shop. He will nowhere so quickly discover his wants as there. Everything he sees appears either necessary, or at least highly convenient; and he begins to wonder (especially if he be rich) how he could have been so long without that which the ingenuity of the workman alone had invented.'[10]

The middle classes were not, in general, intent on aping their social betters; instead they were equipping themselves for a more comfortable life, while at the same time expressing their status in an increasingly fluid social environment. In this new world, in contrast to the courtly society of England's past – a society that at the time still held sway in France, Spain and the Austrian Empire – social standing did not mean ostentation, but expressed itself in taste and the acquisition of high-quality goods. The purchase and possession of goods began to be viewed differently. High-quality items were both a way to a comfortable and decent life by enhancing the home, and a mark of social standing, and so consuming became a social virtue not a vice. Rather than emulating the luxury of the aristocrats, these new consumers were creating a new world. In the telling phrase of one historian these 'social groups are not so much looking above as they are looking ahead'.[11]

Contemporary writers began to see that consumption helped the national economy; the British overwhelmingly bought home-produced goods like furniture, crockery and cutlery rather than imported luxuries like French jewellery or Venetian glass, thereby boosting domestic manufacture and commerce. The philosopher David Hume was one of the first to argue for the virtue of consumption, claiming that acquiring goods 'improved knowledge and increased sociability.'[12] Consumption forced producers to refine and improve the ways of making goods, which would in turn stimulate arts and sciences. The desire to acquire goods, Hume argued, also gave people an incentive to work, which could otherwise only be provided by force.

The arguments in favour of consumption reached their apogee with Adam Smith, who in 1776 argued that while humans have selfish tendencies, they also take pleasure from seeing others thrive. Smith also argued that humans do not just go out and buy all at once for the present, they consider things in the context of their lives, over time. So they will, if possible, buy goods that are durable in the same way they decide on investment in goods, property, enterprises and education.

The desire for more comfort was a catalyst for innovative technologies in lighting, heating, furniture, pottery, glass and cutlery. The ability to buy books now extended to working families who were thereby able to provide their children with some basic education. Even the construction of houses improved, making ordinary people even more inclined to furnish their dwellings well. Gilbert White noted in his parish of Selborne in Hampshire in 1788 that mud dwellings for the poor had been replaced by brick and stone houses with 'upstairs bedrooms, and glass in the windows'.[13] Josiah Wedgwood also saw an improvement from the subsistence farming of his youth: 'the workers earning nearly double their former wages, their houses mainly new and comfortable, and the lands, roads and every other circumstance bearing evident marks of the most pleasing and rapid improvements'.[14]

The purchase of clocks and watches in particular revealed both the growing affluence and the care with which people used their money. Considering that the pendulum clock had only been invented by Huygens in 1657, ownership of clocks spread very quickly: 54 per cent of household inventories in Kent listed clocks in the years 1720–49. Pocket watches started to become fashionable around 1700 and by 1775 over 150,000 were being made in Britain every year. Watches were expensive but working people regarded them as status symbols – sailors at the end of a voyage or good fishing trip, farm workers at harvest, inheritors of small amounts of money, all bought watches for themselves and to pass on to their children.[15]

So the British consumer on the eve of industrialisation was, for the most part, a sober and discriminating buyer, interested in high-quality goods that would last, give pleasure and comfort for a lifetime, and could even be passed on to future generations. However, in the late eighteenth century that attitude began to change and the most obvious indication of it can be found in the consumption of food. Sir Frederick Eden, writing in the 1790s, cited the example of a forty-year-old gardener who earned 30d a day – a typical London labourer's wage. He was able to afford one loaf of wheat bread, half a pound of meat, several ounces of cheese, a pint of beer, and some tea and sugar per day, as well as new shoes and clothes from time to time. Two of his four children went to school. He bought coal in the winter, and rented a house with a garden where he grew fresh vegetables.[16]

Note how the income of a fairly lowly worker brought not only a varied and plentiful diet but also allowed for what would have been regarded as luxury items a century before. Tea, sugar, coffee, chocolate, tobacco and spices were shipped in from foreign parts by the same ships that took British manufactured goods to overseas markets. In the 1630s around 300,000 kg of tobacco was imported annually from North America to Europe, mainly to the Dutch Republic and England. By 1700 consumption was around 35 million kg and by 1790 it had reached 60 million kg. Imports of tea rose from almost zero in 1700 to 1 million kg in 1720 and then 14.5 million kg per annum by the 1790s. Coffee consumption rose too, reaching 50 million kg in Europe in the 1780s – a fifty-fold increase in sixty years.

Along with tea and coffee came sugar. This was not an inevitable mixing: the Chinese drank tea and grew sugar from the tenth century but never used them together. But Europe got a taste for sugar: around 1650, roughly 20 million kg were imported per year; by 1770 this had risen to 200 million kg, and had doubled again by 1820. In 1797, Sir Frederick Morton estimated that workers in southern England were spending 11 per cent of their wages on sugar, treacle and tea.[17]

While these luxuries were becoming standard items, some staple foods were adapted to the changing needs of a society on the move. Bread had traditionally been made from coarse grains, including rye, which would keep well and could be made or bought twice a week. But in the course of the eighteenth century people began to prefer finely ground wheat bread which didn't keep and was sold fresh and preferably hot as a kind of convenience food. When wheat grain became scarce in 1801 Parliament passed the Stale Bread Act, which temporarily outlawed the sale of fresh hot bread, seeing it as a waste of scarce resources.

As high wages continued while more efficient production drove down prices throughout the later eighteenth century, people could afford to buy more. This was particularly true of cotton. Robert Heaton, a Yorkshire farmer in the second half of the century, kept records of his payments to servants and noted that his women servants, for example, had significant disposable income which they spent on clothing. The fall in textile prices had begun in the early eighteenth century; from 1600 to 1730 the price of woollen broadcloth had declined from 138d to 54d per yard, the price of baize from 36d to 10d, linen from 24d to 13d, fustian from 31d to 10d, and calico or cotton from 28d to 24d. Low prices and high wages also drove specialisation in the chain of clothing supply: ready-made garments – coats, suits, petticoats, gowns, shirts and breeches – began to appear in drapery shops after 1700 as middle-class families were able to buy in clothes rather than make them.[18]

The ability to make lighter, thinner cloths helped this decrease in price as producers were getting more yardage from the same amount of raw material. But more significant cost reductions came from better trading networks, lower transaction costs and the concentration of industries in particular regions. From the 1770s the Industrial Revolution drove all of these factors further and added the crucial ability to produce the same amount of cloth at higher quality with fewer workers. By the 1790s, when Arkwright's mechanisation of spinning spread across the industry, the price of high-grade yarn had fallen by 90 per cent in a decade, and by the 1830s labour costs per pound of yarn were around one-tenth of their level in 1770. Cotton cloth was affordable for virtually everyone in Britain.[19]

The consumption of good quality, durable yet convenient clothing and textiles, began to be replaced with an emphasis on low-priced, colourful, fashionable yet disposable clothing. Cheap, easy to clean and colourful, cotton did not need to last; instead its versatility and low price gave birth to rapidly changing fashions. When everyone could afford cotton then tasteful people distinguished themselves from hoi polloi by changing their clothes from one season to the next. By the late eighteenth century Manchester weavers and calico printers would eagerly await the arrival of the London stagecoach bearing the latest designs, so they could adapt their looms and printing machines. The wider range of buyers that could afford disposable clothing was less concerned with quality and more interested in appearance; makers responded by focussing on how to make goods attractive for customers.

By the late eighteenth century, as standardisation in production and the powered mechanisation of industry took hold, the appeal of inexpensive disposable goods spread out from textiles to other industries. Clever craftsmen made veneers look like solid wood, and cotton shine like silk; wallpapers were made to look like Italian marble (nobody was fooled but the point was to appreciate the deception), and elaborate rugs covered cheap wooden flooring. Makers were naturally only too happy to see the lifespan of goods reduced so that the market regenerated itself. But fashion didn't necessarily mean a drop in quality. Cotton cloth was made progressively finer by improved technology and the arrival of Jacquard and Dobby looms gave manufacturers the ability to weave complex and sumptuous patterns into cloth at low cost. Earthenware could be made to a high standard and was in many ways better than the pewter or wood of preceding centuries. Thanks to technically savvy entrepreneurs like Josiah Wedgwood, pottery improved in quality and became more affordable. These new goods were more convenient too: washing cotton, for instance, was easy, reducing the need for labour in the household and allowing further specialisation of labour. The move from high-quality utilitarian goods to inexpensive, convenient and disposable products was a key development that prepared the way for the mass production and mass consumption that followed on from industrialisation.

Along with this gradual but fundamental change in consumption came a retail revolution. From about 1650 to 1750 markets, fairs and direct sales by artisans were supplemented by shops and peddlers stocking a range of goods. Traditionally towns had held markets where butchers, bakers, barbers, metalsmiths and drapers sold their wares from stalls. But while markets still dominated, by 1700 almost every English town had at least one shop selling a range of goods, an innovation that soon spread out to villages. And as people worked longer hours, shops were certainly more convenient than buying direct from suppliers, even if the prices were higher.

Selling goods had been traditionally restricted by guild rules, but clothing-makers managed to separate retailing from guild control. Draper's shops began to sell ready-made clothes as well as cloth. Other trades followed suit and by the mid-eighteenth century a small town of 1,500 population would typically have several blacksmiths, carters, and perhaps a cooper, drapers, milliners and tailors;

bakers, butchers and grocers; ironmongers and stationers. Coal and timber merchants were common, as were pedlars selling produce door to door. By 1752 Britain had one retail shop for every fifty-two people.[20] While shops were first and foremost a functional innovation, the concept of shopping as a leisure activity was arguably first exploited by Josiah Wedgwood, whose luxury emporiums in London began the creation of shopping as entertainment, social occasion and pleasure. Shopping became a leisure activity similar to visiting coffee houses, theatres, concert and dancing halls.

Already by the middle of the eighteenth century British life had become commercialised to a previously unknown degree. A patchwork of regional agrarian economies had been gradually integrated into a single commercial capitalist market system which fed both increasing consumption and higher productivity. How long Britain could have continued to produce more goods from its traditional organic economy is open to question; there is no doubt, however, that the introduction of production based on steam power came at a propitious moment. British consumers were ready and eager to buy goods that were mass-produced, while retaining a degree of quality and utility; just as important, they had the disposable income necessary to stimulate further increases in demand, thereby fuelling continuous investment in innovation.

21. Money for Industry

Money in the hands of consumers drove demand which in turn brought increases in industrial production, but industries also needed money in the form of investment. Even though many of the inventions in the early phase of the Industrial Revolution were on a small scale, their exploitation required investment in new machines and processes; and as the scale of production grew, innovators and industrialists needed ever-greater financial backing. This meant more money up front for ironworks, mines, mills and foundries from investors prepared to wait years for returns. The earliest capitalist entrepreneurs were helped by the relatively low cost of industrial start-ups. In the 1790s a cotton-spinning mill with 1,000 spindles cost around £3,000 to build and equip, one with 2,000 spindles around £5,000, money that could probably be met by a small group of wealthy investors; by the 1830s as the industry was scaled up cotton mills were costing £20,000 to £50,000 and could only be realistically backed through the financial system.[1]

We should remember too that Britain prospered because industrial entrepreneurs such as Boulton, Arkwright, Wilkinson and Wedgwood were able to marry craft industries with technical innovations in order to produce goods on an industrial scale. Developing an invention from the initial patent to a productive, profit-making machine or process demanded a new set of skills and experiences, and a new scale and system of finance. The prototype of the Fourdrinier paper-making machine, for example, was invented in France and patented in England in 1801; developing and building a prototype cost £46,000 with a further

£12,000 spent on improvements before production began in 1808. The machine was to be the basis of all paper-making for the next 200 years but the upfront costs eventually bankrupted its small group of investors.[2] This was a salutary lesson but of course many expensive investments bore fruit and repaid their backers handsomely. Watt's steam engine was patented in 1769, and although it only began to pay back Matthew Boulton's investment in the 1790s, in the long term the engine made them both wealthy men.

In theory the degree of investment needed by industry was not a problem for Britain – there were plentiful savings put aside by merchants, traders, farmers and small-scale manufacturers, while the needs of industry never rose above around 11 per cent of GNP. Potential investments were also helped by the financial stability created by the Bank of England. The national debt grew to worrying amounts at times like the American War of Independence (1775–83), and attempts to reduce debt by taxing goods could be painful for industry, but overall British commerce benefitted from a stable financial structure and a stable rate of interest. The introduction in 1757 of the Consolidated Stock (the Consol) at 3 per cent meant that interest on government bonds remained stable, dictating wider interest payments and encouraging holders of cash to make long-term investments.

The key problem was the lack of a national system for channelling savings to the places where they were needed. There was virtually no retail banking system to take deposits from savers in order to lend to borrowers.[3] Instead Britain's commercial finance was concentrated in London, where bankers made returns by lending to merchant traders and to the government, channelling the cash reserves built up by individuals and businesses into secure government investment. The system was designed primarily to serve the needs of the state and to provide a stable system of national finance. In this it was extraordinarily successful, giving a stable underpinning for the growth of British economic, trading and military power. Industrialisation, on the other hand, was concentrated in the Midlands and north of England, in central Scotland and South Wales. As well as being beyond the reach of London banks, the new industrialists had no track record for bankers to rely on.

These difficulties were compounded by the restrictions of the 1720 Bubble Act, which effectively outlawed the formation of corporations with shareholders. Any grouping of investors had to be a partnership, with a maximum of six members, each of whom was responsible for the losses of the whole – a restriction that also applied to banks. This discouraged investment from third parties so, for much of the eighteenth century, investments in industry were made through family, social and faith networks. The only other sources of major capital financing were fellow industrialists. Richard Arkwright, for example, was refused capital by the Nottingham bank of Ichabod and John Wright, and instead formed a partnership with industrialists Samuel Need and Jedediah Strutt, both of whom had made money from the stocking trade. Correspondence between members of the Birmingham Lunar Society, as another example, shows how Matthew Boulton, James Keir, Josiah Wedgwood and John Roebuck put money into each other's businesses, while also investing further afield.[4] The use of so-called merchant capital spread further with merchants and industrialists investing in industries in which they had no expertise. Merchants making profits from tea, for example, were largely responsible for the large-scale investment in the South Wales coal and iron industry.

Before we see how a banking system developed to enable more third-party investment, we should take note of the historic shift that was taking place, led once again by the artisan industrialists. Historically most makers of goods had been self-employed, owning their own premises and tools and either buying their own raw materials or working through the putting-out system. But the mechanisation of production went hand in hand with the development of a new system in which one person owned the premises,

Land and Money

One of the abiding myths of British history is that the Enclosures – the taking of common land into private ownership – drove up agricultural productivity and pushed peasants off the land and into cities. This then enabled the countryside to support a large urban population while also freeing up workers for the new factories. The Enclosures were therefore a key driver of the Industrial Revolution. However, the relations between land, food and urban expansion were almost the exact opposite. First, the doubling of agricultural productivity (i.e. output per acre *and* output per agricultural worker) happened from 1600 to the 1730s, well before the peak period of Enclosures began, while during the time of Enclosure the rise in productivity slowed to around 10 per cent. Second, Britain's urban population was much higher by proportion than elsewhere in Europe well before the Enclosures (London's population increased from around 50,000 in 1500 to 500,000 in 1700). In fact, the increase in urban population led by London was driven by the growth of craft manufactories and burgeoning world trade, and this in turn provided an incentive for farmers to increase food production; in other words, in a complete reversal of the traditional explanation, it was the cities that led the countryside.[5]

How, then, did farmers raise their productivity so dramatically in the period from 1600 to 1730? The answer lies partly in the security given to farming families through copyholder and beneficial tenancies which had developed over the preceding century through the Court of Chancery.[6] Copyholders became legally entitled to manage their own affairs without oppressive interference from the manor house and could profit from the sale of surplus produce, while the growing urban populations gave a ready market for farm produce.

The market provided the incentive, but how was increased productivity achieved? Although nutritious crops like beans and root vegetables were introduced, of more importance were improvements to the land itself. Records show that farms spent more labour on measures to improve the soil than on any other activity.[7] These were energy-intensive processes; making lime, for example, used up vast amounts of coal which Britain had in abundance.

The increase in food production between 1600 and 1730 came without a significant rise in the agricultural workforce. Throughout human history the production of surplus food almost always encouraged families to have more children, who were seen as the future labour force; the subsequent increase in population gave more mouths to feed and so nutrition returned to the level of subsistence. So why was this time different? It seems likely that both social attitudes and the new commercial system in which farms operated played a role. Historians have long noted that in Britain and northern Europe, from the Tudor period onwards, women married much later than in southern Europe, and in many cases (up to 20 per cent) chose not to marry at all.[8] This cultural difference is thought to stem from the relative independence of young women. The rise in prosperity in the seventeenth and eighteenth centuries did not, as might be assumed, lead to British women deciding that they should marry and have large families; instead it made them more financially independent and kept the fertility rates low.[9] So greater prosperity in the countryside brought more independence, not more children.

The other reason why the agricultural workforce remained stable was the increasing commercialisation of British life. Farmers were producing more food in deliberate response to a growing market; their principal incentive was financial gain and so they were highly motivated not to spend their gains on more children. It was this revolution in attitude that produced the agricultural productivity that freed up more people to work in craft manufacturing and eventually in industry.

equipment and raw materials and paid others to do work for him. The entrepreneur would invest his own money and would take the profits made by the enterprise. Capitalism was not invented by the British industrialists – it had originally developed in northern Italy in the fifteenth century – but they fostered the establishment of the capitalist as the basis of the new industrial economy.

A rough and ready capitalist system developed as people like Arkwright, Boulton and Wedgwood became owners and large scale in the businesses that they ran. But while technical innovations improved productivity and the growing market presented opportunities, making industry pay was no simple matter. Few industrial entrepreneurs had experience or expertise to call on and the biggest danger was over-expansion and resultant drying up of cash. As with today's innovators, the first industrialists needed to produce on as large a scale as they could, as quickly as they could, to keep ahead of their competitors; but bills from suppliers came in well before payment from customers. Manufacturers were also vulnerable to piracy of patents, abuse of credit, legal challenges, destruction of machines, underhand dealings, cartels and even, in Arkwright's case, death threats. Lots of companies went under and even those that thrived had to be helped through their cash-flow problems by sympathetic customers. The ironmaster John Wilkinson was supported by his customer Boulton & Watt on more than one occasion, as shown in this letter of 21 June 1792 from James Watt:

Dear Sir,

In reply to yours we send you inclosed our draft on Mrs Matthews value £1,000, the receipt of which please acknowledge.

B. and W. never were lower in cash than at present, for by our long absence in London our Customers were not craved, so that we have not received for castings this year the half of what we now send you. Mr B. is gone to Birmingham to procure you another £1,000 on his own account and will write you. Wishing you happily

over this crisis and that you may reap much profit and satisfaction
from your new Estates,

> I remain,
>> Dear Sir,
>>> Yours sincerely,
>>>> JAMES WATT

Mrs Watt says that if you do not call at Heathfield and stay a day
with us on your way down she will conclude you have quarrelled
with her.

Richard Arkwright became a villain to some and a hero to others
for his aggressive business practices. He made the cotton-spinning
mill into a profit-making business, and was the first to show that
investing in a large-scale enterprise could bring rewards, but only
with careful control over the financial aspects of the business.
Arkwright learned that extending long-term credit to customers – a
common practice given the dearth of currency and banking – could
lead to disaster, while he implemented systems for keeping track
of the money tied up in stock and processed goods. Those who
failed to follow suit went under, despite the opportunities of the
growing market.

For the embryonic capitalist industrial system to grow, it
needed a banking system to channel investment, while employers
needed banks in order to pay their workers. But even on the most
basic level of supplying coinage and notes the banking system
was, before the mid-eighteenth century, wholly inadequate. The
Bank of England was charged with issuing coins and banknotes
and was required to hold enough gold to redeem all the notes it
issued; this remained insufficient for the country's needs until the
end of the eighteenth century.

Lack of small-value coinage bedevilled the burgeoning retailers,
who had to operate by continually extending credit, while industrialists taking on workers in Birmingham, Staffordshire or
Lancashire were condemned to spend their time in search of shillings to pay wages, or operating the infamous truck system, where

wages were paid in goods from the factory shop. Some, such as John Wilkinson and a few Northumberland mine-owners, even resorted to minting their own coins or tokens.

In the early to mid-eighteenth century merchants in country towns, exasperated at the lack of circulating currency, began to accept bills of exchange bearing the name of a reputable London banking house in return for small currency, while taking commission along the way. A de facto national banking system thereby began to develop. By the 1760s private banks of this type became widespread, emerging not from financiers venturing out from London, but through local enterprises such as goldsmiths, cloth-makers, associations of cattle drovers and wool-traders offering a banking service to fellow traders. Taylors and Lloyds, Quaker iron-makers of Dale End in Birmingham, moved into banking and by 1765 were paying interest to depositors while taking interest on loans; the Miner's Bank of Truro was established in 1759 followed by Praed's Cornish bank in 1774. Scores of others began taking deposits, issuing currency and paying interest while taking commission and making loans. According to Bailey's British Directory the number of banks outside London grew from 119 in 1784, to 230 in 1797, rising to 800 by 1808.[10]

Country banks helped the concentration of industry in the north and Midlands by getting funds to the places and enterprises where they were needed. Banks in rural areas would receive cash deposits from farmers following the summer harvests; this was then sent to their correspondent bank in London, and then recycled to industrial centres hungry for funds to settle their accounts at the year's end. All this was feasible because market towns in Britain had, over the previous centuries, developed into effective commercial centres with an infrastructure of markets, notaries, merchants and middlemen in place. Industrialisation wrenched the country into a different era, but many of its citizens were already commercially astute.

The increase in the number and spread of banks eased the problems of currency circulation and allowed businesses to pay large sums to each other via banker's drafts. At the same time banker's bills were issued to depositors by country banks and were passed around as a kind of ersatz currency, being redeemable for coins and notes at any time. This system worked well as long as the Bank of England kept enough money in circulation to redeem any demands. That didn't always happen and bankers who had tied up their money in long-term investments occasionally faced demands for cash that they could not meet. In 1772, 1793 and in 1814–16 many small banks were forced under, taking their clients with them. It was only in 1826, following another banking collapse, that Parliament approved the setting up of joint-stock banks owned by shareholders with limited liability. Large-scale banks with big capital reserves could then emerge in the industrial cities, for example the Manchester and Liverpool District Banking Company. The culmination of the process came in 1854 when joint-stock banks came into the Clearing House, which allowed cheques to be exchanged between banks. The shoe was then on the other foot and the 'new' industrial-based banks like Lloyds took over 'old' London banks, creating national organisations.

The effects of the Industrial Revolution spread far beyond technology and industry: industrialists adopted capitalism as their method of finance and organisation; they forced the financial system to change to accommodate their needs; they built the banking system that they needed; and they integrated these different elements into a system of industrial and commercial finance that spread to the rest of the world.

22. Adam Smith and the Industrial Economy

The Industrial Revolution came about in the real world, created by practical men with no formal training beyond apprenticeships. They wanted to make money and had little interest in economic theory. But the same changes that set the stage for the Industrial Revolution – new attitudes to work, innovation, prosperity, the improvement of one's lot – also created the need for an understanding of the economic forces at work in society. The resulting theory may not have impinged on the early phases of the Industrial Revolution, but by the early nineteenth century economic theory was steering the hand of government, helping it to set the framework for a sustainable industrial society.

Economic theory emerged in late eighteenth-century Britain because, for the first time, human beings were acting as independent economic agents. This new situation has been described by the leading economic historian Robert Heilbroner as 'The Economic Revolution'. Increasing prosperity, specialisation and novelty in work, widespread disposable income and, above all, a revolution in social attitudes meant that people were, for the first time, making decisions based on economic choices.[1]

For most of human history, societies had followed customs that enabled them to share resources and responsibilities, jobs and rewards, while maintaining social cohesion. This sounds a little high-flown, but in practical terms communities came together in order to develop ways of dealing with a potentially hostile world. Societies were held in place through a combination of inherited customs and coercion from above. In medieval Europe it was important that the daughters of spinners became spinners too, and the sons of weavers became weavers. Custom and coercion also applied to ways of working; anyone stepping outside their customary role by making a different type of cloth, or using more efficient machinery, for example, would face severe punishment.

By the eighteenth century the social and economic changes that swept through Britain brought about a new kind of society and a new kind of economic actor. British people became free to work as they chose, to buy and sell goods, and to invest in the hope of return. This was a liberating but also worrying prospect. How, after all, would society function, how would it hold itself together, how would it prosper and increase, if everyone could do as they pleased? As the eighteenth century progressed, these abstract questions began to need practical answers. Would it, for example, benefit the nation to maintain punitive tariffs on imports of cotton, or keep restrictions on the number of apprentices, or the price of bread or wheat? There was no real explanation of how the economic system worked, of how a nation's wealth could be gained and sustained in a world no longer ruled by custom or enforced authority.[2]

This was the heyday of the Enlightenment when scholars all over Europe looked for patterns and meanings in every part of the natural world and in every area of human existence and endeavour. The way was open for someone to investigate and codify the laws underlying economic behaviour and to explain their implications for national economies. Adam Smith took the first giant strides; in 1776 he published *The Wealth of Nations*, which effectively gave economics its terms of reference and its language as well as making it an essential subject for every thinking person.

Adam Smith was born in Kirkcaldy in Fife in 1723; at seventeen he won a scholarship to the University of Oxford and in 1751, aged just twenty-eight, he was appointed professor of logic and then of moral philosophy at the University of Glasgow. By 1757 he was dean of the university and a leading figure in the so-called Scottish Enlightenment. The first question Smith addressed was: if everyone can do as they like, what will hold society together; without a central force in place, how will society ensure that all the things that must be done are done? His answer came in the shape of his most famous and lasting idea, the invisible hand. Here is how he introduced the concept:

> By preferring the support of domestick to that of foreign industry, he intends only his own security; and by directing that industry in such a manner as its produce may be of the greatest value, he intends only his own gain, and he is in this, as in many other cases, led by an invisible hand to promote an end which was no part of his intention. Nor is it always the worse for the society that it was not part of it. By pursuing his own interest he frequently promotes that of the society more effectually than when he really intends to promote it.[3]

The end that is promoted is the situation 'that is most agreeable to the whole of society'. In this way commercial capitalism is seen as a kind of being of 'perfect liberty' in which everyone is free to do as they wish and in the process they bring about a situation that is the best for all. But Smith also realised that this situation is not a final fixed end; society is ever-changing.

Before we look at the other side of this coin, we should pause to take in the full force of this new vision of society. For most of human existence people believed in life as a cycle of existence anchored in a world in which little changed. Christians in Europe had long believed that the world would continue as it was until God brought it to an end.[4] But just as Isaac Newton had shown that while the rules that governed the universe were constant the universe itself was continually changing, so Adam Smith presented a vision of society in which constant economic laws brought about continual change.

However, if the invisible hand meant that individual actions inevitably brought about a good society, then at the same time a series of laws acted as restraints on these actions. While butchers and bakers were free in theory to produce as much as they could and charge any price, the market itself automatically dictated both quantity and price. Produce too much and you overfill demand and the price drops; charge too much and someone else will produce the same for less and undercut you. According to Smith these were the inviolable laws of the market and they brought society the right amount of goods at a fair price. The market also regulated the incomes of the producers since they could only earn such profits as the market deemed fair, while if incomes were driven down producers and investors would leave the sector, forcing a shortage and a consequent rise in prices.

But the market was not simply a regulator of a static situation; it promoted the growth in productive capacity that Smith witnessed in eighteenth-century Britain. How did it do this? Smith argued that, like pieces of cloth or ingots of iron, people too could be produced to order. At the time, most children died in infancy, and Smith believed this was due to poverty; he also believed that it was the natural desire of people to increase their wages in order to accumulate wealth. So, as the wealth of society in general increased, the number of children surviving into adulthood would also increase; this would then bring more people into each industry. This would tend to hold wages down but the overall effect would be an ever-increasing number of productive people and therefore an ever-growing economy.

Smith's vision was optimistic; he believed that if these market mechanisms were allowed to operate the result would be beneficial for the whole of society, including the poorest. This was a self-evident good because: 'No society can surely be flourishing and happy, of which the greater part of the numbers are poor and miserable.'[5] However, Smith also saw a limiting factor to economic growth. This was to be dramatically expounded by Thomas Malthus who argued in 1798 that population would grow exponentially, while resources grew arithmetically, and that therefore humanity would always tend to find itself in shortage.[6] Both men believed that as the population grew and the economy expanded, it would nevertheless eventually come up against the natural limits of the economy, which were dictated by the productive capacity of the land. At this point, if population continued to grow, then the living conditions of individuals and profitability of enterprises would stagnate or even fall. As Smith wrote: 'In a country which had acquired that full complement of riches which the nature of its soil and climate, and its situation with respect to other countries, allowed it to acquire; which could, therefore, advance no further, and which was not going backwards, both the wages of labour and the profits of stock would probably be very low.'[7]

In other words Smith understood the limits of the existing organic economy; what he did not foresee was the coming transition to a coal-based economy that would blow away the limits to growth that he described. In the same year in which his masterpiece was published, his fellow Scot James Watt was busy erecting his first two improved steam engines; the economic world was about to change again.

In fact Smith's prescription was soon undercut in other ways by industrialisation; in the 1770s iron and cloth producers met regularly to fix prices and rig the market, and within a few decades some individual enterprises became big enough to influence the market in their own favour – self-interest no longer automatically fed the common interest. Government intervention against price fixing, for example, was necessary and the market, therefore, was not a natural phenomenon but a construct held in place by continual adjustment of rules and regulations. The 'free' market was anything but; in fact it was a reflection of the society of the times. Nevertheless, while some of Smith's extrapolations may look misguided his genius lay in showing how the market could be understood. And while he was set against interference with the market, he saw the chief danger coming from the industrialists themselves.

David Ricardo, who was Smith's successor as the most influential economic thinker of the time, saw economic society as sets of interest groups each doing battle with the other.[8] In Ricardo's time the dominant groups were not labour and capital, but landowners and industrialists, whose different interests were highlighted by the passing of the 1815 Corn Law. The law restricted imports of corn until home-grown corn reached a price of £4 per quarter-ton; this protected the landowners' market, but raised prices of bread for ordinary people. The consequence was profound as charging people more for staple foods reduced demand for manufactured goods. The issue remained at the forefront of British economic politics until the laws were finally repealed in 1846. The arguments for and against the Corn Laws showed that, in the new world of self-interested economic actors operating in an industrial economy, it was incumbent on the government to intervene in order to construct a suitable legal and fiscal framework, to regulate imports and exports, and above all to be alert to changing economic circumstances. The new world was one of rapid change.

Smith, Malthus and Ricardo were all writing in the midst of the greatest economic revolution in history and yet none of them could sense the earthquake beneath their feet. All three were extremely perceptive about the economic conditions that had existed for most of human history and about the economic developments in Britain. They all saw a society in danger of stretching its natural resources to the limit – what none of them saw was that those limits were about to be blown open for the first time in human history.[9] In fact the coming of industrialisation enabled the economy to enter an entirely new phase that overthrew the predictions of Smith and Malthus. How was this possible? As we have seen, the essential answer is that in an organic economy humans must gain all their needs through growing crops and rearing animals and through sources of energy such as timber. The land can produce only so much food and fuel and this places limits on economic growth. Industrialisation, however, gave humans access to another source of energy in the form of coal. Food still had to be derived from the land's resources but these did not need to be used for heating, cooking, clothing or building. Indeed the conversion of natural resources into food could be made much more efficient through fertilisation and through improved transport and distribution systems, all fuelled by coal. This left increasingly large parts of the economy available to produce goods, again using fossil energy. The productive capacity of the economy is hugely increased by using energy beyond the natural resources of human and animal muscle.

Once the invention of the steam engine allowed coal to be used to produce mechanical energy, the total amount of energy available to the economy was vastly increased, while the amount of energy available to industrial production was also immensely greater than in an organic economy. A natural organic economy requires a delicate balance to be maintained if it is to be sustainable, otherwise it enters a cycle of a system of negative feedback – the greater the productivity, the nearer the economy gets to the natural limits of the land. In an industrial or mineral-based economy, on the other hand, there is positive feedback – each step that brings greater productivity opens the way for more innovation and makes the next step easier to take. Though this vast change took some time to work through, once people began to use coal to produce usable energy, the limits of economic growth imposed by the organic economy were blown away.

VIII. Work

'The workshop may, without any great feat of imagination, be considered as an engine, the parts of which are men.'

ADAM FERGUSON, 1767

23. The Nature of Work and the Rise of the Factory

Industrialisation utterly changed the nature and meaning of work. Timekeeping, the factory system, regular hours, fixed holidays and large work-based organisations, as well as the separation of owner-ship, management and labour all came into being. Industrialisation was not just about the mechanisation of industrial production; it placed human beings in a totally different relation to their work, which became a central element in their social and cultural iden-tity. The consequences were profound and long-lasting and have been felt well beyond the workplace. Family life, for example, was profoundly altered as mature women and children, while initially used in factories, were increasingly driven out of formal work.

While these changes were made visible by industrialisation, the Industrial Revolution was itself part of a bigger process which catapulted humanity into the modern age. We have already seen how Britain became a dynamic commercial, trading and manu-facturing society before the great watershed of the 1770s; this brought profound changes in the nature of work which were cemented as industrialisation became embedded in society and workers had to organise their lives around the requirements of machinery.[1]

The major changes to work patterns which took place from roughly 1650 are best viewed through the prism of the household. Before then the vast majority of households lived in a state of 'subsistence plus' – they had enough for their basic needs with a little left over for extras. In the typical rural family with a small amount of land the man did the ploughing, made implements and fixed buildings; the woman harvested, ran the dairy, and prepared the food, while the children gathered produce and looked after animals. The woman might also do some spinning and the man some weaving or nail-making. Any surplus they made could be traded for goods that could not be made at home. Not every household had enough land to support itself, but every working man and woman was capable of a range of tasks that made the household as self-sufficient as possible. This situation was not confined to Britain in the late Middle Ages; it was the dominant state of being for most of human history.[2] Every member worked for the good of the household, which was the essential economic unit, so that changes to the household economy had profound effects.

Over the two centuries from 1650 English households began to earn more than they needed for basic living, which allowed some members of households to focus on a single activity. The wide distribution of relative prosperity among the population was crucial since no one could give up self-sufficiency unless they could buy in goods and services from elsewhere. A woman could not stop making bread to focus on millinery unless someone nearby was prepared to sell bread to her. A farmer could not stop making lime to concentrate on forging knife blades unless he was sure he could buy in lime from elsewhere. So, while it was easy for one person to set up as a specialist milliner, her survival depended on others specialising in all the trades that she needed to satisfy her wants. Everyone had to move together to make the system work, in a process we might call 'mutual specialisation' – and this, for the first time in human history, is exactly what happened.

We have seen how Britain moved from an economy dominated by the English wool trade to a widely based craft-industrial economy in which goods were produced in small workshops, homes, forges and occasional mills. The historic importance of these craft industries was that they allowed the process of mutual specialisation to emerge gradually – though in terms of human history it was a remarkably rapid process – as households could shift the emphasis of their work without becoming instantly dependent on others. Farmers in Staffordshire could do more nail-making as demand increased, perhaps saving time on gathering wood for fuel by buying in coal; a woman could develop her skill in making clothes, and buy in bread or ready-butchered meat from a village shop. The eventual result was a society of workers with specific occupations, rather than a nation of households with simple basic needs to fill.

Though these changes took two centuries to work through, the process reached the critical point of self-sustainability in the first half of the eighteenth century. Over just a few decades people changed from organising their work on the basis of their household's needs, to orienting themselves to the demands of the market. To Adam Smith, writing in 1776, this seemed logical, even inevitable: 'It is the maxim of every prudent master of a family never to attempt to make at home what it will cost him more to make than to buy. The tailor does not attempt to make his own shoes but buys them from the shoemaker. The shoemaker does not attempt to make his own clothes but employs a tailor.'[3]

Rational it may have been, but it was nevertheless utterly revolutionary. The effect of specialisation was to make each household as well as the economy as a whole more productive. One reason was simple logistics; a person working continuously at one task – weaving, for example – will produce more than five people only giving weaving one-fifth of their time and breaking off to perform other tasks. But the time spent at work increased by around 25 per cent from 1760 to 1830, and there was also an intensification of work. It seems that people began to work longer and harder because they knew that they would be able to use their surplus income to buy in goods. Workers also had the newly available possibility of advancement, which drove the desire to acquire skills. Some historians see the change in work habits as being forced on the labouring classes, with the previous custom of working at your own time and pace replaced by the needs of the capitalist owner.[4] There is no question that working people traded control over their work for the greater financial rewards of the factory; their motivation for doing so will always be open to question – some workers were coerced, but in many cases households made conscious choices to change their work patterns.

Industrialisation also brought about a new mobility of labour. People moved from country districts to towns and cities in search of work, while others travelled great distances to exploit their skills, or to find employment. Ironworks were among the earliest to attract workers from far afield. In the early eighteenth century the Backbarrow Iron Company in south Cumbria drew labour from South Wales, Yorkshire, Staffordshire and Shropshire; ironworks established at Invergarry in the Highlands imported workers from Barnsley and South Wales and charcoal burners from Ireland. At about the same time Abraham Darby took workers from Bristol to Coalbrookdale having previously brought Dutch workers to Bristol. The Coalbrookdale Company built houses for their workers and kept expanding through the century: in 1782 the parish of Madeley, which contained the works and housing, was home to 2,690 people in 440 houses; by 1793 the figures were 3,677 people in 754 houses. John Wilkinson's works at Bradley, Staffordshire brought in workers from South Wales and Shropshire, swelling the population from 3,000 in 1780 to 12,000 in 1821. In the mid-eighteenth century workers moved from these early ironworks in the Midlands to the Carron Ironworks at Falkirk, which became the largest smelting plant in Europe, and in 1784 Richard Arkwright invited workers from Perth to join him in Derbyshire the following year. The *Derby Mercury* recorded the result:

A few Days since, between 40 and 50 North Britons, with Bagpipes and other music playing, arrived at Cromford, near Matlock-Bath, from Perth, in Scotland. These industrious Fellows left that place on account of the Scarcity of Work, were taken into the Service of Richard Arkwright, Esq. in his Cotton Mills and other extensive works, entered into Present pay, and provided with good Quarters. They appeared highly pleased with the Reception they met with, and had a Dance in the Evening to congratulate each other on the Performance of so long a Journey.'[5]

The specialisation of work also laid the ground for the factory system as it enabled at least one household member to devote all their waking hours to paid employment – in fact the early factories were unattractive to many workers precisely because they were so demanding. Nevertheless, there were enough families who had either already become specialist wage earners, or who were willing to give it a try, or who needed the money, to make the system work.

Specialisation utterly changed the nature but also the meaning of work; people in certain crafts had previously identified themselves through their work, but now virtually everyone did that. The new mechanised economy exploited this change and built a society that catered for the needs of workers who would be enclosed in mills and factories for twelve hours a day. Towns were remodelled with factories and housing placed cheek by jowl; transport systems were reconfigured; shops, amusements, parks, holiday resorts were all brought into being to fit around the new ways of working. And, eventually, the bringing together of workers would lead to an alteration in the political, as well as the urban, landscape of Britain.

New attitudes to work provoked a less tolerant view of others and their place in society. While the pre-industrial world had seen the state as an organic whole in which each should be valued and cared for, this turned into a belief that each should make their contribution. Individual dynamism was the key to success in life and for the whole economy; each should look to himself and the nation should not be supporting those who could not help themselves. The notion that the poor were not simply people who had fallen on hard times but were different from others was spelled out by the economist and writer Joseph Townsend in his 1786 *Dissertation on the Poor Laws*: 'The poor know little of the motives which stimulate the higher ranks to action – pride, honour and ambition. In general it is only hunger which can spur and goad them on to labour.'[6]

The changing attitudes could only come about once it was possible to separate out the working and non-working; while households had worked together this distinction did not exist, but once paid employment dominated, then non-working people were seen as a burden rather than a potential source of wealth production.

Factories provide the abiding image of the Industrial Revolution, and while they remained a small part of British production until the middle of the nineteenth century, their influence was profound and long-lasting.[7] Textile mills in particular provided a new model of how productive work could be organised. Mechanised machinery within a large factory gave astonishing gains in productivity over hand-operated devices in small workshops: one large spinning mule, powered by steam and staffed by half a dozen overseers, could produce as much thread as several thousand hand-spinners, and of better quality, while a single steam engine could power a dozen mules or several hundred looms. The economic case for more factories grew so persuasive that factories became the central element in a new kind of society in which work, communities, towns, roads, railways and the entire geography of Britain and the lives of its citizens began to be organised to answer their demands.

While the word factory had been used for centuries to mean a collective place of productive work, the modern sense developed as a manufactory comprising a variety of devices all powered by a single source. The first purpose-built large-scale factory was a silk-spinning mill founded by Thomas Cotchet in Derby in 1704, swiftly followed by another built by the Lombe brothers in 1721. The latter was five storeys and seventeen metres high, thirty-three metres long and twelve metres wide.[8] Lewis Paul and John Wyatt built spinning factories powered by waterwheels in Birmingham in 1741 and Northampton a year later, though we know little about their construction. Though a few silk mills followed the Lombes' example, the great age of factories came with the mechanisation of cotton spinning in the 1770s and 1780s.

The textile factory came about in two ways: first the gradual combining of individual workers in shared spaces; and secondly through the giant step made by Richard Arkwright. Around Manchester in particular, carders, spinners and weavers began to join forces with their colleagues, or even hire other workers, and move their work from their homes into converted barns, mills and workshops. These small workshop-cum-factories were private concerns and left few records of their existence except when they came up for sale: a building sold in Heaton Norris in Lancashire in 1780 housed thirteen spinning jennies of up to 120 spindles each, seven looms, three carding machines, twenty slubbers' wheels (for making the rovings used to spin from) and various other items; a building in Altrincham, Cheshire was advertised for sale in the *Manchester Mercury* in 1782 as being 'four Stories high, with a Cellar under, and containing on the Inside, 46 feet in length, and 25 feet in breadth, laid out in proper Rooms and Apartments, for the Spinning, Carding and manufacturing Cotton'. The building came with a warehouse, a waterwheel and an acre of land.[9] From roughly 1780 to 1810 so-called jenny shops and small mills proliferated. But people with access to capital soon began to see how putting spinning machines and looms into large powered sites and hiring labour to run them, could bring decent profits. In economic terms the textile factories were a development of the putting-out system – instead of clothiers taking raw materials to the workers, they brought the spinners and weavers to the machines. The advantages were clear, since in a factory the machinery could be kept safe and the workers could be regulated and supervised.

While these developments were under way in and around Manchester, in the early 1770s Richard Arkwright showed that it was possible to construct a purpose-built factory, install a single power source, equip it with cotton-spinning machinery, hire, train and in some cases house and feed a workforce, and still make a handsome profit. The coordination of separate tasks and processes is perhaps the area of the factory which is easiest ignored, and yet most crucial. Arkwright and his successors had to ensure that each stage was completed effectively without causing either a pile-up of materials through going too quickly, or a bottleneck through working too slowly. He also needed his workers to be flexible and to understand the need for an effective throughput, while keeping them focussed on single tasks when necessary. In all of this the workers themselves played a key role. The system did place them in dangerous situations, but it also revealed their adaptability to changes in conditions and technical innovations.[10] A lot of factory work was monotonous and some was dangerous, but mechanisation also led to the emergence of the technically ingenious industrial working class, many of whom took enormous pride in their ability to master the needs of increasingly complex machinery.

Powered machinery: Mechanisation spread through craft industries as devices, like this wheel-cutting machine, were converted from manual to steam power.

Other factory owners not only modelled their textile mills on Arkwright's Cromford system, they also used his machinery under licence. The converted workshop soon gave way to the purpose-built factory. However, by the late 1780s textile factory owners began to free themselves from the Arkwright system in two ways. First they successfully challenged his patents, and second they began to install steam engines rather than waterwheels as their central power source. Factories could now be built near to transport to take finished goods out, and, crucially, near to centres of population. Factory owners had no need to follow Arkwright, Strutt and David Dale in building settlements for workers, they simply built their factories in existing towns, which duly expanded to house the workers. Britain's geography began to be remodelled around the needs of these new producers of wealth.

The momentum of factories was remorseless as inventors devised and adapted machinery to fit within the factory system. The powered loom is a stark example: in 1806 the cotton industry employed 90,000 factory workers and 184,000 hand-loom weavers; by 1820 there were 126,000 factory workers and the number of hand-loom weavers had grown to 240,000; but by 1850 as mechanised looms spread there were 331,000 factory workers and 43,000 hand-loom weavers; and by 1862 there were 452,000 factory workers and just 3,000 hand-loom weavers – hand-weaving had virtually disappeared. The overall growth of cotton mills followed a similar path; in 1782 there were two cotton mills in the Manchester area; by 1830 there were ninety-nine, and by 1835 there were 1,262 cotton mills in the UK, 683 of them in Lancashire. By 1837 the Factory Inspector had registered a total of 4,283 mills under the 1833 Factory Act.[11]

A reference-book entry for 1812 shows that the template for the cotton-spinning factory was by then well established:

A large cotton mill is generally a building of five or six stories high: the two lowest are usually for the spinning frames, if they are for water twist, because of the great weight and vibration caused by these machines. The third and fourth floors contain the carding, drawing and roving machines. The fifth storey is appropriated to the reeling, doubling, twisting, and other operations performed on the finished thread. The sixth, which is usually the roof, is for the batting machine, or opening machine, and for the cotton pickers, who for a large mill are very numerous.[12]

Arkwright's Cromford mills, which are still standing, were dwarfed by their later imitators. In 1823 Richard Guest wrote of 'Those vast brick edifices in the vicinity of all the great manufacturing towns of south Lancashire, towering to the height of 70 or 80 feet, which strike the attention and excite the curiosity of the traveller, now performs labours which formerly employed whole villages.'[13] The Orrell mill in Stockport, built in 1834, was seven storeys high, and contained more than 150,000 spindles driven by two 80 h.p. engines and complete with a lift or hoist system to move goods and people between floors.

The wool trade eventually followed cotton and the towns of Yorkshire's West Riding began to sprout the same great mills and expanding towns as Lancashire. The population district of Huddersfield, for example, had grown to 108,000 when the journalist and author Angus Reach reported in 1850: 'The population of Huddersfield and the surrounding districts are almost entirely engaged in the manufacture of wool . . . The town has sprung up almost entirely within the last sixty years. Previous to that time it was but an insignificant cluster of irregularly built lanes.' Bradford had also grown from 'a mere cluster of huts: now the district of which it is the heart contains upwards of 132,000 inhabitants'.[14]

The change in work patterns and in attitudes to work also had profound effects on the British family and society. While specialisation had begun the process of change, the factory system and the mechanisation of productive work led to a complete recasting of people's roles. Factories began by employing large numbers of women and children. Factory owners preferred women to men;

they could pay them less, they were less likely to be rebellious and they were nimble-fingered in dealing with fine cotton thread. But during the early nineteenth century it became less acceptable for mature, married women to work in factories. The Victorian ideal of the domestic family saw work for women as a pre-marriage phase, and older working women became objects of scorn or pity.[15] The increasing survival of children beyond infancy meant that women were needed at home and the respectable middle-class home-keeper was then contrasted with the unrespectable 'factory girl'. These were a new social phenomenon – financially independent and out to enjoy urban life, they were frowned on by Victorian society and considered unsuitable as potential brides. Mary Merryweather, a Quaker philanthropist and nurse, was hired in the early nineteenth century to help the girls in the Courtauld factories. She found them too eager to marry, unsteady and idle, and lacking in sanitation. Though championing women's rights in general, she described them as 'coarse, noisy girls, with no womanly reserve or modesty'. Nevertheless the textile industry relied on young women to make up the major part of its workforce – in 1850 Angus Reach recorded woollen mills in Halifax employing ten women for every man.[16]

While changes in employment disadvantaged married women, the horrific treatment of children is the darkest chapter in the early industrialisation of Britain. First-hand evidence to parliamentary commissioners, the testimony of inspectors and campaigners, and the portrayals of child paupers in the pages of Dickens, Kingsley and others have left us with a body of deeply disturbing evidence. While we need to set these stories within their historical context, we should never lose sight of the wilful cruelty and neglect that was visited on the helpless and the ease with which it was justified.

The background to child labour in factories was the huge increase in the numbers of British children – taking England alone, the juvenile population increased from roughly 2 million in 1750 to 4.5 million in 1821.[17] This rapid increase meant that there were many more families with a large number of children and more mouths to feed. In the early industrial period the poorest families were the most likely to send children out to work, but this pattern was complicated by individual family choices: the presence of younger children, for example, meant the older children would have to go out to work; and even well-paid families in certain trades were eager to get their children into work. Miners' children could earn good wages working underground – in 1752 John Brabbon earned £19 a week as a coal-hewer while his ten-year-old son brought in almost £10 a week as a pony-driver, both at Whickam colliery in Northumberland; and in 1841 a Durham colliery manager said his miners were 'very anxious, and very dissatisfied if we do not take the children'.[18] Parents often lied about their children's ages, while older children falsely obtained working certificates for their younger siblings.[19]

While some families chose, or were forced by circumstance, to send their children to work, the worst exploitation came through use of so-called pauper or parish apprentices. A mill-owner could make a one-off payment of £5 to a workhouse overseer, provide a set of clothes and essentially take ownership of a child pauper. Thousands of children were brought from workhouses in cities and towns to mills often hundreds of miles away, where they were given bed and food in return for work. A 1757 law allowed apprentices the right of settlement in any parish after forty days' residence, which had the effect of dramatically increasing the number of poor children taken out of London to work in Lancashire mills and as domestic help in the booming cities of the north. In 1795 Dr John Aikin expressed his concerns: 'In these [factories] children of a very tender age are employed; many of them collected from the workhouses in London and Westminster, and transported in crowds, as apprentices to masters resident many hundreds of miles distant, where they serve unknown, unprotected, and forgotten by those to whose care nature or the laws had consigned them.'[20]

This process was not confined to Lancashire; Robert Owen took over the works at New Lanark from his father-in-law David Dale in 1799:

. . . at that period I found there were 500 children, who had been taken from poor-houses, chiefly in Edinburgh, and these children were generally from the age of 5 and 6, to 7 and 8. The hours of work at that time were 13, inclusive of meal times, and an hour and a half was allowed for meals . . . their limbs were very generally deformed, their growth was stunted, and, although one of the best schoolmasters upon the old plan was engaged to instruct those children regularly every night, in general they made very slow progress.'[21]

Robert Blincoe, a one-time pauper apprentice, later gave some details of life at the Litton mill in Derbyshire: 'Palfry, the Smith, had the task of riveting irons upon any of the apprentices, whom the masters ordered, and those were much like the irons usually put upon felons. Even young women, if suspected of intending to run away, had irons riveted on their ancles, and reaching by long links and rings up to the hips, and in these they were compelled to walk to and from the mill to work and to sleep.'[22]

In 1832 Elizabeth Bentley, a doffer at a wool mill in Leeds from the age of six, described one method of discipline: 'I have seen the overlooker go to the top end of the room, where the little girls hug the can to the backminders; he has taken a strap, and a whistle in his mouth, and sometimes he has got a chain and chained them, and strapped them all down the room.'[23]

In 1810 two Manchester JPs inspected the Merryweather Weaving Factory in Ancoats, Manchester:

. . . we found the Rooms in general tolerable, but crowded with too many Looms; that there were no Rules put up in this Factory . . . The Potatoes for Dinner were boiling with the Skins on, in a State of Great Dirtiness, and Eight Cow Heads boiling in another Pot for Dinner; a great Portion of the Food we were told was of a liquid Nature; the Privies were too offensive to be approached by us; some of the Apprentices complained of being overworked.'[24]

When mills closed down or were short of work, mill-owners often advertised groups of apprentices 'To be disposed of' to anyone who would take them. In 1816 the transportation of parish apprentices was limited to forty miles and their use in factories generally declined.[25] This mirrored the general decrease in the use of children, which came partly through technology – the piecers who tied up broken thread, for example, became redundant once this could be done automatically – and partly through changes in social attitudes. There were regular factory Acts through the nineteenth century but legislation tended to echo the changing realities rather than lead the way, while small workshops and manufactories, potteries and match-making factories were unregulated before 1870, and child chimney sweeps were not prohibited until 1875.

Aside from factories the most disturbing workplaces for children were coal mines. Children had worked in mines for centuries but the huge demand for coal made their situation worse. Five-year-old children worked as trappers, sitting in the dark all day to open ventilation doors, before graduating to pony-drivers and eventually coal-face workers. In the pits of West Yorkshire and Lancashire the seams were too narrow to use ponies, so the coal was hauled from the face to the shaft by children. A horrific incident at the Silkstone colliery in Bradford in 1838, in which rainwater flooded a shaft, saw twenty-six children drowned. The resulting Royal Commission into child labour in mines heard from Patience Kershaw: 'I hurry in the clothes I have now got on, trousers and ragged jacket. The bald place on my head is made by thrusting the corves. I hurry the corves a mile or more underground and back; they weigh 3 cwt. I hurry eleven hours a day. I wear a belt and chain at the workings to get the corves out. The getter that I work for sometimes beat me if I am not quick enough.' One commissioner reported: 'When a child has to drag a carriage loaded with coals through a passage not more than eighteen inches in height some ingenuity is required to get his body and the carriage through the narrow space. In some pits I have had to creep on my hands and knees, the height being barely twenty inches, and then have gone still lower on my breast, and crawled like a turtle.'[26] The children often worked in a knee-deep sludge of water and coal dust and sometimes had to crawl on inclines of one in three. The Mines and Collieries Act of 1842 outlawed the use of all girls and boys under ten in underground working; for once legislation was ahead of practice.

Various factory Acts prescribed education for children but without saying how this was to be gained. Nevertheless industrialisation began the creation of the modern idea of childhood, and the transition from dependency to adulthood, as a time of learning rather than working. While the earliest factories depended on child labour, this era was short-lived. Textile mills relocated to towns and cities, technology improved, skills levels increased and the demand for child labour shrank. As adult wages improved people did not need to send their children out to work.

While children were gradually eased out of the industrial workplace, conditions for all workers remained difficult and dangerous. The finest cotton threads stuck together if the temperature fell below 24°C so the spinners kept the heat levels high. Lack of ventilation allowed infectious diseases to spread and this, combined with the noise from the machinery and the open moving parts, made work uncomfortable and potentially dangerous.

The structure of the factory, with its shop-floors, overseers, managers and owners, gave birth to and reflected the class structure of society. The early factory owners emerged under the old dispensation and became, either by default or intention, the lords of their industrial manors. Building a mill in a small town or village, employing local and immigrant workers, and accumulating wealth and social standing made these industrial pioneers into patriarchs who ruled their empires from on high. Factories needed their workers to attend regularly and work continuously. Owners like the Strutts were typical in holding back one-sixth of wages, which would then be paid quarterly in reward for good behaviour. They drew up a book of punishable offences including: 'Being absent without leave; Going to Derby Fair; Absent due to drink; stealing thread; Stealing candles or oil; Wasting yarn; neglecting cleaning and oiling; tying bad knots.' From the offences committed it is clear that there were occasional high spirits among the apprentices: 'Riding on each other's backs; Striking T Ride on the nose; Throwing tea at Josh Bridworth; Using ill language; Throwing water on Ann Gregory very frequently.'[27] These employees had not, in general, broken any law but their employers assumed the right to punish them.

The most successful early industrialists like Arkwright, Boulton, Strutt and Wedgwood treated their apprentices and other workers with firmness and decency. Young people were made to work hard but many were trained in their trade, with Boulton, for example, also providing instruction in the arts of drawing and design. He even started an insurance scheme for workers, one of the first in the world, to cover sickness, injury or death. Wedgwood imposed severe rules against lateness, drunkenness and misbehaviour, usually the loss of hours and pay; he was the first to introduce time cards and a clock.

However well or badly workers were treated, the factory saw the beginnings of an industrial class system with the owners and workers on either side of an unbridgeable social divide. While in previous times an apprentice would aspire to become a master, such a path was to become increasingly difficult. Instead a middle class emerged that was quite separate from shop-floor workers, and as the century progressed members of each social class had, at best, nothing to do with each other, and at worst a mutual contempt.

A new type of society emerged as the factories offered stability and wages in return for workers keeping regular hours, obeying sets of rules, and working at new levels of intensity. In effect people traded the insecurity, continual near-poverty, and relative freedom of low-level working for secure, better-paid, more highly controlled employment. Society itself became much more controlling, regulated and disapproving of those, such as the poor and dissolute, who did not conform to its standards and requirements. In return Victorian society offered a degree of widespread material well-being that, fragile though it may look to us, was beyond the experience of any previous human society. The Victorian age also saw the separation of the domestic sphere from the public sphere, the home from the workplace. This was the culmination of the change from the self-sufficient household of earlier times; now the ideal household comprised a man out at work, a woman as home-maker and children in education.

The huge upheaval brought on by industrialisation inevitably led to social unrest. The most serious threat to the cotton industry came in 1779, when Arkwright's new mill at Chorley was destroyed, along with nine other local mills (see p. 199). There were fears of a general insurrection and the army had to intervene, but disruption did not lead to full-blown revolution. In fact the rioters of 1779 argued that they were on the side of the law since, by throwing people out of work, the machines would ruin the country. In 1780 the Lancashire Court of Quarter Sessions gave a historic judgement in favour of the new machines, declaring:

> that the invention and introduction of the machines for carding, roving, spinning and twisting cotton has been of the greatest utility to this country by the extension and improvement of the cotton manufacturers and the affording labour and subsistence to the industrious poor . . . that it is impossible to restrain the force of ingenuity where employed in the improvement of manufactures . . . that if the legislature was to prevent the exercise of them in this kingdom, it would tend to establish them in foreign country's, which would be highly detrimental to the trade of this country.

While violent protests against machines continued, the 1780 ruling marked the point where new machinery, and innovation in general, was supported by law. This seems a logical or even inevitable part

Atrocious Murder

'On Tuesday evening last, about half past six o'clock, as Mr WILLIAM HORSFALL, a very extensive Woollen Manufacturer, at Marsden, about seven miles from Huddersfield, was returning from the market at that place, he was assassinated on the public road, on Crossland Moor:

'The circumstances, as stated to us by an eyewitness of this most barbarous Murder are these:– Mr Horsfall and a Manufacturer, of the name of Eastwood, had left Huddersfield together, and at a short distance before they came to the fatal spot, Mr Eastwood stopped to water his horse, while Mr Horsfall rode leisurely along the road; soon after he had passed the Warren Inn, a distance of about a mile and a half from Huddersfield, and on the Manchester road, four men, each armed with a horse pistol, appeared in a small plantation, and placed the barrels of their pistols in appertures in the wall, apparently prepared for that purpose; the muzzle of two of these pieces Mr Horsfall distinctly saw, but before he had time to extricate himself from his perilous situation, they all four fired, and inflicted four wounds in the left side of their victim, who instantly fell from his horse, and the blood flowed from the wounds in torrents. A number of passengers both horse and foot rushed almost instantly to the spot, and, after disentangling his foot from the stirrup, he was with some difficulty got to the inn.'[28]

William Horsfall, who died of his wounds, was a virulent anti-Luddite who became a noted target of activists. On 8 January three men were hanged for his murder. The Horsfall case became notorious as people were appalled by the murder, and the authorities became more assiduous in their quashing of Luddite dissent.

of industrialisation, but we should remember that patent laws and guild regulations had, for centuries, made illegal devices that threatened livelihoods. The world had turned.

The most notable organised rebellion came from the Luddites who operated in Nottingham, West Yorkshire and Lancashire in 1811 and 1812. A letter to a Huddersfield mill-owner in March 1812 was typical:

> Information has just been given that you are a holder of those detestable Shearing Frames and I . . . give you fair Warning to pull them down . . . If they are not taken down by the end of next week, I will detach one of my Lieutenants with at least 300 men to destroy them [and burn] your Buildings down to Ashes and if you have the Impudence to fire upon any of my Men, they have orders to murder you, & burn all your housing.[29]

William Felkin recorded his experience as a special constable aged seventeen chasing a Luddite across Nottingham rooftops in 1811:

> . . . who entered a house alone in Rutland Street, Nottingham, one evening; proceeded up the stairs and smashed the material parts of a frame in a minute or two . . . threw himself on the roof; passing along others he saw in the dim light that the earth had been lately turned up in a garden below, and leaped from the eaves of a three-storey house upon it. The frame-breaker quietly passed through a kitchen where a family were at table, and escaped. In a few minutes the shouts of a sympathising crowd were heard at New Radford, half a mile from the scene of the adventure.[30]

William Cobbett, who had been sympathetic to the protest of the Luddites but who believed destruction of machinery was no answer, wrote 'A Letter to the Luddites': 'By machines mankind are able to do that which their own bodily powers would never effect to the same extent. Machines are the product of the *mind* of man; and their existence distinguishes the civilised man from the savage.'[31] The murder of William Horsfall by four Luddites in 1812 (see capsule text p.330) was a shock to the nation; seventeen Luddites were hanged at York in 1813 and many more transported and, while protests continued, the movement dwindled.

Workers did not simply get together to wreck machinery; mills and large-scale mines employed large numbers of workers, and gave the possibility of collective action in support of better pay. In 1792 local dignitary Henry Blundell became concerned about miners in Wigan who had gathered 'to demand an extravagant advance in wages. They have given only til tomorrow at 3 o'clock to consider of it and if their demand is not complied with, they threaten to destroy the Works by pulling up the engines, throwing down the wheels and filling up the pits.'[32] The authorities soon realised that large numbers of workers coming together gave potential for political subversion, and industrial workers began to be seen as a potentially dangerous class of people. The 1799 and 1800 Combination Acts made it illegal for workers to combine to press for improvements in pay or conditions. The Acts were repealed in 1824 but a new Act in 1825 restricted trades unions to bargaining over pay and conditions.

It is clear that the shock of industrialisation caused enormous hardship for many and it took decades to put right the abuses while holding on to the gains. But over time, and in an echo of the old guild system, workers created their own forms of mutual support including Friendly Societies, unions, federations and cooperatives. The change to an industrial economy powered by coal was far from smooth; it plunged working people into an era of rapid change that made many worse off, while also losing control of their own destinies. In the long run it freed the nation from fear of want, but the long run was a long time coming for those at the bottom. Protests to halt innovation were doomed to fail, but workers were able to organise successfully to bring about improvements in conditions. By the late nineteenth century the trade unions went so far as to form their own political party, eventually winning the power to govern the country. This was only possible because industrialisation brought workers together where they could fight for their common concerns.

24. Life in the Industrial City

Along with the treatment of children in factories, the appalling living conditions in early industrial cities remain central in our collective memory of industrialisation. There are enough accounts of the filth, overcrowding and destitution experienced in these cities to fill this volume and several more. Many writers focussed on endemic diseases: 'In one place we found a whole street following the course of a ditch, because in this way deeper cellars could be secured without the cost of digging, cellars not for storing wares or rubbish, but for the dwellings of human beings. Not one house of this street escaped the cholera.'[1]

> The lodging homes, near the extremities of the town, produce many fevers, not only by want of cleanliness and air, but by receiving the most offensive objects into beds, which never seem to undergo any attempts towards cleaning them, from their first purchase till they rot under their tenants . . . The horror of those houses cannot easily be described; a lodger fresh from the country often lies down in a bed filled with infection by its last tenant, or from which the corpse of a victim to fever has only been removed a few hours before.[2]

In 1835 Alexis de Tocqueville gave his impression of Manchester: 'A sort of black smoke covers the city. The sun seen through it is a disc without rays. Under this half-daylight 300,000 human beings are ceaselessly at work.'[3] And Friedrich Engels described housing in the central London district of St Giles: 'The houses are occupied from cellar to garret, filthy within and without, and their appearance is such that no human being could possibly wish to live in them. But all this is nothing in comparison with the dwellings in the narrow courts and alleys between the streets, entered by covered passages between the houses, in which the filth and tottering ruin surpass all description.'[4]

In the mid-nineteenth century Angus Reach visited the wool towns of the West Riding: 'Conceive acre on acre of closely built and thickly peopled ground, without a paving stone upon the surface or an inch of sewer beneath, a deep trodden-churned slough of mud forming the only thoroughfares . . . Conceive, in short, a whole district to which the above description rigidly and truthfully applies and you will, I am sorry to say, have a fair idea of what constitutes a large proportion of the operative part of Leeds.'[5]

And so on and on. A picture of wretchedness continues as if a malign force of nature was let loose, with everyone and anyone helpless to do anything that would help. The result of the brilliant, ground-breaking innovations of Newcomen, Hargreaves, Cort, Watt and Trevithick was, it seems, to bring humanity into a catastrophically worse state of existence. Was this what industrialisation was to offer the world?

Why then did this happen; why did the emergence of industry based on steam power lead to such a degradation of urban life? The underlying force was the unprecedented increase in population, but we also need to put life in industrial cities into its historical context. Cities were continually overwhelmed by sheer numbers of inhabitants but, from the late seventeenth century onwards, people began to understand the problems of urban life and to take measures to overcome them. This was a historic change from the fatalism of earlier times and led eventually to cities coping adequately and even triumphantly with vast populations. The first clue to this change lies in the contemporary accounts. The lack of clean water, fresh air, light, the disposal of sewage, clean bedding, proper housing and decent food were all pointed out because they were important to human health. This all seems like common sense but writers, physicians and campaigners were pointing out the lack of these basic requirements precisely because they had not previously been considered. The call for clean bedding, for example, went against an old belief that covering the sick in clean linen would draw out their vital energies, while the build-up of waste and filth in yards and alleys was previously disregarded. In the early sixteenth century the Dutch writer Erasmus wrote to Cardinal Wolsey about the reasons the English suffered from the sweating sickness and bouts of plague: 'The floors are commonly of clay, strewed with rushes, which are occasionally renewed, but underneath lies unmolested, an ancient collection of beer, grease, fragments of fish, spittle, the excrement of dogs and cats and everything that is nasty.'[6]

The growing towns and cities of the late eighteenth century carried over habits that were unchanged for centuries: a gutter running down the street would act as a water supply *and* sewer; narrow streets cut off supplies of air and light; animals were slaughtered in the streets and timber houses were continually vulnerable to fire. Diseases that we associate with the tropics, including cholera, typhus and plague, were rife, and malaria was endemic in areas of Britain. But as the cities grew, so too did the realisation of the dangers of open sewers, lack of air and light, filthy clothing and foul water. The old recourse to seeing sickness and death as the will of God, or simply part of nature, gave way to a desire to know practical cause and effect.[7] The impulse to improve urban conditions was given impetus by the Great Fire of London in 1666, after which the 13,200 wooden houses that had burnt down were replaced by 9,000 brick dwellings. The London Rebuilding Act of 1667 formalised this rule and, at the same time, alleys were cleared and streets widened. In 1766 an Improvement Act saw the Fleet ditch covered in, drains and sewers installed and streets paved with large stones; the City of London was expanded, as was Westminster, so that there was more room between streets. William Hutton, visiting from Birmingham in 1783, wrote 'the stranger will be astonished at the improvements which have been introduced in the last 35 years and how money could be procured to complete them . . . every street and passage in the whole city, and its environs, has been paved in one regular and convenient stile'.[8]

Between 1785 and 1800 Parliament passed 211 Acts allowing different bodies to raise taxes for paving and other parochial improvements. In 1776 a Street Improvement Act was passed for Manchester: while in 1775 Methodist minister John Clayton wrote that the streets of Manchester were 'no better than a common dunghill . . . our very churchyards are profaned with filth', by 1786 a Mr Henry reported to the Manchester Lit and Phil that 'Within these few years also the great alterations that have been made in the town by widening and providing for the ventilation of the streets, together with the commodiousness of our modern houses etc., may have contributed to restrain the increased mortality which might otherwise have been apprehended from its enlargement.'[9]

As fast as improvements could be made, there were more people to accommodate. Nevertheless in 1780 the quantity and quality of Manchester's water supply was increased, and in 1791 an Act of Parliament granted funds and gave authority for the lighting and policing of the town, including a twice-weekly removal of waste and cleaning of the streets. In 1816 a water company began supplying piped water through iron pipes (for those who could afford to be connected). In the 1820s Manchester gained gas street lights. In 1786 an Improvement Act granted Liverpool £150,000 to widen its streets; in this great port the wealthy Corporation lavished money on public buildings but was tardy in improving the living conditions of its people, including the notorious cellar dwellings. Only in the mid-nineteenth century did Liverpool gain a decent clean water supply. Improvements, it seemed, depended on local authorities seeking powers to act. Birmingham was more enlightened; here an Act of 1769 allowed the widening of the streets and gave permission for a levy to be raised for scavenging the streets of waste; further powers were granted in 1773 and 1780. By the 1790s Bristol was similarly improved, with the streets cleaned twice a week and further wooden buildings prohibited.

The curse of malaria was finally removed from Portsmouth when the town was paved and drained in 1769 with similar actions and effects in nearby Southsea in 1793. Locks on the River Ouse enabled York's sewage to be washed away where 'Before the river was frequently very low, leaving a quantity of sludge and dirt in the very heart of the city, also the filth of the common sewers which it was unable to wash away [whereas now] the lock kept the river high, broad and spacious.'[10]

Medieval towns were built on or near natural supplies of water, but, as they expanded, systems of cisterns, pumps and pipes had to be installed. New houses with large windows gradually replaced wooden hovels; coal-fired heating allowed warmth, better cooked food, hot water for washing, and therefore clean clothing. This may not have been sophisticated medicine but it was certainly a better approach than the bloodletting, patent cures and spa waters that had preceded it.

As people understood the virtues of well-built houses and clean streets, they reported the squalid conditions of the shanty towns, but they also gave praise where it was due.

By the mid-nineteenth century, in some districts at least, building had caught up with population increase: 'The houses inhabited by the factory hands of Huddersfield consist in most cases of a large parlour-kitchen opening from the street, with a cellar beneath it, and either two small bedrooms or one large one above. In some instances a scullery is added to the main apartment . . . and a plentiful supply of water is in general conducted into every house.'[11]

By the standards of modern Europe early industrial towns were overcrowded, smoky, and vulnerable to infectious disease, but they were no longer simply carrying on where medieval towns had left off. People understood the need to have good living conditions, and urban authorities tried, for the most part, to bring these about. They were, though, victims of their own success; better living conditions brought more people and more potential over-crowding and this could never be completely solved, only amelio-rated. Nevertheless there was a deeply significant alteration in human conception; as one historian has put it: 'Cleanliness may be next to godliness but it is often its rival; we have built drains instead of cathedrals.'[12]

One effect of larger cities was the separation of the social classes. In late medieval towns the wealthy had to live cheek by jowl with the poor, often sharing the same streets, churches and public spaces in something of a jumble. But the expansion of towns allowed districts to become separated, particularly into working-class and middle-class districts.

Industrial towns were dirty and unhealthy, but city life was liberating and exciting; you could even, within limits, choose your employer; you might be able to buy an education through evening classes, and you could certainly find entertainment and compan-ionship. And while towns might have seemed soulless places to begin with, a sense of community developed around workplaces, Friendly Societies, chapels and later trade unions, as well as neigh-bourhoods. Private space was more confined in cities but public space was more available to all. As cities improved, parks, gardens, squares, meeting rooms, inns and shops became places of social interaction and enrichment. The industrial city gradually learned how to serve its people.

The Population Paradox

The sustained increase in the world's population from around 1 billion in 1800 to 6.5 billion today began in the industrial towns and cities of Britain. The population of England in 1750 was 5.7 million, a 10 per cent increase over the previous century, but the next fifty years saw an increase of over 50 per cent to 8.6 million, while the following fifty years saw a doubling to take the population to 16.7 million by 1851. From 1750 onwards Britain appeared to break out of the 'natural' limits to population growth predicted by Malthus and population increase became sustainable over the long term. For the first time in history an increase in population was generated from within a long-existing economy and was sustained. The process clearly began at the same time as the Industrial Revolution, but how did it come about and how was it connected to industrialisation?

The growth of urban centres, initially aided by migration of people from the countryside, rapidly became self-sustaining. Towns and cities grew because more people were being born and slightly fewer people were dying prematurely.[13] More children were being born because women were marrying earlier and because the proportion of stillbirths went through a dramatic decrease. In the seventeenth and early eighteenth centuries, England's estimated stillbirth rate was around 80 to 90 per 1,000 births; by the mid-nineteenth century this had fallen to around 40 per 1,000.[14] Close analysis of the reasons for infant mortality presents another factor. The proportion of infants who died from so-called endogenous factors – i.e. weakness and frailty at birth – also fell from 88 per 1,000 in the late seventeenth century to 33 per 1,000 in 1825–37; however, infant deaths from so-called exogenous factors – i.e. disease – rose from 88 to 111 per 1,000 over the same period.[15] Meanwhile average life expectancy increased by about three years to 40.8 years from 1800 to 1831; by 1871 it had only reached 41.3 years.

What do these figures tell us? Most importantly, the number of babies being born in a healthy condition was increasing and this increase was enough to overcome the rise in childhood diseases, while the small increase in life expectancy was a minor factor.[16] So, why did this happen and why did the consequent rise in population become sustainable? The overwhelming reason for both was improved nutrition. In the second half of the eighteenth century mothers were eating better and therefore carrying more pregnancies to successful term, while also giving birth to infants with a better chance of immediate survival. However, the population increase did bring about pressures which acted in the opposite direction. Overcrowding in cities was undoubtedly responsible for the rise in infant deaths caused by disease and infection, which also held the average life expectancy down – local figures indicate that life expectancy in some inner cities plunged to as low as twenty-eight years. In that sense a Malthusian limit was coming into play as disease bore down on crowded populations.

Nevertheless the increase in population was sustained over the medium and long term for the same reasons we have seen elsewhere in this book. The increasing use of coal for energy accompanied by notable increases in agricultural productivity allowed Britain to feed a growing population; there were difficulties along the way, but the population increase that began in the late eighteenth century was sustained through the nineteenth century with Britain able to feed millions more people. This remarkable achievement was possible because, as we have seen elsewhere, a coal-powered energy economy freed up more land for food production and, at the same time, vastly increased the productivity per acre by putting energy in the form of fertilisers, transport and machinery into agricultural production.

As well as increasing food production, coal energy allowed living conditions to improve through brick housing, iron bedsteads and bigger glass windows, while steam power brought employment and wages that could be spent on better nutrition and housing. Industrialisation made possible a better life, but the possibilities took time to be realised, and in the meantime people suffered a serious deterioration in living conditions.

Epilogue:
Britain in the 1830s

By the 1830s the British were, with some exceptions, convinced that they had created a new world that was of immense benefit to the country and to humankind. Steam-driven mills, factories and workshops had grown up, employing hundreds of thousands of workers and producing seemingly endless amounts of everything that humanity could possibly need, while the problems of slums and child labour were recognised, if not yet fully addressed. In 1830 Thomas Macaulay declared: 'We might with some plausibility maintain that the people live longer because they are better fed, better lodged, better clothed, and better attended in sickness, and that these improvements are owing to that increase in national wealth which the manufacturing system has produced.'[1]

Fifteen years earlier Patrick Colquhoun had given this paean to British industry:

> It is impossible to contemplate the progress of manufactures in Great Britain within the last thirty years without wonder and astonishment. Its rapidity, particularly since the commencement of the French revolutionary war, exceeds all credibility. The improvement of the steam engines, but above all the facilities afforded to the great branches of the woollen and cotton manufactories by ingenious machinery, invigorated by capital and skill, are beyond all calculation; and as these machines are rendered applicable to silk, linen, hosiery and various other branches, the increased produce, assisted by human labour, is so extensive that it does more than counter-balance the difference between the price of labour in this, and other countries.[2]

And in 1835 Edward Baines pointed to the specific contribution made by the cotton industry: 'Each workman performing, or rather superintending as much work as could have been done by *two or three hundred men* sixty years ago . . . When it is remembered that all these inventions have been made within the last seventy years it must be acknowledged that the cotton mill represents the most striking example of the dominion obtained by human science over the powers of nature, of which modern times can boast.'[3]

The opening of the Liverpool to Manchester railway in September 1830 was perhaps the event that publicly sealed the arrival of the new steam-powered age, but by then the textile and other trades showed that the basic technologies required to convert Britain from an organic to a coal-based economy were in place. Atmospheric steam engines were being superseded by high-pressure engines that could drive locomotives and ships as well as powering factories and pumps; inventors had devised ways of powering almost every aspect of manufacture; iron was cheap and plentiful and was replacing wood and brass in machine components, rail tracks and even ships' hulls.

Britain's first census of 1831 shows that while this process was well under way, it still had a long way to go. Just 10.4 per cent (314,106) of working men over twenty were employed in manufacturing, compared to 32.6 per cent (980,750) working in agriculture, and 32.0 per cent (964,177) in retail trade and handicrafts.[4] Over the following decades steam-powered machinery found its way into more and more trades, and while this took time to work through, by the 1830s the conversion to a mineral-based economy was progressing apace. Crucially, it was clear to inventors, investors and industrialists that continual technical innovations were the key to industrial success.

British inventors of the late eighteenth century were primarily from an artisan background, able to build devices in small workshops and with few resources, and needing little theoretical knowledge to support their practical genius. But the world moved on and further improvements in technology required a more sophisticated theoretical understanding. On the other hand scientists who were traditionally concerned with studying the natural world began to give serious attention to the new forces that industrial technology had unleashed. In 1824 the French scientist Nicolas Sadi Carnot published his *Reflections on the Motive Power of Fire*, which gave birth to the science of thermodynamics, and a basic understanding of this new discipline became essential for all mechanical engineers; by the 1830s Michael Faraday was following up his discovery of electromagnetism to produce both electromagnetic induction and an electric motor. Science and technology were increasingly married to the benefit of both.

Much has been written about Britain's lead in bringing industrialisation to the world, and its subsequent decline as an industrial nation. The dominant pre-industrial culture of the nation was certainly commercial, but it was centred on world trade flowing through London, and was intricately tied up with the established social hierarchy of court and counties. Industrialisation emerged from an entirely different British culture, centred around Nonconformists who had been excluded from the establishment. Once the industrialists were brought into the fold they too succumbed, sending their children to schools and universities where they studied Ovid and Seneca at the expense of Faraday and Carnot. It wasn't all like this of course, and the tradition of British engineering endured for another generation through the likes of Isambard Brunel and Robert Stephenson. Nevertheless the dominant culture was preserved and emulated by the newly empowered. The British middle classes distinguished themselves from those beneath by looking to the disdain of the old aristocracy, rather than the inventiveness of their industrialists, for social guidance. This attitude did not hold in America or Germany, each of whom, by the late nineteenth century, had overtaken Britain.

The central argument of this book is that the Industrial Revolution was, in essence, the transition from an organic economy to an economy based on energy derived from fossil fuels, as well as being the beginning of a sustained period of innovation that has lasted to the present. The importance of that transition will not be lost on readers for whom population growth and climate change represent a potential catastrophe for humankind. Understanding the Industrial Revolution should at least enable us to appreciate the central role that energy holds in every aspect of modern life. Life before industrialisation was, for most people, a continual struggle to survive; without reliable sources of energy we cannot live secure and comfortable lives. Any answer to the twin problems of global resources and climate change must begin with that stark truth.

Notes

Introduction

1   Restoring a balance with nature is now seen as a necessary element in humanity's future; we should be aware that in the past this was achieved by extremely high infant mortality and stillbirth, disease and famine. See Wrigley (2004) Chapter 12, 'Population'. See also Diamond (1997) p. 197 *et seq.*

2   Zinsser (1934) p. 10: 'Civilizations have retreated from the plasmodium of malaria, and armies have crumbled into rabbles under the onslaught of cholera spirilla, or of dysentery and typhoid bacilli. Huge areas have been devastated by the trypanosome that travels on the wings of a tsetse fly, and generations have been harassed by the syphilis of a courtier. War and conquest and that herd existence which is an accompaniment of what we call civilization have merely set the stage for these more powerful agents of human tragedy.' On p. 8 Zinsser argues that in the precarious balance with nature 'man may be defined as a parasite on a vegetable'.

3   See Thomas (1971).

4   Matthias (1983) pp. 1–3. Ashton (1948), Wrigley (1988), Allen (2009), Mokyr (1990) and most scholars of the period discuss this problem from different points of view.

5   For example, Colquhoun (1815) p. 68.

6   This central argument, and the separation of the organic economy supplemented by coal for thermal energy, from the industrial economy which uses coal for mechanical energy, was first proposed by Wrigley (1988). Modern scholarship on the economic history of the Industrial Revolution stems from Wrigley's insight.

Prologue: Britain on the Verge

1   Figures: Allen (2000) pp. 8–9; quoted in Allen (2009) Table 1.1.
2   Figures: Matthias (1983) pp. 87–8, Table IV.
3   See Morriss (2011).
4   Defoe (1726) p. 208.
5   R. Floud & D. N. McCloskey (1981) p. 64.
6   Allen (2009) p. 18.
7   Wrigley (1988) p. 13.
8   Wrigley (1988) p. 50 *et seq.*
9   Wrigley (1988) p. 54 quoting Unger (1984).
10 See Hatcher (1984–93) Vol. 1.
11 DeVries (2008) pp. 92–104.
12 Brown (2011) Chapters 6 and 7.
13 Matthias (1983) pp. 142–3.
14 Walvin (1999) p. xii. The first Atlantic slave voyage was made by Sir John Hawkins in 1562–3; the Society for the Abolition of Slavery was founded in 1787 and slave trading across the Atlantic abolished by Britain and the United States in 1807. Slavery was abolished in the US in 1865 and in Brazil in 1888.
15 Benjamin Franklin, marginalia in *An Inquiry*, Franklin Papers 17, 341–2, quoted in Uglow (2002) pp. 167–8. The exact date of writing and of Franklin's recollections are not known.
16 Allen (2009) pp. 12, 259–62.
17 Allen (2009) pp. 54–5.
18 Thomas (1971) Chapter 14, 'Witchcraft in England: the Crime and its History'.
19 See Richards (1929).
20 Hatcher (1984–93) pp. 419–20.
21 Visit www.glassmaking-in-london.co.uk/ravenscroft.
22 Defoe (1726) pp. 212–13; Ginsburg (1991) p. 53.
23 Each of these four has been given prime importance by a different scholar in recent years. For full discussions of each see Wrigley (1988), Mokyr (1990), De Vries (2008) and Allen (2009).
24 See Humphrey et al. (1998).
25 Mokyr (1990) Chapter 9, 'China and Europe'. By the fourteenth century China had adjustable iron ploughs, seed drills, rakes, harrows, insect and pest control and veterinary medicine; iron production using blast furnaces had been running for nearly 2,000

years; a plethora of devices and materials were used in China that were virtually unknown in Europe, including draw-looms, cotton gins, water-powered trip hammers, water clocks, compasses, cavel-built ships with multiple masts, rudders and buoyancy chambers, porcelain, wheelbarrows, lacquer, crossbows, horse collars, matches, umbrellas, paper, moveable type, and so on. But the arrival of the Ming dynasty in 1368 saw a long period of 'orderly' government. Technical innovation halted and then went into reverse and by 1600 China was not just behind Europe, but behind where it had been 200 years before. Ming China was prosperous and fostered great engineering projects like the Great Wall and the Forbidden City, but there was a technology retreat. Ocean-going ships were no longer built, clocks disappeared, and machines used for reeling silk had disappeared by the eighteenth century.

26 The Albion Mill powered by steam engines was near William Blake's home in London; the 'dark satanic mills' in the poem 'Jerusalem' (written around 1804) may, though, refer to the churches of the established Anglican order which Blake disdained, or even to the megaliths of Britain's pagan past. See Porter (1974) p. 198.

1. The Watershed

1 The opening of the Liverpool to Manchester railway in 1830 was attended by national figures including the prime minister, the Duke of Wellington. This was the symbolic acceptance by the ruling class that industrialisation was of vital importance to the nation.

2. Inventors and Inventing

1 The term proto-industrialisation, coined by Mendels (1972), is widely used to describe these eighteenth-century developments. The word is controversial since it implies a direct line of development to the industrial economy that followed and I have avoided it. For arguments against the concept, see Coleman (1983). See also Matthias (1983) p. 15; Allen (2009) Chapter 5.

2 Mandeville (1714, 1724) quoted in Allen (2009) p. 251.

3 Allen (2009) Table 10.4; see also Mokyr (2002) Chapters 5 and 10.

4 Dutton (1984) pp. 104–8.

5 Triewald (1734) quoted in Rolt (1963) p. 56.

6   See Mokyr (2002) Chapter 10 on obstacles to change.
7   Quoted in Hart (1856).
8   Dr Williams's Centre for Dissenting Studies, Queen Mary, University of London at www.english.qmul.ac.uk/drwilliams.
9   See Whatley (1997).
10 Dutton (1984) pp. 132–40.

3. Navigating the Patent System

1   For patent developments up to 1800 see MacLeod (1988); for developments during the Industrial Revolution see Dutton (1984).

4. Fuelling the Revolution

1   See Hatcher (1984–93) Vol. 1 for exhaustive detail on the pre-industrial development of coal. Figures in this chapter are from Hatcher.
2   Allen (2009) Table 4.1.
3   Addy (1969) pp. 19–20.
4   Defoe (1724) Letter 1, p. 66.
5   Plattes (1634) quoted in Hatcher (1984–93) p. 428.
6   Harrison (1577) Chapter 8.
7   Quoted in Carey (1987) pp. 280–1.
8   Wrigley (1988) pp. 53–5. Readers interested in the analysis of industrialisation through the production and use of energy should read Wrigley (2010).
9   Wrigley (2004) pp. 78–9.
10 Wrigley (1988) p. 79(n), quoting Ubbelohde p. 63.
11 For contemporary illustrations see Addy (1969) pp. 59–61.
12 Davy (1816).

5. Watermills and Wheels

1   Allen (2009) Table 7.1, p. 173.
2   Gimpel (1976) p. 1.
3   See Brown (2011).
4   Addy and Power (1976) p. 27.
5   Fairbairn (1861, 1863). The Catrine Mills and all aspects of water power are covered extensively in Brown (2011).

6. Steam before Newcomen

1 Humphrey et al. (1998).

2 Ramsay's son William wrote of him that James I 'sent into France for my father, who was then there, and made him page of the bedchamber and groom of the privy chamber, and keeper of all his majesties' clocks and watches'. Wm. Ramesay, *Astrologia Restaurata* (1653) p. 28.

3 Published in 1663 as part of 'A Century of the Names and Scantlings of the Marquis of Worcester's Inventions', quoted in Rolt (1963) p. 25.

4 Patent No. 175, awarded to Morland on 14 March 1674.

5 Calendar of State Papers, Domestic, 16 Dec 1682.

6 Desaguliers, *Experimental Philosophy* (1744) quoted in Rolt (1963) p. 39.

7 Switzer (1729) quoted in Rolt (1963) p. 40.

7. The Newcomen Engine

1 See Lidstone (1871).

2 See Rolt (1963) and Preston (2012) for modern biographies of Newcomen; also Stuart (1824) p. 55 *et seq.*

3 Triewald (1734) translated and quoted in Rolt (1963) p. 51.

4 Pole (1844) p. 12.

5 Triewald (1734) translated and quoted in Rolt (1963) p. 61.

6 Ibid. p. 61.

7 Switzer (1729) quoted in Stuart (1824) p. 56.

8 Hutchinson (1794) quoted in Rolt (1963) p. 68.

9 Stukeley (1776) p. 52.

10 Quoted in Kirke (1913).

11 Quoted in Raistrick (1953) p. 135.

12 Rolt (1963) p. 122.

13 *Monthly Chronicle*, Vol. II, p. 169.

14 See Smiles (1861–2) and Skempton (2002).

8. James Watt's Revolution

1 James Watt lacks a full modern biography. Elements of his life have been compiled from his own writings and those of John Robison,

David Hart, John Stuart and others in the eighteenth century and George Williamson in the nineteenth. Fellow Scot Andrew Carnegie weighed in, while H. W. Dickinson's biography dates from 1936 and L. T. C. Rolt's from 1962. His story is told in some detail in Uglow (2002). The papers of James Watt and his family formerly held at his home Doldowlod House (referred to as the Doldowlod Papers) are now at Birmingham Central Library. Selected letters quoted can be found in Tann (1981).

2 Defoe (1724) Letter 12, p. 604 *et seq.*

3 Quoted in Dickinson (1936) p. 18.

4 James Watt, Notebook of Experiments on Steam, Doldowlod Papers.

5 Quoted in Rosen (2010) p. 106.

6 Roebuck to Watt, 30 Oct 1768, quoted in Uglow (2002) p. 133.

7 Sketchley's Birmingham Directory, 1767, quoted in Uglow (2002) p. 17.

8 The different Soho buildings can cause confusion; the Soho Manufactory was built in 1761; the Soho Foundry was built for the production of engines in 1795 by the firm of Boulton & Watt; Soho House was Matthew Boulton's family home from 1766 to 1809.

9 Boulton to Watt, 17 Feb 1769.

10 Watt to William Small, 28 April 1769.

11 Watt to William Small on his thirty-fifth birthday, 19 Jan 1771.

12 Watt to William Small, 11 Dec 1773.

13 William Small to Watt, 5 Feb 1769.

14 Soon after he arrived in Birmingham Watt joined the Lunar Society (they met on the full moon to make it easier to travel home). Members of this famous gathering included Erasmus Darwin, Matthew Boulton, William Small, James Keir, Thomas Day, Richard Lovell Edgeworth, Samuel Galton, Josiah Wedgwood, William Withering, Joseph Priestley, Jonathan Stokes and John Whitehurst. The importance of the group was not just their meetings but their continual correspondence and support for each other. See Uglow (2002).

15 Quoted in Rolt (1962) pp. 63-4. Joseph Harrison was senior mechanic at Boulton & Watt's works at Soho; Isaac Perrins was an independent engine erector.

16 Boswell (1791), Vol. II, p. 459.

17 J. Hornblower Snr, 23 Dec 1776.

18 Addy (1969) pp. 16-17.

NOTES | 353

19 Boulton to Watt, June 1781.

20 Watt to James Watt Jnr, 1808.

21 Watt to Boulton, Sept. 1786.

22 P. Drinkwater to Boulton & Watt, 20 Oct 1791; see Fitton (1989) p. 65.

23 James Watt brought the Berthollet method of producing chlorine to Britain; this was a fundamental process in the chemical industry of the following century.

24 Boulton to Watt, 28 May 1788. The governor had a long practical legacy in engines and other mechanical devices. Its theoretical legacy is even more interesting, since James Clerk Maxwell used its example to explore dynamic feedback systems in his 1868 paper 'On Governors' (Proceedings of the Royal Society, London, pp. 270–83). Natural dynamic feedback is at the heart of analyses of ecosystems.

25 Jonathan Hornblower was the elder son of the Jonathan Hornblower who befriended Watt in Cornwall; the younger son was Josiah.

26 Boulton to Watt, 7 July 1781.

27 Watt to Boulton, late 1782.

9. Richard Trevithick: Steam into Motion

1 See Hodge (1973) for details of Trevithick's life and work.

2 Wilson to Watt, 1784; Rosen (2010) Chapter 12.

3 Ferguson (1980) p. 54.

4 See Bathe (1935).

5 Watt to Boulton, Sept. 1786.

6 Stephen Williams is the passenger; see Burton (2011) p. 70.

7 Hodge (1973) p. 18.

8 Ibid. pp. 20–1.

9 Ibid. p. 21. There is now a Trevithick Trail, which follows the line of the world's first steam locomotive run, just south of Merthyr Tydfil.

10. The Rise of Cotton

1 Figures: Allen (2009) Chapter 8.

2 For history of the wool trade see the following:
Lloyd (2005); Mantoux (1928) pp. 47–74 and throughout; Power (1941); Keen (1968) p. 90 et seq. refers to wool from England, Scotland and Spain being woven in Flanders.

3   See Raistrick (1953a).

4   Harrison (1577).

5   Pepys, *Diaries*, 5 Sept. 1663 and 1 July 1661.

6   Collinges (1675).

7   The parish church of St John's in Halifax has a grave in the south porch, dating from 1150, marked with a pair of croppers' shears; this is the earliest evidence of wool trade in the area.

8   Defoe (1724) Letter 8, p. 495. Shalloon is a lightweight worsted fabric used for coat linings; from the French *chalon*, after Chalons-sur-Marne.

9   See Baines (1985).

10 The cotton trade is detailed in every major work on the Industrial Revolution. See esp. Allen (2009) pp. 182–216; Fitton (1989); Matthias (1983); Berg (1985); Mantoux (1928) pp. 197–271; Power (1969).

11 Roberts (1641) p. 17.

12 Stripes and checks could be woven into the cotton so were not covered by the prohibition on printed cloth.

13 British imports of raw cotton reached 8.2 million kg in 1785 and 360 million kg by the 1850s. See Matthias (1983) Appendix, Table 34.

14 Bamford (1844) p. 1.

15 Radcliffe (1828) p. 65.

16 Kidd (1993) p. 27.

17 Quoted in Aspin (1981) pp. 29–30.

18 Slavery became an issue in the industry when cotton supplies were disrupted during the American Civil War (1861–5). Once Lincoln made his declaration of emancipation, Lancashire cotton workers and many mill-owners publicly supported the Union cause, though the war was harming their trade. See Walvin (1999) for the movement of slaves to the cotton fields of the Deep South.

11. Spinning and Weaving

1   For the history of spinning see Leadbetter (1979).

2   For full details of the mechanisation of spinning see Catling (1970, 1986).

3   Boulton to Watt, August 1781, quoted in Fitton (1989) p. 12.

4   Quoted in Downs (2010) p. 11.

5   Arkwright to Strutt, 2 March 1772, quoted in Fitton (1989) pp. 31–2.

6   Quoted in Catling (1970, 1986) pp. 31–2.

7   Quoted in Catling (1970, 1986) p. 34.
8   For the history of weaving see Benson and Warburton (1986) and Aspin (1981) pp. 19–21.
9   Quoted in Aspin (1981) pp. 19–20.
10   Quoted in Downs (2010) p. 33.
11   For details of Lee's life and work see Harte (1989).
12   For William Gardiner see Felkin (1867).

12. Richard Arkwright: The King of Cotton

1   The definitive modern biography of Arkwright and his son Richard is Fitton (1989).
2   Fitton (1989) p. 12.
3   Fitton (1989) p. 26.
4   Elizabeth Grant, quoted in Fitton (1989) p. 31.
5   Arkwright family papers, quoted in Fitton (1989) p. 28.
6   Quoted in Fitton (1989) p. 28.
7   Quoted in Fitton (1989) p. 30.
8   Letter quoted in full in Fitton (1989) pp. 31–3.
9   Quoted in Fitton (1989) p. 39. The Strutt Collection is in Derby Central Library.
10   Quoted in Fitton (1989) p. 39.
11   John Byng, *The Torrington Diaries 1781–94* (republished 1935), quoted in Fitton (1989) p. 152.
12   The Atholl MSS collection at Blair castle, quoted in Fitton (1989) p. 152.
13   Wedgwood to Thomas Bentley, quoted in Fitton (1989) p. 51.
14   Masson Mill now contains a museum with a collection of working spinning frames, as well as looms and other devices which have been brought from elsewhere.
15   Watt to Joseph Wilkes, 1784, quoted in Fitton (1989) p. 69.
16   Quoted in Fitton (1989) p. 72.
17   Evidence to the Royal Commission of Inquiry into Factories prior to the 1833 Factory Act, quoted in Fitton (1989) p. 153.
18   T. Rees, *The Cyclopædia; or, Universal Dictionary of Arts, Sciences, and Literature* (1802–20).
19   John Byng, *The Torrington Diaries 1781–94* (republished 1935), quoted in Fitton (1989) p. 152.
20   Atholl MSS, Box 65, Bundle 5, 171, quoted in Fitton (1989) p. 184.

21 *Macclesfield Courier*, 13 June 1818.

22 *Manchester Mercury*, 27 March 1787, quoted in Fitton (1989) p. 185.

23 *Gentleman's Magazine*, 1793, p. 506.

24 Quoted in Fitton (1989) p. 219.

13. Arkwright on Trial

1 For full details of the first three trails see Fitton (1989) Chapter 4 'Arkwright on the Offensive', and for the final trial see Chapter 5 'The great patent trials: *Rex* vs *Arkwright*'.

2 Quoted in Fitton (1989) p. 93.

3 Quoted in Fitton (1989) p. 95.

4 Quoted in Fitton (1989) p. 97.

5 Quoted in Fitton (1989) p. 102.

6 Quoted in Uglow (2002) p. 396.

7 Quoted in Fitton (1989) p. 128.

8 Quoted in Fitton (1989) p. 136.

9 Quoted in Fitton (1989) pp. 138, 139. A copy of the broadsheet was found in the papers of Richard Guest II.

14. Manchester: The First Industrial City

1 De Tocqueville (1835) pp. 107–8.

2 Hall (1998) Chapter 10.

3 For full details of the history of Manchester see Kidd (1993).

4 Richard Cobden was perhaps its best-known advocate.

5 Aikin (1795) pp. 3–4.

6 Wrigley (1988) p. 84.

7 Moffit (1925) p. 298 quoting Richard Brooke (1775–1800) *Liverpool As It Was*.

8 Kidd (1993) pp. 24–5.

9 Nathan Mayer Rothschild was one of the five sons of the Frankfurt founder of the banking dynasty, Mayer Amschel Rothschild, four of whom were sent abroad to establish businesses across Europe. The later mid-Victorian warehouses were among the glories of the city; a surviving example is now the Britannia Hotel on Portland Street.

10 Bamford (1849) p. 278 quoted in Kidd (1993) p. 29.

11 Honeyman (1982) p. 62 *et seq.*

12 Hall (1998) pp. 339–40.

13   Aikin (1795) p. 178.
14   Aikin (1795) p. 172.
15   Aikin (1795) p. 176.
16   Advocates of Manchester point out that it had the world's first railway station, and municipal airport; that the atom was first split, and the world's first computer built, in the city. More recently the development of graphine in Manchester put it at the forefront of material technology.

15. Abraham Darby's Blast Furnace

1   For the history of smelting of iron and other metals see Tylecote (1976) esp. Chapter 9.
2   Historical Manuscripts Commission 13th Report, Vol. II, p. 275.
3   Daniel Defoe, quoted in VCH Worcestershire, Vol. I, p. 272 and Vol. III, p. 412 (1901–13).
4   For the history of the Darby family and business see Raistrick (1953).
5   Quoted in Lewis (1971) p. 10.
6   Plot (1686) p. 128.
7   Thomas Fuller, quoted in Galloway (1898) I, p. 205; see also Hatcher (1984–93) Vol. I, p. 454 *et seq.*
8   Tylecote (1976) p. 105.
9   Quoted in Addy and Power (1976) p. 23; see also Ashton (1924) p. 50.
10   Tylecote (1976) p. 106.
11   Flinn (1984) Table 7.11, p. 242.

16. Henry Cort and Cheap Iron

1   Charcoal was in plentiful supply in the Baltic region, while the quality of Swedish ore made bar-iron easier to make. Iron made up 75 per cent of Swedish exports in 1720. See Tylecote (1976) p. 94.
2   Journal of the House of Commons xxiii, 20 April 1737, p. 854.
3   Whitworth (1766), quoted in Ashton (1924) p. 88.
4   Quoted in Ashton (1924) p. 90.
5   For details of Cort's life and work see Mott and Singer (1983).
6   Cort was granted Patent Nos. 1351 and 1420. Full details are given in Mott and Singer (1983) Appendix 2.
7   David Hartley, Dr J. Black et al., *Brief State of the Facts relating to a*

new method of making bar iron (1787): description by David Hartley.
See Mott and Singer (1983), p. 45.

17. Crucible Steel

1 Tylecote (1976) p. 126 *et seq.* Eighteenth-century steel was slightly
   higher in carbon than modern mild steel.
2 Leader (1901); see also Swank (1884).
3 Samuel Smiles (1863).
4 Addy (1969) p. 52.
5 See Addy (1969) for details on the Walker family. Their journals are
   in Rotherham Archive.
6 Young (1768–70), quoted in Addy (1969) p. 14.

18. Rivers and Roads

1 See Hatcher (1984–93) Vol. I.
2 Atkinson (1966).
3 Matthias (1983) p. 102 *et seq.*
   Maps of turnpike development are adapted from Daunton (1995)
   pages 300 to 302.
4 Blind Jack Metcalf's life was first recorded in 1795 in an anonymous
   biography *The Life of John Metcalf, commonly called Blind Jack of
   Knaresborough*; recent biographies are by Hogg (1967) and Kellett
   (2007).
5 Young (1768–70), quoted in Gradwin and White (1967) p. 10.
6 Gifford (1990) p. 111.
7 Quoted in Ashton (1948) p. 242.
8 Quoted in Ashton (1948) p. 243.
9 *Cumberland & Westmoreland Antiquarian and Archaeological Society,*
   1982–3, extra series, xxiv, p. 12.
10 Defoe (1724) p. 66.

19. Canals and Locomotives

1 Smiles (1861–2) 'James Brindley'.
2 Uglow (2002) p. 112.
3 Burton (2011).
4 One branch of the canal went direct to Elsecar where a Newcomen

engine was installed in 1795; the engine ran until 1923 and is still in position.

5   For more on William Smith, see Osborne (1998) Chapter 4.

6   Pennant (1779) p. 55.

7   Bye (2003).

8   Quoted in Addy and Power (1976) pp. 61–2. There is a further letter from Blenkinsop to the agent of Sir John Sinclair dated 1814 answering questions about the possibility of running a railway from London to Edinburgh; see Ward and Wilson (1971) p. 105.

9   The Mumbles to Swansea service ran until 1960, latterly as an electric tram service, making it the longest continual railway service in the world.

10   See www.welshwales.co.uk/mumbles_railway_swansea.

11   See Davies (1977, reissued 2004) for the life of George Stephenson.

12   Northumberland Co. Record Office, Cully MSS, Folder 35; Addy (1969) p. 63.

13   *Observer*, 25 April 1830.

14   Quoted in Carey (1987) pp. 304–6.

15   *Sheffield Telegraph*, 30 June 1923; see Addy and Power (1976) p. 70.

16   Matthias (1983) Chapter 10.

17   Welsh coal was preferred by the navy as it raised steam well, did not produce ash and, crucially, did not smoke – warships did not want to advertise their presence to the enemy.

20. Producers and Consumers

1   Allen (2009) Figure 2.1.

2   See De Vries (2008) p. 52 *et seq.*

3   Mun (1664), pp. 180–1.

4   See, for example, De Vries (2008) p. 44 *et seq.*

5   Home consumption of sugar in 1669 was 2.13 lb per person per year; in 1750 it was 16.94 lb; and in 1790, 24 lb. Imports of tea, including smuggled tea, are estimated in 1700 at 0.01 lb; 1750, 1.1 lb; 1790, 2.1 lb.

6   Weatherill (1988).

7   De Vries (2008) p. 44 *et seq.*

8   Defoe (1726) p. 73.

9   Mandeville (1714, 1724) p. 69.

10   Steuart (1767) pp. 53–4 and throughout.

11   De Vries (2008) p. 52.
12   Hume (1752) p. 287 *et seq.*, quoted in De Vries (2008) p. 65.
13   White (1788) quoted in Downs (2010) p. 21.
14   Quoted in Downs (2010) p. 21.
15   De Vries (2008) pp. 1–3.
16   Eden (1797) Vol. II, pp. 433–5, quoted in Allen (2009).
17   Ibid.
18   Shammas (1990) p. 98.
19   Allen (2009) Figure 8.2.
20   Mui and Mui (1989) pp. 135–47.

21. Money for Industry

1   Matthias (1983) Chapter 5.
2   Mokyr (1990) p. 249.
3   See Matthias (1983) Chapter 5; Pressnell (1956); Cameron et al. (1967).
4   Uglow (2002) throughout.
5   The key proponent of this interpretation is Robert Allen; see Allen (1992) and Allen (2009) Chapter 3.
6   The Crown was keen to protect the so-called yeoman farmers against overbearing feudal lords. But after the Civil War Parliament gradually reversed the position and gave big landowners extensive rights; many became fabulously wealthy as a result – this was the era of the building of the great stately homes.
7   14 per cent for soil improvement compared to 12 per cent for harvesting and 9 per cent for ploughing; see Wrigley (1988) p. 44.
8   See Hajnal (1965).
9   The age of marriage fell among working-class women at the end of the eighteenth century as economic conditions worsened and the range of employment choices narrowed.
10   Pressnell (1956).

22. Adam Smith and the Industrial Economy

1   See Heilbroner (2000).
2   See Mandeville (1714, 1724).
3   Smith (1776) Book IV, Chapter 2, pp. 291–2.
4   See Brown (2000).

5   Smith (1776) Book I, Chapter 8, p. 78.
6   See Malthus (1799).
7   Smith (1776) Book I, Chapter 11, p. 144 (unabridged edn).
8   See Ricardo (1817).
9   See Wrigley (1988) pp. 22–3.

23. The Nature of Work and the Rise of the Factory

1   De Vries (2008) Chapter 3; see also Wrightson (2002) Chapter 14.
2   Many societies needed to expand their communal sufficiency beyond the household, generally to the village; in medieval Europe the most interesting exceptions to this household economy in Europe were monasteries and other religious houses. The Benedictine Rule, drawn up in the sixth century for the guidance of abbots and their flocks, was the first work schedule in history; but the monastery was a self-sufficient community.
3   Smith (1776, OUP edn) Book IV, Chapter 2, p. 292.
4   See, for example, Thompson (2002).
5   *Derby Mercury*, 12 May 1785, quoted in Fitton (1989) p. 77.
6   Townsend (1786) p. 23.
7   See Ward (1970) for early accounts of factories.
8   The building was damaged by fire in 1910 but restored and now houses the Derby Industrial Museum.
9   Berg (1985) pp. 225–8.
10 See Fitton (1989) for a full biography of Richard Arkwright. For the difficult relations between owners and artisan workers in the eighteenth century see Darnton (1984), also Safley and Rosenband (1993).
11 Quoted in Ward (1970) p. 39.
12 T. Rees's *Cyclopedia* (1802–20) 'Manufacture of Cotton' (1812).
13 Guest (1823) pp. 46–8.
14 Reach (1850) Letter XIV quoted in Ward (1970) p. 161.
15 See Davidoff and Hall (2002) for a full discussion of changes to family life in this period.
16 See Davidoff and Hall (2002) for a full discussion of women in the workplace. Reach (1850) Letter XIV, p. 1.
17 See Wrigley (2004) for a full discussion of population changes.
18 Wrightson (2002) p. 311.
19 Reliable birth dates were not registered until 1846 (1854 in Scotland).

20   Aikin (1795) p. 219.

21   Robert Owen, 26 April 1816, in evidence given to a House of Commons committee chaired by Robert Peel.

22   John Brown, A *Memoir of Robert Blincoe* (1828) p. 71; see Burnett et al. (1984) and Humphries (2011) for autobiographies of child labourers.

23   'Report of the Parliamentary Committee on the Bill to Regulate the Labour of Children in Mills and Factories' (1832) quoted in Carey (1987) pp. 295–8.

24   Ralph Wright and Thomas Bellamy, Manchester JPs, 1810; see Honeyman (2007) p. 193.

25   Destitute children then became an increasing problem in the nineteenth century. People used forced adoptions to acquire servants while 80,000 pauper children were sent to Canada as agricultural and domestic servants in the half-century after 1868.

26   Quotes from Thomas (1945) pp. 49–50, 52–54.

27   Strutt Papers, Derby County Library.

28   *Leeds Mercury*, April 1812, quoted in Aspin (1981) p. 8.

29   Quoted in Crump (1931) p. 229.

30   Felkin (1867) p. 234.

31   Cobbett (1816).

32   Letter from Henry Blundell to Henry Dundas, Home Secretary for Troops, 1792, quoted in Addy and Power (1976) pp. 95–6.

24. Life in the Industrial City

1   Dr Hawkins, quoted in Thomas (1945) p. 15.

2   Dr Ferriar, report to the committee for the regulation of the police in Manchester, quoted in Downs (2010) p. 80.

3   De Tocqueville (1835) pp. 107–8.

4   Engels (1845) p. 27.

5   Reach (1850) quoted in Aspin (1981) p. 11.

6   Quoted in Buer (1926) p. 92.

7   See Thomas (1971).

8   Quoted in Buer (1926) pp. 82–3.

9   Clayton, 'Friendly Advice to the Poor' (1755), and Henry, report to Manchester Lit and Phil (1786) quoted in Buer (1926) p. 84.

10   Quoted in Buer (1926) p. 87.

11   Reach (1850) quoted in Ward (1970) p. 163.

12   Buer (1926) p. 95.

13   Because the figures are derived in a number of different ways, all of which are to some degree unreliable, the contribution of each of these factors is the subject of fierce debate. I am using the interpretations of the Cambridge Group of the History of Population and Social Structure. See Wrigley (2004) for a full discussion.

14   Figures of stillbirths were not kept by parish registers and the definition is itself contentious. One exception was the parish of Hawkshead in Cumbria which recorded 106 'abortive' children in its burial register between 1658 and 1705; in the same period 1,299 children were baptised, giving a stillbirth rate of 75 per 1,000.

15   Wrigley (2004) p. 425.

16   Wrigley (2004) p. 337; life expectancy, Wrigley (1988) p. 88.

Epilogue: Britain in the 1830s

1   Macaulay (1830).

2   Colquhoun (1815) p. 68.

3   Baines (1835) p. 215.

4   Wrigley (1988) p. 85.

Select Bibliography

The central argument of this book, that the Industrial Revolution should be defined as the conversion to an economy based on coal-derived energy to drive machines, was proposed by E. A. Wrigley (1988) and enlarged in his 2010 book. Modern economic interpretations of the Industrial Revolution begin with Wrigley's work which has been taken on and challenged by Allen (2009) and De Vries (2008) among many others. The social aspects of the period, in particular the role of the household economy, have been particularly illuminated by Humphries (2011). While economic and social studies of the period have undergone a revival, the history of technology in the late eighteenth century remains highly fragmented. Studies of invention such as Mokyr (1990) and, again, Allen (2009) are fascinating, but authoritative accounts of leading figures are lacking – Fitton's 1989 biography of the Arkwright family is a lonely exception. Short biographies and accounts of industries have been published, or reissued, principally by Shire Publishing; otherwise local history societies remain a fertile source of material – the best book on the crucial technical developments in the cotton industry is by Catling (1970) now kept in print by Lancashire County Council. The history of technology has been better served by the revival of industrial museums, particularly in the old industrial heartlands, with working machinery often on display.

John Addy (1969) A Coal and Iron Community in the Industrial Revolution, 1760–1860, Longman, London.

John Addy and E. G. Power (1976) The Industrial Revolution, Longman, London.

John Aikin (1795) A Description of the Country from Thirty to Forty Miles Around Manchester, John Stockdale, London, facsimile reissue, Kelley, New York, 1968.

Robert C. Allen (2000) Enclosure and the Yeoman, OUP, Oxford.

Robert C. Allen (2009) *The British Industrial Revolution in Global Perspective*, CUP, Cambridge.

T. S. Ashton (1924) *Iron and Steel in the Industrial Revolution*, Manchester University Press, Manchester.

T. S. Ashton (1948) *The Industrial Revolution*, OUP, Oxford.

T. S. Ashton and J. Sykes (1929) *The Coal Industry of the 18th century*, Manchester University Press, Manchester.

Chris Aspin (1981) *The Cotton Industry*, Shire, Oxford.

Frank Atkinson (1966) *The Great Northern Coalfield 1700-1900*, Durham County Historical Society, Durham.

Edward Baines (1835) *History of the Cotton Manufacture in Great Britain*, London.

Patricia Baines (1985) *Flax and Linen*, Shire, Oxford.

Samuel Bamford (1844) *The Autobiography of Samuel Bamford 1788 to 1872*, reissued 1967, Cass, London.

Greville and Dorothy Bathe (1935) *Oliver Evans: A Chronicle of Early American Engineering*, Philadelphia Historical Society, Philadelphia.

Anna Benson and Neil Warburton (1986) *Looms and Weaving*, Shire, Oxford.

J. Benson and R. G. Neville (eds) (1976) *Studies in the Yorkshire Coal Industry*, Manchester University Press, Manchester.

Maxine Berg (1985) *The Age of Manufactures*, Collins.

James Boswell (1791) *Boswell's Life of Johnson*, 6 Vols., ed G. B. Hill, 1934-50, OUP, Oxford.

H. V. Bowen and P. L. Cottrell (1997) 'Banking and the Evolution of the British Economy, 1694 to 1878' in Alice Teichova et. al. (eds), *Banking Trade & Industry: Europe, America and Asia from the thirteenth to the twentieth century*, CUP, Cambridge.

John Brewer & Roy Porter (1993) *Consumption and the World of Goods*, Routledge, London.

John Brown (1828) *A Memoir of Robert Blincoe*, Doherty, Manchester.

Jonathan Brown (2011) *Water Power and Watermills*, Ramsbury, Crowood.

Peter Brown (2000) *Augustine of Hippo*, 3rd edn, University of California Press, Berkeley.

Mabel C. Buer (1926) *Wealth, Health and Population in the Early Days of the Industrial Revolution*, Routledge, London.

J. Burnett, D. Vincent and D. Mayall (1984) *The Autobiography of the Working Class: an annotated critical bibliography*, Harvester, Brighton.

Anthony Burton (2000) *Richard Trevithick, Giant of Steam*, Aurum, London.

Anthony Burton (2011) *Canal 250: The Story of Britain's Canals*, History Press, Stroud.

Sarah Bush (2000) *The Silk Industry*, 2nd edn, Shire, Oxford.

S. Bye (2003) 'John Blenkinsop and the Patent Steam Carriages' in *International Early Railway Conference, 2001*, Newcomen Society, Bury St. Edmunds.

R. E. Cameron et al. (1967) *Banking in the Early Stages of the Industrial Revolution*, New York.

John Carey (ed.). (1987) *The Faber Book of Reportage*, Faber, London.

Harold Catling (1970) *The Spinning Mule*, David & Charles, Newton Abbot, reissued Lancashire County Council, 1986.

William Cobbett (1816) 'Letter to the Luddites' in *Political Register*, Vol. 31, 30 November 1816.

D. C. Coleman (1983), 'Proto-industrialization, a concept too many' in *Economic History Review*, second series, Vol. 36, pp. 435–48.

John Collinges (1675) *The Weaver's Pocket Book*, Maxwell, London.

Patrick Colquhoun (1815) *A Treatise on the Wealth, Power and Resources of the British Empire*, 2nd edn, Mawman, London.

W. B. Crump (1931) *The Leeds Woollen Industry, 1780–1820*, Thoresby Society, Leeds.

Robert Darnton (1984) *The Great Cat Massacre and Other Episodes in French Cultural History*, Basic, New York.

M. J. Daunton (1995) *Progress and Poverty: An Economic and Social History of Britain 1700–1850*, OUP, Oxford.

Leonore Davidoff and Catherine Hall (2002) *Family Fortunes: Men and Women of the English Middle Class, 1780–1850*, 2nd edn, Routledge, London.

Hunter Davies (1977) *George Stephenson: A biographical study of the father of the railways*, Quartet, London.

Humphry Davy (1816) *The Papers of Sir Humphry Davy*, Emerson Charnley, Newcastle.

Daniel Defoe (1724) *A Journey Through the Whole Island of Great Britain*, Penguin, London, 1971.

Daniel Defoe (1726) *The Complete English Tradesman*, Create Space edn, 2011.

Thomas Deloney (c.1590) *The pleasant history of John Winchcombe called in his younger days Jack of Newbury*, reprinted by W. Hall, Newbury, c.1890.

Jan De Vries (2008) *The Industrious Revolution*, CUP, Cambridge.

Jared Diamond (1997) *Guns, Germs and Steel*, Chatto & Windus, London.

H. W. Dickinson (1936) *James Watt, Craftsman and Engineer*, CUP, Cambridge.

Jonathan Downs (2010) *The Industrial Revolution*, Shire, Oxford.

Harry Dutton (1984) *Patent System and Inventive Activity During the Industrial Revolution, 1750–1852*, Manchester University Press, Manchester.

Sir Frederick Eden (1797) *The State of the Poor*, 3 Vols., London.

Madeleine Elsas (ed.) (1960) *Iron in the Making: Dowlais Iron Company Letters 1782 to 1860*, County Records Committee of Glamorgan County Council.

Friedrich Engels (1845) *The Condition of the Working Class in England*, OUP, Oxford, 2009.

William Fairbairn (1861, 1863) *Treatise on Mills and Millwork*, London.

John Farey (1827) *A Treatise on the Steam Engine*, Longman, London, re-issued David & Charles, 1971.

William Felkin (1867) *The History of the Machine-Wrought Hosiery and Lace Manufactures*, London.

Adam Ferguson (1767) *Essay on the History of Civil Society*, Edinburgh, CUP edn, Cambridge, 1996.

Eugene S. Ferguson (1980) *Oliver Evans, Inventive Genius of the American Industrial Revolution*, Hagley Museum, Wilmington.

R. S. Fitton (1989) *The Arkwrights: Spinners of Fortune*, Manchester University Press, Manchester.

Michael W. Flinn (1984) *The History of the British Coal Industry, Vol. 2 The Industrial Revolution*, Clarendon, Oxford.

R. Floud & D. N. McCloskey (1981) *The Economic History of Britain since 1700*, 2 Vols., CUP, Cambridge.

Gilbert J. French (1859) *The Life and Times of Samuel Crompton*, London and Manchester.

Robert Galloway (1898) *Annals of Coal Mining and the Coal Trade*, Colliery Guardian, London.

Don Gifford (1990) *The Farther Shore, A Natural History of Perception, 1798–1984*, Faber, London.

Jean Gimpel (1976) *The Medieval Machine: The Industrial Revolution of the Middle Ages*, Gollancz, London.

Madeleine Ginsburg (1991) *The Illustrated History of Textiles*, Studio Editions, London.

David Gladwin and Joyce White (1967) *English Canals, A Concise History*, Oakwood, Usk.

Richard Guest (1823) A *Compendious History of the Cotton Manufacture*, Manchester.

J. Hajnal (1965) 'European Marriage Patterns in Perspective' in D. V. Glass and D. E. C. Eversley (eds) *Population in History*, Aldine, Chicago.

Peter Hall (1998) 'The First Industrial City, Manchester 1760–1830' in *Cities in Civilisation*, Weidenfeld & Nicolson, London.

Robert Hart (1856) 'Reminiscences of James Watt', *Transactions of the Glasgow Archaeological Society* Vol. 1 No. 1.

Negley Harte (1989) 'William Lee and the Invention of the Knitting Frame' in John Millington & Stanley Chapman (eds) *Four Centuries of Machine Knitting*, Knitting International.

William Harrison (1577) 'Description of Elizabethan England', in Holinshed, *Chronicles of England*, London.

John Hatcher (1984–93) *The History of the British Coal Industry, Vol. 1, Before 1700* Clarendon, Oxford.

Geoffrey Hayes (2010) *Beam Engines*, Shire, Oxford.

Robert L. Heilbroner (2000) *The Worldly Philosophers*, 7th rev edn, Penguin, London.

James Hodge (1973) *Richard Trevithick, An Illustrated Life, 1771 to 1833*, reissued Shire, Oxford, 2010.

Gary Hogg (1967) *John Metcalf, called Blind Jack of Knaresborough*, Phoenix, London.

A. H. Holdsworth (1841) *Dartmouth, the Advantages of its Harbour as a Station for Foreign Mail Packets*, Onwhyn, London.

Katrina Honeyman (1982) *Origins of Enterprise: Business Leadership in the Industrial Revolution*, Manchester University Press, Manchester.

Katrina Honeyman (2007) *Child Workers in England, 1780–1820*, Ashgate, Farnham.

David Hume (1752) *Essays Moral, Political and Literary, Vol 1., Of Commerce*, reissued Longman, London, 1989.

John W. Humphrey, John P. Oleson, Andrew N. Sherwood (eds) (1998) *Greek and Roman Technology, A Sourcebook*, Routledge, London.

Jane Humphries (2011) *Childhood and Child Labour in the British Industrial Revolution*, CUP, Cambridge.

William Hutchinson (1794) *History of the County of Cumberland*, Jollie, reissued E. P. Publishing, Carlisle, 1974.

E. L. Jones and M. E. Falkus (1979) 'Urban Improvement and the English Economy in the 17th and 18th centuries' in *Research in Economic History*, 4, 193–233.

Maurice Keen (1968) *History of Medieval Europe*, Penguin, London.

Arnold Kellett (2007) *Blind Jack of Knaresborough*, Denton, Knaresborough.

Alan Kidd (1993) *Manchester*, Ryburn, Keele.

Henry Kirke (1913) 'Dr Clegg, Minister and Physician in the 17th and 18th centuries' in *Journal of the Derbyshire Archaeological Society*, Vol. 35.

Ann Kussmaul (1990) *A General View of the Economy of England 1538–1840*, CUP, Cambridge.

Eliza Leadbetter (1979) *Spinning and Spinning Wheels*, Shire, Oxford.

Robert Leader (1901) *Sheffield in the 18th century*, Sheffield Independent Press, Sheffield.

Brian Lewis (1971) *Coal Mining in the 18th and 19th centuries*, Longman, London.

Thomas Lidstone (1871) *A few Notes and Queries about Newcomen, who made the first steam engine*, Pardon and Son, London.

T. H. Lloyd (2005) *The English Wool Trade in the Middle Ages*, CUP, Cambridge.

Thomas Macaulay (1830) *Edinburgh Review*, Edinburgh.

Christine MacLeod (1988) *Inventing the Industrial Revolution: The English Patent System, 1660–1800*, CUP, Cambridge.

Thomas Malthus (1799) *An Essay on the Principle of Population*, OUP edn, 2008.

Bernard Mandeville (1714, 1724) *The Fable of the Bees*, J. Roberts, London.

Paul Mantoux (1928) *The Industrial Revolution in the Eighteenth Century*, revised edn, Methuen, London, 1961.

Peter Matthias (1983) *The First Industrial Nation*, 2nd edn, Routledge, London.

F. F. Mendels (1972) 'Proto-Industrialization' in *Journal of Economic History*, Vol. 32, 241–61.

Louis Moffit (1925) *England on the Eve of the Industrial Revolution, A study of economic and social conditions from 1740 to 1760 with special reference to Lancashire*, reissued Cass, London, 1963.

Joel Mokyr (1990) *The Lever of Riches: Technological Creativity and Economic Progress*, OUP, Oxford and New York.

Roger Morriss (2011) *The Foundations of British Maritime Ascendancy: resources, logistics and the state, 1755–1815*, CUP, Cambridge.

R. A. Mott and Peter Singer (1983) *Henry Cort, The Great Finer: Creator of Puddled Iron*, Metals Society, London.

Hoh-Cheung Mui and Lorna H. Mui (1989) *Shops and Shop-Keeping in*

Eighteenth-Century England, McGill-Queen's University Press, Montreal.

Thomas Mun (1664) *England's Treasure by Forraign Trade*, Blackwell edn, 1926.

Dr T. Nash (1782) *Collections for the History of Worcestershire*, reprinted with contributions by K. Tomkinson, Kidderminster, 1984.

Roger Osborne (1998) *The Floating Egg: Episodes in the Making of Geology*, Cape, London.

Robert Owen (1816) *An address delivered to the inhabitants of New Lanark*, London.

Thomas Pennant (1779) *The Journey From Chester to London*, London.

Samuel Pepys (1663) *The Diaries*, Penguin edn, 2003.

Gabriel Plattes (1634) *Practical Husbandry Improved*, London.

Robert Plot (1686) *The Natural History of Staffordshire*, Oxford.

William Pole (1844) *A Treatise on the Cornish Pumping Engine*, London.

Peter Porter (1974) *The English Poets: from Chaucer to Edward Thomas*, Secker & Warburg, London.

E. G. Power (1969) *A Textile Community in the Industrial Revolution*, Longman, London.

Eileen Power (1941) *The Wool Trade in English Medieval History*, OUP, Oxford.

L. S. Pressnell (1956) *Country Banking in the Industrial Revolution*, Clarendon, Oxford.

Eric Preston (2012) *Thomas Newcomen of Dartmouth and the Engine that Changed the World*, Dartmouth History Research Group, Dartmouth.

William Radcliffe (1828) *Origin of the New System of Manufacture, Commonly Called Power Loom Weaving*, Lomax, Stockport.

Arthur Raistrick (1953) *Dynasty of Iron Founders, the Darbys and Coalbrookdale*, Longman, London.

Arthur Raistrick (1953a) *The Role of the Yorkshire Cistercian Monasteries in the History of the Wool Trade in England*, International Wool Secretariat, London.

Angus Reach (1850) *The Yorkshire Textile Districts*, reissued Royd Press, Hebden Bridge, 2007.

David Ricardo (1817) *Principles of Political Economy and Taxation*, Dover edn, 2004.

Richard Richards (1929) *The Early History of Banking*, King, London.

Lewes Roberts (1641) *The Treasure of Trafficke, or a Discourse of Forraigne Trade*, London.

Eric Robinson (1969) 'James Watt: Engineer by Act of Parliament' in Donaldson (ed.) *Bicentenary of the James Watt Patent*, University of Glasgow Press, Glasgow.

John Robison (1818) *Articles written for the Encyclopaedia Britannica on Steam and Steam Engines*, Edinburgh.

L. T. C. Rolt (1962) *James Watt*, Batsford, London.

L. T. C. Rolt (1963) *Thomas Newcomen: The Prehistory of the Steam Engine*, David & Charles, Newton Abbott.

William Rosen (2010) *The Most Powerful Idea in the World*, Cape, London.

Thomas Max Safley and Leonard N. Rosenband (eds) (1993) *The Workplace Before the Factory: Artisans and Proletarians 1500–1800*, Cornell University Press, Ithaca.

Carole Shammas (1990) *The Pre-Industrial Consumer*, OUP, Oxford.

A. W. Skempton (ed.) (2002) *A Biographical Dictionary of Civil Engineers in Great Britain and Ireland, Volume 1: 1500–1830*, Institute of Civil Engineers and Thomas Telford Limited, London.

Samuel Smiles (1861–2) *Lives of the Engineers*, John Murray, London.

Samuel Smiles (1863) *Industrial Biography: Iron Workers and Tool Makers*, London, reissued David & Charles, Newton Abbott, 1967.

Adam Smith (1776) *The Wealth of Nations*, London and Edinburgh, unabridged edn, Cosimo, New York, 2011; selected edn, OUP, Oxford, 1993.

Sir James Steuart (1767) *Inquiry into the Principles of Political Economy*, Edinburgh.

Robert Stuart (1824) *A Descriptive History of the Steam Engine*, reissued, Nonsuch Publishing, Stroud, 2007.

William Stukeley (1776) *Itinerarium Curiosum*, 2nd edn, London.

James M. Swank (1884) *History of the Manufacture of Iron in all Ages*, Philadelphia.

Stephen Switzer (1729) *Hydrostaticks and Hydraulicks*, London.

J. Tann (ed.) (1981) *The Selected Papers of Boulton & Watt, Volume 1*, Diploma Press, London.

Keith Thomas (1971) *Religion and the Decline of Magic*, Weidenfeld & Nicolson, London.

Maurice Thomas (1945) *Young People in Industry, 1750–1945*, Nelson, London.

E. P. Thompson (2002) *The Making of the English Working Class*, revised edn, Penguin, London.

Alexis de Tocqueville (1835) *Journeys to England and Ireland*, English edn, Faber, 1958.

Joseph Townsend (1786) *Dissertation on the Poor Laws*, London.

Martin Triewald (1734) A *Short Description of The Fire and Air Machine at The Dannemora Mines*, English translation published 1928, Newcomen Society, London.

R. F. Tylecote (1976) A *History of Metallurgy*, Metals Society, London.

Alfred Ubbelohde (1963) *Man and Energy*, Penguin, London.

Jenny Uglow (2002) *The Lunar Men*, Faber, London.

R. W. Unger (1984) 'Energy Sources for the Dutch Golden Age' in *Research in Economic History*, IX, pp. 221–53.

R. W. Vernon, G. McDonnell and A. Schmidt (1998) 'An integrated geophysical and analytical appraisal of early iron-working: three case studies' in *Historical Metallurgy* 31 (2), pp. 72–5.

James Walvin (1999) *The Slave Trade*, Sutton, Stroud.

J. T. Ward (1970) *The Factory System, Vol. 1 Birth and Growth*, David & Charles, Newton Abbott.

J. T. Ward and R. G. Wilson (eds) (1971) *Land and Industry; The Landed Estate and the Industrial Revolution*, David & Charles, Newton Abbott.

Lorna Weatherill (1988) *Consumer Behaviour and Material Culture in Britain 1660–1760*, Routledge, London.

Christopher A. Whatley (1997) *The Industrial Revolution in Scotland*, CUP, Cambridge.

Richard Whitworth (1766) *Advantages of Inland Navigation*, Baldwin, London.

Keith Wrightson (2002) *Earthly Necessities*, Penguin, London.

E. A. Wrigley (1988) *Continuity, Chance and Change: The Character of the Industrial Revolution in England*, CUP, Cambridge.

E. A. Wrigley (2004) *Poverty, Progress and Population*, CUP, Cambridge.

E. A. Wrigley (2010) *Energy in the Industrial Revolution*, CUP, Cambridge.

Arthur Young (1768–70) A *Six Months Tour Through the North of England*, 4 vols., Strahan, London.

Arthur Young (1769) A *Six Weeks Tour Through the Southern Counties of England and Wales*, Strahan, London.

Hans Zinsser (1934) *Rats, Lice and History*, Little, Brown, New York.

Index

11/6/14